THE INMATE WITHIN:

Prison Ministry a Haven of Hope

Peter K. Einstein

Peter and Fran Einstein

This book is dedicated to...

Fran, my wife. You have been my partner in life and ministry through both the sunshine and the rain. God has used both elements to nurture and grow us into something that looks more like Him, and less like us. You are my helpmeet, my completer. Thank you for your perspective, patience, and love throughout this spiritual journey.

The Inmate Within is also dedicated to those men and women, inside and outside the prison system, who choose to labor selflessly "in the vineyard" for the Kingdom of God. May you never minimize your efforts or doubt the impact of the ministry you have been given. Remember that, throughout the ages, our Creator, in His infinite wisdom, continually has used ordinary people to accomplish extraordinary things. Step out in faith, never wavering. Be obedient to the calling of God on your life. Never give up.

With Great Appreciation

Give thanks to the Lord for He is good
and His love endures forever

(Psalm 107:1).

There are numerous individuals who, individually and collectively, have impacted my life and ministry. All of you, in some way, have been used by God to influence and help direct the writing of my first full-length book, *The Inmate Within: Prison Ministry, a Haven of Hope.*

To the Einstein and Wilson families: Thank you for your patience and understanding all these years, as God continues to shape and mold a rebellious spirit into someone who looks a bit more like Him and a lot less like the "old me."

Special thanks to the members and congregation of Carlisle Alliance in Carlisle, Pennsylvania, my home church. Your prayers and financial support, throughout the twenty-five-plus year adventure that is SonPower Ministries, have been priceless.

To my pastor, Tim Keller: I appreciate your care, your candor, and most of all, your friendship, particularly during our impromptu "iron-sharpens-iron" conversations.

Without the pastors of our supporting churches, who welcome us and help to financially fortify SonPower Ministries, it would be very difficult to travel, as "stateside missionaries," throughout the prison system. I am grateful to you all.

Pastor Jim Law introduced Fran and me to ministry within the state penitentiary system. We owe you a debt of gratitude. I miss those early road trips; however, I am thankful that we still share the vision of spiritual care for incarcerated men and women.

Since its inception, SonPower Ministries has always had an active board of advisors. I would like to recognize the current board for their efforts in helping to guide and direct the ministry's evolving mission, and for holding me accountable to the standard of Christ in my life. Board advisors for 2017 are Steve Bloom, Pastor Rich Cline, Matt Eisenberg, Phil Flaharty, Pastor John Gill, and Marlin Herr.

A special thanks to Deputy-Warden Jeff Ilgenfritz (retired), Cumberland County Prison, Carlisle, Pennsylvania, for taking time to provide clarification, more detailed information, and answers to my many "prison questions." Also, my deepest appreciation to CCP Warden Earl Reitz and Deputy-Warden Mike Carey for your hospitality and support of SonPower Ministries' evangelism and discipleship efforts through the years.

Fran and I would not be able to minister so frequently and effectively throughout the state penitentiary system were it not for the efforts of the prison facilities' chaplains. May God continue to bless your unique mission field. Each of you holds a special place in my heart.

To Jeff Benzon Photography, Mechanicsburg, Pennsylvania, your photographic assistance in the prison scenes for this book is truly an invaluable asset in portraying the story of *The Inmate Within.*

A number of individuals, throughout the United States and beyond have supported SonPower Ministries' throughout our twenty-five-plus years of service. You are too numerous to mention, but are all greatly appreciated.

Original, contemporary music has always been the "spiritual ammunition" which has set the stage for presenting the Word of God since the inception of this ministry. To co-producers Keith Mohr (*Work To Do* CD) and Pastor Selara R. Mann, Jr. (*Jubilation Journey* CD)…and to *all* my studio and live-performance musician friends…I couldn't have ministered as I do without your time, talent, and creativity.

To Cynthia A. Sudor, CARACYN Publishing—my most sincere gratitude. Cynthia, your vision for the global impact of this book was far greater than my own. Your guidance and direction have been invaluable in transforming me from a writer to an author. You are, indeed, a mentor. But much more than that, you are a valued and trusted friend.

Testimonials

"*God has blessed Pete and Fran Einstein with a long and fruitful ministry to incarcerated men and women. The experience they have gained from those years is insightful as well as thought-provoking.* The Inmate Within: Prison Ministry, a Haven of Hope *provides a colorful picture that is helpful, not just for those contemplating ministry within the prison environment, but also for those desiring to better understand the goings-on behind those imposing (prison) walls. Pete's constant awareness and reliance upon the God's Holy Spirit working in the midst of his ministry efforts is an added insight from which readers will benefit.*"

Mark Kimmel
Senior Vice President, Finance and Administration
The Navigators
Colorado Springs, Colorado

"*Pete Einstein brings to the reader a book that is not only well-written, but one that gives a realistic glimpse into a world that many people would like to forget exists. Throughout the chapters of* The Inmate Within, *Pete intimately describes the underbelly of prison life, and the many challenges facing incarcerated men and women. But he also gives heartwarming accounts of hope and 'spiritual successes' which occur in prison chapels across the United States. At a time when prisons are a 'hot topic' of sometimes controversial conversation, Pete's intelligent writing brings a voice of sanity to the platform.*"

Rev. Debra L. Reitz
Facility Chaplaincy Program Director/Volunteer Coordinator
State Correctional Institution at Muncy
Muncy, Pennsylvania

"It is because of God's grace that freedom rings in prisons throughout America. And it is because of the steadfast efforts of believers such as Pete and Fran Einstein that thousands of inmates are answering the call to new life in Jesus Christ. The Inmate Within *chronicles the journey of a couple, favored by God, simply for 'putting their shoulders to the plow' in obedience to a unique calling. This riveting biography of how God has, and continues to use, their ministry of music and testimony in the often-forgotten prison population is an excellent portrayal of enduring love and service."*

Marcia J. Sinkovitz, M.S., LPC
Director, Leading Inmates in Faith & Education, Inc.
Newville, Pennsylvania

"What happens behind foreboding prison walls when the steel gates close? Pete Einstein, one of America's most experienced and faithful prison ministers, shares the gritty truth. Throughout the pages of The Inmate Within: Prison Ministry, a Haven of Hope, *Pete relates, in intimate detail, his courageous journey in carrying the Gospel of Jesus Christ—the only key that unlocks the bondage of souls—into the darkest of places."*

Honorable Stephen Bloom
Pennsylvania State Representative
199th Legislative District
Carlisle, Pennsylvania

"I met Pete and Fran Einstein more than twenty years ago and experienced, first-hand, the call of God upon their lives as we co-labored in prison ministry throughout Pennsylvania. In his first book, The Inmate Within: Prison Ministry, a Haven of Hope, Pete captures the very depth of ministry to incarcerated men and women in an expressive and insightful manner… exploring the spiritual, clinical and mental aspects of the ministry process. The Inmate Within is a must-read for anyone involved in prison ministry, for 'inquiring minds,' and for those wrestling with bondage and strongholds in their own hearts."

Pastor Jim Law
President, Second Chance Ministries International
Author, Rebellion to Righteousness, Hope for the Next Generation
Baton Rouge, Louisiana

"You will thoroughly enjoy reading this book! The Inmate Within: Prison Ministry, a Haven of Hope, is a testimony of selfless ministry, not only to countless men and women behind prison walls, but to the chaplains, correctional officers and prison officials, as well. Pete documents his ministry experiences in such a way that you, the reader, literally are transported to another world… a different culture, with its own rules, regulations and, often, skewed perceptions of life and living. But for the prison ministry veteran, the ministry neophyte, the curious or the misinformed, the message of The Inmate Within is clear: intentional interaction, relationship-building and the sharing of one's faith rings the bell of evangelism and ushers in hope—a new birth in Jesus Christ."

Apostle Otha Ulysses Bell, Jr.
Speaking the Word of Faith Prophetic Teaching Ministries
Georgetown, Texas

THE INMATE WITHIN:
PRISON MINISTRY, A HAVEN OF HOPE

ISBN 978-0-9897591-1-3
Printed in the United States of America

©2017 by Peter K. Einstein
www.theinmatewithin.com

CARACYN Publishing LLC
1205 Ridge Road
Grantville, PA 17028
717-469-7329
www.caracynpublishing.com

Names in this book have been changed to protect the identities of incarcerated men and women.

Table of Contents

The Inmate Within: Prison Ministry, a Haven of Hope
Peter K. Einstein, Author

i

Foreword

I first met Pete and Fran Einstein in 2001 as they participated in college-level studies provided by Christ Quest Institute, Phoenix. Arizona. At that time, Pete was learning and applying scriptural principles to better develop Christlikeness within the context of marriage. He and Fran were embarking upon a journey, which is still ongoing, of spiritual maturity, employing principles and insights from their studies. Pete had established the foundation of SonPower Ministries and as it grew, he and Fran were able to incorporate some of these learned principles to minister to men and women within the prison system. Pete's book, *The Inmate Within: Prison Ministry, a Haven of Hope,* chronicles those ministry efforts in a way that introduces the reader not only to life within prison walls, but also gives insight to our own lives, where we are sometimes "in prison" behind invisible bars which impact us in countless ways.

I see this book as a valuable resource for one or all of the following five categories of reader.

First, *The Inmate Within* inspires and provides food-for-thought for those whom God may be calling to serve Him through ministry to those who are imprisoned. For those preparing for or already engaged in ministry to the incarcerated, the text is an excellent handbook and reference.

Second, this book can serve as an in-depth source of information to increase understanding for those readers seeking greater knowledge of the world of incarceration and the "prison culture."

Third, men and women who are currently imprisoned can use the principles demonstrated in *The Inmate Within* to better prepare themselves spiritually for release back into society. While imprisoned, inmates can also better understand and appreciate the dedication of those who minister to them for their spiritual well-being.

Fourth, for those who are "imprisoned" in their minds and hearts—but not confined to an actual jail cell—the truths and examples demonstrated time and again within the chapters of this book can encourage a healthy spiritual a path to freedom.

And, Fifth, last, but certainly not least, *The Inmate Within: Prison Ministry, a Haven of Hope* is a "spiritual testament" for those readers seeking the ultimate freedom—a personal relationship with Jesus Christ.

Readers will be riveted by Pete's vivid, real-life experiences and examples of prison ministry and spiritual redemption. By incorporating his wealth of colorful, in-depth information and insights, the reader will be able to judge not others, but examine their own inclinations and motivations. Readers will be empowered to fully understand that feeling 'imprisoned" by the events of this life can be overcome.

There are many benefits from the practical wisdom and spiritual counsel throughout the pages of *The Inmate Within*.

Ken Nair
Founder and President
Christ Quest Ministries
Phoenix, Arizona

Preface

My Unplanned Path to Prison Ministry

Isn't it fascinating how *the things of life* help to prepare us for *the living of life?*

Our environment, upbringing, temperaments, talents, and convictions, combined with specific life experiences and interests, collide in a cosmic coincidence which, as we acquire wisdom and insight, proves to be no coincidence at all. I never had intentions in the grand scheme of my life to become intimately involved in any sort of ministry. And I certainly didn't go looking for prison ministry; it found me. But it was not until I had experienced what bondage and imprisonment looks and feels like *outside* those steel bars—*inside* of me—that I was able to be used by God to minister to incarcerated men and women within prison walls.

This is a story of hope and redemption—otherworldly grace, mercy, and unmerited favor that we can never earn. We can't work hard enough for it and we can't purchase it at any price. We can't wish upon a star for it, but we *can* pray for it. Our lives are a continuing saga; an unfinished work. The words in this book speak to the human condition and where the spiritual heart takes us with or without a firm foundation of faith. As our lives travel to some sort of earthly destination, what path will we choose to arrive at such a place? Will it be a course that leads to destruction, or one that leads to freedom and new life? As you read this book, you will have the opportunity to examine these questions, and more, as they pertain to your own life.

My life journey took me through the world of music; from a self-taught ten-year-old percussionist, to a skinny, white, teen-aged singer in a black soul group, to the bright lights of Hollywood. My continual search for love, acceptance, and power led me down the slippery slope of alcohol and drug abuse, sexual immorality, aberrant theology, New

Age occultism, reincarnation—even witchcraft. But instead of finding illumination at the top of the mountain, I spiraled deeper and deeper toward the pit of Hell.

The Bible says, "The steps of a good man are ordered by the Lord…" (Psalm 37:23). Looking back on my life, I realize that the breath of God was a cool breeze in the midst of the tempests and storms that tossed me to and fro. He alone kept me from self-destruction as I careened down the long and winding road of a decadent life, in search of some sort of personal epiphany, but finding nothing. God began a supernatural "personalized" process of molding, shaping, and healing that continues to this day. He made me fit for *His* service and then nurtured in me a more caring, others-centered heart that was ready to serve even "the least of these," the men and women populating our county jails, state prisons, and federal penitentiaries.

Yes, prison ministry found me. And God, in His infinite wisdom, used a man who had never been incarcerated in a jail cell, but had known bondage in many other ways within himself, as an example of how *He works inside and outside the steely, cold prison bars.* Through His grace and mercy He can set *all* the captives free for eternity. Although to the rest of the world an individual might appear "free" from the outside, that same person may be experiencing some sort of hidden bondage that prevents him or her from living life to the fullest.

My hope is that the message throughout this book will engage you in such a way that you, too, will feel the power and presence of God as you explore the deeper meaning of this text. You can find comfort in the realization that your trials and tribulations in an increasingly dark world are *not* too tough to handle, *not* too much to bear, and that there *is* light at the end of that tunnel. And that light can lead to the beginning of a whole new life for us. It is a life that honors God in all we think, say, or do.

I pray that the timeless spiritual principles which are renewing the minds and hearts of many incarcerated men and women throughout this nation and the world would be a healing balm for your wounds, as well. Most of us envision prison as a foreboding place with high walls, iron bars, and razor wire. But there is also the *prison within* that we will experience at some point in our earthly lives. I am a testament to successfully breaking out of that personal hell and finding peace in the presence of God. His grace is more than sufficient. What God accomplished in me He can accomplish for you.

Truth—or reality, as God sees it—can take us from wallowing in the mire of our self-centered past to the expectation of a bright and glorious future of serving others. Perhaps you are, or will become, interested in pursuing ministry to the incarcerated in some way. Perhaps you are simply interested or intrigued by the predicament of prison life. Or maybe you have experienced, directly or indirectly, the costs of indiscretion—whether it be the consequences of crime or the ravages of sin—and you seek healing and restoration in your soul.

This book is for you. Read it, and through it be released, refreshed, and restored. Be prepared not just to be changed, but to be transformed by the renewing of your mind. Open your heart, discover your strengths, call upon a power beyond yourself to equip you to step out in faith to do something, knowing beyond a shadow of a doubt that yours is a life worth living—in freedom and victory.

Peter K. Einstein
Carlisle, Pennsylvania

Prologue

Just another Sunday in the "Big House." Another "three hots and a cot." Another 24 hours of prison bars and, if you're lucky, an opportunity to spend some time with fellow inmates.

But this Sunday morning *could* be different. Something positive and uplifting *could* be on the horizon, because of a choice you made. This Sunday morning, SonPower Ministries is in the house. In the past, you heard the upbeat music drifting down the hallways. And you listened as the brothers on the block recounted the powerful message that was preached when this man—this "Son-of-Power"—and his wife visited the prison. In the past, you chose not to be a part of it. But, today, you made the decision to participate….to find out what this "Jesus-thing" is all about.

At least this morning's chapel service will offer a break from the same, old routine. Perhaps you *will* find time to catch up with your homies caged in the far reaches of this hellhole. An opportunity to interact with them might present itself, at some point, before, during or after the service. Before leaving your cell, you "clean-up" as best you can…washing the stink from another sleepless night into the small metal, wall-mounted basin. You brush your teeth and tuck a sweaty, soiled and faded blue shirt into matching, over-sized denim trousers.

Now, the prisoners on the block are on the move. You shuffle, single-file, down a barren corridor, with the duty officer barking orders to, "Hug the wall," as a cordon of inmates approaches from the opposite direction. Your eyes hone in on the passers-by, your senses heightened. Last week, during a similar hallway trek, a disgruntled prisoner, seeking revenge or payback, broke ranks and lunged across the corridor, gut-shanking the guy in line right behind you. You watched impassively as that sorry soul doubled over and fell onto the cold, linoleum floor. Word reached you through the grapevine that his injuries were bad enough to send him to the prison infirmary for some "vacation time." You thought then, as you do now, *"There's got to be something better than this!"*

And then you hear it. Almost a whisper in the distance, at first, but building in rhythm and intensity, as you draw nearer to the "church" sanctuary. It's that guy "from the outside"—the one you heard about—ministering today. And it seems he's brought some musical "ammunition" with him! Some guys who have heard him preach before say this Pete Einstein is for real. We'll see. One thing is for sure… if the message is as fresh and soulful as the melodies which are energizing your senses, this SonPower Ministries' service could be a life-changer…or, at least, a pleasant diversion from your daily drudgery.

"Ok, Lord," you whisper to yourself. "I'm ready for something better…something finer…something more meaningful in my life."

Entering the chapel, you march down the aisle, stopping at one of many tired, hardwood church pews to assume your assigned position. But, instead of sitting, you remain standing, clapping your hands and swaying in time to the music—surrounded by a sea of fellow blue-clad inmates expressing the same sense of joy, relief…*and hope.*

Caught up in the moment you wonder, "Is *this* the beginning of that 'new day' you've been searching for behind these prison walls?"

PART ONE

SETTING THE STAGE
FOR EFFECTIVE MINISTRY

Chapter One

AN INMATE PROFILE:
THE PRISON SYSTEM

*"For my thoughts are not your thoughts,
neither are your ways my ways declares the Lord."*

(Isaiah 55:8)

As a nation, we seem to have a morbid fascination with "the prison experience."

In popular music and videos, the "thug life" on the streets of America is romanticized to such a degree that we are developing a generation of young people who do not shrink from, but run toward, a gangster lifestyle that revolves around guns, drugs, wanton sex, and a sub-culture that glorifies it all. It has gone so far that, in some circles, "getting paid," or "taking what I think should be mine" from an innocent victim, has become an inalienable right. The "taker" is perceived to be strong; the victim is perceived to be weak.

The irony and sad reality of such a pursuit is that very often those attempting to live up to this misguided criminal persona do, in fact, end up somewhere in the prison system. Documentaries and television programs—even reality-type shows—give viewers a tantalizing glimpse into the lives of incarcerated men and women. And we, as a nation, are content to engage on the other side of the TV or movie screen, drawn in as inquisitive bystanders, but thankful we aren't inside the steel cages with "those people." Without God-given discernment, some viewers buy into the fantasy and do not think twice about the reality—that our actions can, indeed, have dire consequences.

God tends to look at the things of this world differently than you and I do. His Word says, "For my thoughts are not your thoughts, neither are your ways my ways declares the Lord" (Isaiah 55:8). God sees sin as sin. First-degree murder or cheating on your tax return are all the same to Him. Scripture shows us that God hates sin, even despises it. Most of us, if questioned, would agree that we too despise sin and all the inappropriate behavior that accompanies the machinations of a dark, twisted mind or a hardened heart. But, more likely than not, we are referring to the really "major" sins—murder, rape, armed robbery—and not what we perceive to be the tiny indiscretions that so easily beset us as human beings. As a society, we tend to categorize sin. And we certainly categorize crime. Just turn on the TV or pick up the daily newspaper and you discover that, across the nation, and even in our own communities, countless individuals have been convicted of kidnapping or aggravated rape and have been given state penitentiary sentences of as much as forty years to life. In contrast, another individual has defrauded the local Little League boosters association of $3,000 and must make full restitution, plus serve three years of probation. More often than not, a judge or magistrate, serving as an officer of the court, oversees legal proceedings to insure the punishment fits the crime and that "justice is served."

Americans like to measure things. We tend to employ facts and figures to substantiate preferences, win arguments, and prove points. Often "just cause" is boiled down to a numbers game and bigger is usually better. Statistics can give us a fundamental understanding and insight regarding a particular subject of interest, and this is especially

4

true when we explore something as enormous as the U.S. prison system. Statistical analysis can, and does, shed light and allow us to gain a cursory grasp of the topic. But herein lies the trap—the snare—in getting too caught up in facts, figures, and percentages: A statistics-only reference relegates flesh-and-blood *people* to the status of *numbers.* And numbers, over time, can become boring…something examined, referred to periodically, and then tucked away safely in a drawer, forgotten.

As we explore further the topics of prison and ministry within, we will see that incarceration can be a dehumanizing experience. So it is incumbent that we, as a nation, recognize the humanity of troubled men and women behind the sometimes heinous crimes that have isolated them from the public-at-large.

As the moral and spiritual foundations of our society continue to weaken, the rate of crime, in general, tends to rise. As the crime rate escalates, the need to house criminal offenders becomes greater. The result—the building, operation, and maintenance of prisons, from the county to the state to the federal levels—has become "big business"… *very* big business. Total expenditures throughout the prison system in the United States eclipse **$48,000,000,000** (that's right, forty-eight-billion dollars) a year! The average cost to house an inmate can vary by state or institution but, for practical purposes, *the expense to incarcerate one inmate in America is more than $31,000 per year.* And those are your tax dollars at work. State senators or representatives who secure the funding to have a county jail or state prison built within depressed areas of their districts become instant heroes to their constituents. If they can manage to land two such facilities, they have a job for life. The prison business has even extended to the private sector, as companies contract with local or state municipalities to build and/or operate facilities on their behalf.

From land acquisition to construction, personnel and staffing to supplies, services, and maintenance, a penal facility can be the economic engine which drives a community. One world on the outside; another society behind prison walls. Approximately one-percent of the U.S. population—some 2,300,000 juvenile offenders and adults—conducts their lives behind prison bars, in isolation from the rest of us. But, at some point in time, 95% of these "shadow world" inhabitants will be released back into the towns and cities in which we live. Doesn't this fact alone call for some sort of meaningful response? If you and I were hurting spiritually, mentally, or physically, wouldn't we want someone to care for and about us?

If you live in the United States, chances are one-in-thirty-one, just over 3%, that the prison experience will touch you in some way. In our country, today, there are *more than seven million adults* who either live life behind bars or who are being monitored via probation or parole procedures after release from county, state, or federal prisons. Men comprise 93% of the prison population versus 7% for women. The average age of a male inmate is 33.5 years old; for females, 34.5 years. If you fall in the age category of 20–25, you represent the most prevalent age group in the penal system. In terms of demographics, more inmates fall into this age category than any other age group (the average age is increased by inmates well into their sixties and seventies).

African-American males comprise 10% of the U.S. population, but comprise 37% of the prison population. White men represent 32% of the prison population and Hispanic males 22%. Among the female population, whites represent nearly 50% of incarcerated women, followed by African-Americans at approximately 25%, and Hispanics at 20%.

At some point, fifty to sixty-percent of released offenders will return to prison. Nationwide studies report that the first year after release is the most critical period regarding recidivism. This is when a person's future regarding repeat offenses and re-entry into the system will be determined. This is what various studies conclude. But the realities and needs of human beings paint a far different picture. God has shown me through twenty-plus years of on-site prison ministry that *the first three weeks after an offender has been released from a penal institution will be the most critical!*

Imagine that you're an ex-offender. You've just received your "Bag and Baggage" call—your discharge announcement—over the prison intercom and are released from a county jail with several pieces of paperwork, some clothing, and your personal belongings. The battery on your cell phone is dead, so you politely ask a visitor in the parking lot if he would allow you to call a friend for a ride to town. You are calling a friend, because your family relationships are in complete disarray—too many bridges have been burned. Your mother is old beyond her years and is fed up with your shenanigans. Since your father walked out on the family when you were three, she has been the sole provider. At present, your mother is taking care of your younger sister's baby girl and raising the child as if she were her own daughter. Your girlfriend stopped visiting and then wrote you a "Dear John" letter. Her new boyfriend sent word that if you tried to contact her when you got out of the joint he would beat you to within an inch of your life. And so you call your friend. He has a vehicle and a low-paying job at the local car wash. He and another guy share an efficiency apartment and have offered to allow you to sleep on the sofa *if* you can come up with fifty bucks a month. Maybe you can land a job at the car wash, but with a lengthy felony record, nothing is certain. The owner's known for giving ex-cons a second chance, so we'll see…

Several days pass. The friend's apartment has roaches and his roommate's snoring seems louder than the whine of a chainsaw cutting through hardwood. Your efforts to secure a good night's sleep are constantly thwarted. But at least you have a roof over your head—a place to stay. If only you could find a job so that perhaps you could finance a place of your own. Negative self-talk begins to crowd in, and with the realities of life come doubts and confusion. You ask yourself, as you've done so many times before, *Why does all this junk keep happening to me? Why can't I catch a break once in a while?* One week goes by, then two. Nothing is falling into place! You can't pay your buddy the rent money so now you're out on the street. *At least if I had a car I could sleep in the damn thing,* you think. There's nobody to call upon—certainly not God. He's never been there for *you.*

And then your thoughts drift to the man who would come into the jail on Wednesdays to lead a Bible study and discussion session. You had gone once or twice, but nothing stuck. That old man was out of touch with the dog-eat-dog world in the streets. You ridiculed the guys who seemed to receive comfort and some modicum of hope from the Bible studies, calling them "punks" and "soft" when they chose to respond to the stressors of prison life in a kinder and gentler way. You clung tenaciously to the truth as you knew it to be; in the end, when push came to shove, life was what you made it, on your own. No supernatural power was going to crack the skies and, in a blinding flash of light, rescue you from this living hell called life.

Week three comes and goes. Now, you're in survival mode. You spend your last ten bucks on crack cocaine. A good hit will give you the confidence you need. Pulling the baseball cap down over your forehead so that your eyes become dark shadows, hand on the revolver in your waistband, you enter the convenience store. It's time to get paid.

There has to be something more to life than this. And there is.

The United States incarcerates more
people, per capita, than any country
in the world.

(Prison Policy Initiative figures)

Chapter Two

SIGHTS AND SOUNDS
OF THE PRISON EXPERIENCE

"Taste and see that the Lord is good;
blessed is the one who takes refuge in Him."

(Psalm 34:8)

Our lives are filled with the experiences of our five senses. These five senses play a critical part of every waking moment. Have you ever wondered what prison *really* looks like? What it *feels, smells, sounds,* even *tastes* like? Prison—both the facility and the ministry—opens up a world of sensory experiences in dramatic fashion. And for some, those experiences are overwhelming.

There is an ironic dichotomy as one approaches any penal institution, particularly in the state penitentiary system. Quite often, a long lane or road branching off a main highway or rural route provides the outsider with a straight shot leading to the facility. The visitor usually is treated to a panoramic, long-range view of the institution a short time before actually arriving. This view is eerily similar at every facility, no matter where the location: a massive complex of buildings and open exercise areas, in a cityscape defined by the architecture of the particular prison. Some buildings are modern prototype structures, others monstrous older edifices—orphans' homes, mental institutions, or tuberculosis sanitariums—converted for a newer form of incarceration.

On a clear day, the most eye-catching feature is the brilliant reflection as the sun lights up a maze of massive, seemingly endless coils of concertina and razor wire which hinder every possible avenue of escape. Topping the incapacitating, electrified fences that adorn exercise areas and courtyard rooflines is row after row of glinting, gleaming streams of wire. Different than the barbed wire made famous for keeping cattle within property boundaries of the farms and ranches in the Old West, this is something far more sinister, more deadly. These are surgically honed blades of steel akin to a futuristic weapon in a sci-fi movie, capable of shredding human flesh upon contact. The message is loud and clear: "No one escapes this place, this fortification, without paying a horrible price, possibly even the loss of your life."

Smokestacks poke skyward above the confines of many facilities, as refuse and other sanctioned materials are disposed of from within the self-contained community. Enclosed guard towers are designed to be conspicuous by their presence, strategically positioned around the perimeters of the prison, providing still another level of security, to keep the "bad guys" inside the fortress.

"Silent spies" are not so conspicuous, but they are everywhere. All-seeing eyes, searching, seeking, finding, and then capturing images—of you—for display on giant monitor screens. Atop buildings. Along fencerows. Slowly turning on towering turrets. Be aware. From the moment you enter prison property, as you exit your vehicle in the parking area and walk toward the visitors' entrance, and throughout your journey within the confines of the facility, you're *always* on *Candid Camera*.

Dirt, dust, and grit swirl and cling to everything and everyone as a first welcome upon arrival. Parking lots, visitors' check-in areas, and staff entrances tend to be asphalt or gravel battlefields littered with cigarette butts, aluminum ring tabs, bits of paper and minute debris from long-distance travels, much of it from inmate visits of days gone by. In stark contrast, colorful flowerbeds and foliage break up what would otherwise be a pretty somber scene. On a typical spring day, whiffs of fresh-bloomed forsythia, mingled with the odor of fossil-fuel dust, fills your nostrils with an aroma that can only be described as interesting and, despite the floral scent, somewhat disturbing.

As you enter the check-in station or guest lobby of most modern-day prisons, not one thing seems new—there is nothing particularly inviting or fashion-forward about the architecture, the design and layout, the furniture or décor. Even the state-of-the-art, computerized system that automatically locks and unlocks the massive gray metal gates and doors appears strangely antiquated. The scene is consistently institutional and efficient. From the steel-framed or molded fiberglass chairs, to the long wooden benches, everything you touch or sit on imparts an unclean film that contaminates every part of your body. That same sense of uncleanliness hangs heavy in the restroom facilities, causing you to wash your hands a bit longer, and a bit more vigorously, than usual. And, noticing the paper towel supply is exhausted, you have no choice but to wipe your hands on your pant legs or search for toilet paper in a nearby stall.

Prison gates have their own distinct dismal sound. If you imagine the sound of a massive chain dropped from atop a one-story building onto a concrete parking lot, combined with the forceful strike of a heavy-duty hammer on steel pipes, then you might approximate the sound of prison gates. Standing, waiting, as the gears slowly grind to open or shut the gate, you are never quite prepared for the loud hollow echo of *Ka-CHUNG*. It is core-shaking, gut-wrenching, metallic, ominous, and often preceded or followed by an annoying, ear-splitting buzzer. It is a sound that clearly sends the message, "You're in *our* environment now. And *we're* in control." *Ka-CHUNG*. The relatively new gates and bars still have a steely sheen, or, if painted a nondescript color, a certain smoothness about them. In contrast, the decades-old rust-pocked and paint-layered doors and cages seem to hold the oils and grit of the stories embedded in them, but left untold, of inmates' lives spent in disquieted solitude. In some cases, you can sense their acrid metallic bite in your nostrils or on the tip of your tongue.

As volunteer ministers, our journey from the entrance to the chapel is a calculated and structured route, most often facilitated by the chaplain, or corrections officer, who accompanies us. In some institutions, the chapel, or *religious center* (with the purpose of conducting services for all theological persuasions) is a free-standing structure. In other prisons, it is a specified meeting area or substantially sized room within a much larger building. The correction officers' and chaplain's task is to get us from the entrance to the chapel in the safest and easiest way possible, particularly if I am pushing a cumbersome wooden-platform dolly loaded with sound equipment.

Much like our journey through life, the excursion through a prison to the chapel—a lighthouse for transformation and new life—can be a varied and interesting sensory adventure.

At times, the process of getting to our destination takes us on a circuitous course within the building, through a seemingly endless maze of concrete-block hallways which themselves are utilitarian, stark, rather barren, usually painted in monotone off-white colors or neutral pastels. The function of these pedestrian passageways is to transport the inmate population from place to place in an orderly, safe, efficient, and uneventful fashion. The corridors tend to be narrower than you might imagine, giving a feeling of closeness that can be unsettling at times. T-intersections, left and right turns, all punctuated by guard stations, or guards standing or seated on raised chairs, some, with arms folded, in front of locked gates. "You will NOT enter here," their body language commands. As the chaplain leads the way, he will have us pause if inmates approach us from the rear, allowing them to pass by in the cramped space between walls. If prisoners file toward us in a single line, correction officers (or COs) caution them to press the wall and remain quiet. But that does not prevent eye contact, with Fran, my wife and prison ministry partner, who often receives unavoidable glances from men who may not have seen a woman other than a uniformed corrections officer or nurse for weeks…or months…or more.

Even the hallways in the more modern facilities seem decrepit—smelling of old, hard times. If in our journey we walk near a kitchen or cafeteria area, the aroma of food being prepared mixes with the sweat and antiseptic cleaner of the block-and-tile concourse. Fran recently described the odor emanating from one state penitentiary dining hall as best resembling the smell of silage, the vegetable mash that farmers feed their livestock during the cold-weather months. In one particular institution, every time we visit, our meandering journey to the chapel never fails to stimulate our senses. To enter the building that houses the worship center, the chaplain "blesses" Fran and me by providing a short-cut to our destination—entering the area via a loading dock where the facility's refuse is loaded onto garbage trucks for disposal. Sensory overload to the nth degree!

In a prison setting, light provides sight, an essential and critical component of a secure environment. No ambient lighting here. Wherever you travel outside or inside the prison, you are accompanied by the harsh glare of illumination. Shadows, amid dusky darkness, or areas devoid of light, are not the friends of correction officers or of weaker inmates among the strong. Throughout the cell blocks, the hallways, the medical and counseling areas, the prison libraries and meeting rooms, efficient lighting is essential and ever-present. Exterior windows providing natural light are designed with panes filled with narrow, thick safety glass, not easily broken. As darkness falls, the penitentiary takes on an otherworldly appearance, as huge, towering lamps bathe the entirety of the complex in an eerie glow, washing every nook and cranny in ghostly whiteness, broken only by the reflection of the never-ending razor wire.

The noise level is yet another prison ministry phenomenon. Although our volunteer efforts do not allow us to venture into areas that house the most troubled inmates, the din of human voices—some near, some far away—and "prison sounds" is omnipresent. Even the quietest conversation is magnified as it reverberates off the hard surfaces of the hallways, cement walls, cell blocks, and multi-purpose rooms. Add the sounds of salutations called out to friends from a distance, the coarse jesting and laughter of inmates traveling to and fro in small groups, the *Ka-CHUNG* as metal security gates open and close, harsh buzzer prompts and indecipherable messages blasting through loudspeakers, and you have a cacophony of sound—a veritable sonic assault on the ears of the uninitiated. But to the prisoner, this aural tapestry is part of everyday life in the Big House, permeating the mind and the heart ad nauseam.

Inside the walls of some of the newer penitentiaries, the grassy areas with gardens of flowers and shrubs could almost be mistaken for the campus of a community college—complete with a network of concrete sidewalks connecting building to building. But despite the niceties, it quickly becomes apparent that this campus is *not* co-ed. And, even more apparent, these "students" are not decked out in the latest fashions, but instead model ill-fitting, institutional garb—brown or light blue or brilliant orange—often emblazoned with a stenciled "DOC" on the backs of their shirts or coats, signifying their status as "enrollees" in the Department of Corrections. Through the eyes of an outsider, the men and women in the more modern prototype prisons seem to have one distinct advantage over those incarcerated in more ancient facilities because, in spite of everyone's best efforts, the older prisons seem to carry the macadam, dust, and dirt from the outside throughout the interior walkways and common areas making for a far more somber atmosphere.

In my quest to be a more compassionate and others-centered person, I am endeavoring, with God's leading, to become a student of people. To this end, I have found no better a classroom for learning than from Fran, and from prison inmates. And so, as we travel and minister throughout the prison system, I try to be a keen observer. I am discovering that, just as it is on the streets of America, in the schools and workplaces across our nation—*and in our own homes*—countenance and body language can provide powerful insight into a person's life story, or show the condition of his or her spirit in the moment. As Fran and I make our way to and from the prison chapel venues, and during the worship concert/services themselves, God gives me ample opportunity to perfect this gift that I seek. Even at a distance, the inmate's story unfolds. What happenstance caused the hitch in his gait or the pronounced limp as he approaches? Or the prisoner being pushed in a wheelchair—did he earn his "additional confinement" during the commission of the crime that landed him here? Was it part of his life before incarceration, or did it happen during his prison stay? Instances of wondering, such as these, take me back to the Scriptures where, in the Gospel of John, 9:2, the disciples ask Jesus, "Rabbi, who sinned, this man or his parents, that he was born blind?" We would be remiss if we did not include Jesus' reply: "Neither this man nor his parents sinned…but this happened so that the works of God might be displayed in him" (John 9:3). And so it is: the truth for society-at-large—every one of us—is truth for the incarcerated, as well.

The lines and wrinkles, stains and scars on inmates' faces, necks, and arms tell personal accounts of lives gone wrong, of wasted talents, missed opportunities, and bad decisions—the consequences for actions taken. And the tattoos—whether homemade "jailhouse tats," or skillfully and professionally inked, they illustrate, in living color, loves won and lost, fierce allegiances, declared hatred (of oneself or others), humor, and heartfelt desires.

As always, the eyes prove to be the real windows to the soul. And yes, it is distressing to see "dead men walking"—when the spark of life has been replaced by the dull, empty, emotionless stare of one who is broken, who has fallen one last time and failed to get back on his feet.

But in this punitive, sometimes unforgiving environment, it brings joy to my heart to observe, in increasing numbers, the smiles in the eyes of my brothers and sisters on the other side of the wall. To see the "heart-light" shining from their crinkled grins is exhilarating, as inmates—perhaps first glancing at the Bible I carry—nod knowingly to Fran and me. As they extend salutations to the chaplain—"Hi, Rev! See you at the service!"—it is not just about pain, abandonment, injustice. These lives are about the hope that only spiritual transformation can bring to the men and women behind bars, to society in general, and to you and me in particular.

Individuals receiving felony convictions
and/or undergoing imprisonment find
employment exceptionally difficult upon
release, costing the U.S. economy between
$57–67 billion dollars annually in lost
economic output.

(Prison Legal News study 2011)

Chapter Three

PRAYER AND PREPARATION FOR MINISTRY

"Put on the full armor of God…"

(Ephesians 6:11–12)

Our lives are a life-and-death spiritual struggle…*every single day*. While we focus our attention on the people and events that shape our daily existence and dominate the evening news, a fierce battle rages in the spiritual realm with the prize being our very souls. Picture in your mind warring angels and insidious demons in mortal combat, with your eternal future—your ultimate destiny—hanging in the balance. Sense God's angelic vanguard, muscles gleaming in holy righteousness, their powerful, swift swords of the Spirit cleaving through the contorted forms of an unholy hoard. Imagine the hissing, screaming minions of Satan, their fangs dripping with the blood of wounded saints—those who fought back valiantly and tasted victory and those who did not experience the abundant life, never realizing they were even in a battle. This image is the reality of the spiritual warfare that has existed since the fall of man in the Garden of Eden. It remains, today, a continuing conflict, championed by some and dismissed by others as simply stories and fables from a bygone era.

God's Word in the Bible tells you and me to "Be strong in the Lord and in his mighty power. Put on the full armor of God, so that you can take your stand against the devil's schemes. For your struggle is… against the rulers…authorities…powers of this dark world…against the spiritual forces of evil in the heavenlies" (Ephesians 6:1-12 NIV). In the midst of life's commotion, perhaps you have felt the debilitating, and sometimes exhausting, effects of this spiritual tug-of-war, but, for one reason or another, have failed to recognize your trials and tribulations for what they are—opportunities for spiritual growth! Particularly in America, the pinnacle of achievement is "the good life." But what is *good to God* and that which is *good in the eyes of the world* can be vastly different. The real fruit of spiritual goodness involves engaging in ongoing struggle in our lives, developing self-discipline, and maintaining a perseverance that will carry us through "the valley of the shadow of death" to a mountaintop victory. We need to understand and accept that this purging and purifying process leads to righteousness (right-living), holiness, and spiritual maturity—noble human characteristics indeed, and pleasing to almighty God. Unfortunately, these attributes tend to fly in the face of the selfish, self-serving, instant-gratification mindset which pervades much of today's society. And living by the world's standards is a trap we have all fallen into at some point in our lives. Experience, and God's Word, have shown me that if we choose the standard of Jesus Christ—the only perfect man to walk the face of this earth—as *the* measuring rule for our lives, over time we shall see good fruit borne from our labors if we don't grow weary and quit…abandon ship…give up.

In case you assume that your spiritual sojourn is (or will be) "all work and no play," I assure you that God, in His infinite grace and mercy, will provide joy within what can seem like a long arduous journey. True joy may not look like the world's happiness, which tends

18

to be based upon ever-changing situations or circumstances, ideally resolved to directly or indirectly benefit us in some way. What I'm referring to is an unspeakable joy that is soul-deep, something we can *never* attain in and of ourselves. It is the essence of a heartfelt attitude which enables an incarcerated man or woman to truly be "free" while serving a life sentence in a maximum-security penitentiary. Joy based upon the grace and mercy of a God who loves us unconditionally provides opportunity for clarity of thought, even in the midst of chaos—the "renewed mind" that the apostle Paul speaks of in Romans 12:2. It allows an inmate to view his or her surroundings not as a dungeon, but as a mission field. It transforms a prison sentence into a time in which to bless others by extending the gift of service—expecting nothing more than to bring glory to God through their actions and, perhaps, to hear the still, small voice of His Holy Spirit whisper the commendation, "Well done, my good and faithful servant."

This same unadulterated joy can inhabit you, me, or anyone who is "free in the outside world," walking unfettered on the streets of our communities, as opposed to those behind prison walls. It flows from the same fountain which bestows grace and mercy to transgressors who reside behind the gated fortresses of our nation's penal institutions. God is no "respecter of persons;" that is to say, He desires to bless all of His creation, you and me, with "…beauty for ashes, the oil of joy for mourning, the garment of praise for the spirit of heaviness" (Isaiah 61:3)—hope in the face of adversity. All this, so that the human spirit may experience a personal relationship with God, that the tragedies of life might be transformed into triumphs, and that *He* may receive the glory.

I never feel more like I'm going to war than when I am preparing to minister within the prison system. It is then that I cover—no, *immerse*—myself in prayer. And, truthfully, if I saturated my mind and spirit with the same sense of urgency and importance as I do prior to and during my prison visits, I would be far better equipped and empowered for all of my *own* daily activities. What about you? Is prayer simply a lackluster "please and thank-you" casually tossed to God from time to time? Is it a brief blessing of the meal before partaking? If you answered yes to the above questions, undoubtedly you are missing out on an opportunity to tap into life-changing, supernatural power. By *not* utilizing the power of prayer fervently and consistently, you're selling yourself—and God—short.

Have you ever overheard someone say, "We have tried everything else, we might as well pray?" I have heard similar phrases spoken concerning lifestyle or relational issues and requests for healing or intersession in homes, in emergency rooms, in ICUs, and within church sanctuaries and corporate boardrooms. Such statements indicate a lack of understanding regarding the power of prayer and illustrate what I call "backwards thinking." Prayer is not a last resort. It should be our *first line* of both offense and defense when facing any situation that comes our way.

What is prayer? *Webster's Collegiate Dictionary* describes it this way: "Prayer is the offering of adoration, confession, supplication (and) thanksgiving to God." To put this dictionary definition into a spiritual perspective, prayer is nothing more and nothing less than an earnest, heartfelt conversation with the creator of the universe! Imagine the powerful implications as you and I become clear channels for communication with the Maker of all things, all peoples, all nations, and all governments. Our human minds cannot fathom the scope and immensity of that kind of power. But it is there for the asking—to heal the hurts, restore the relationships, answer the tough questions—all by sending out a petition, a request: a prayer.

Throughout our ministry, I have been asked to pray for a given person or for some pressing need. The request is often accompanied by a statement from the individual that he or she wants me to intercede on their behalf because "I don't know how to pray." This often supposes that I, or anyone else who stands in the gap between God and man for another, has some mystical power, some elevated title or special vocabulary that might better convince God to grant their petitions and deliver the desired results. Particularly during my weekly ministry within the county prison system, I encounter young men and women who have no spiritual foundation and, therefore, prayer *is* a foreign concept. After explaining that the power of answered prayer comes from developing and nurturing a personal relationship with God through the shed blood of His Son, Jesus Christ, I then can illustrate the simplicity of the prayer process.

Prayer does *not* have to be an exercise in elaborate, scripture-ridden oratory. I remember a dear man in our church who passed away a number of years ago. He was a retired pastor and missionary and I would always smile when he prayed aloud. The style most comfortable for him might best have been described as "Old King James." To his thinking, there never was such a thing as a "short" prayer and the language he employed was often far beyond the grasp of the common man. He might begin a prayer with, "O gracious and most merciful God, Lord most high, the One who hast made the Earth and all things therein. Heavenly Father, thou dost knowest…" The man could pray! But few others could duplicate the way in which he communicated with God. I'm sure many people listening to him were thinking, "I could *never* pray like that." And that may be true. But the reality remains that, first and foremost, the human heart yearns for love and acceptance…and God knows this. Therefore the style and words used when we come before Him in prayer are not nearly as important as a broken and contrite heart, pleading for healing, hope, and restoration.

Representing the gut-level essence of human need, a prayer could be as simple as, "God, I messed up again. I've tried but I can't change on my own. I need Your help!"

Whether we are free to move within society or incarcerated in an institution, we all embody *the inmate within*. God knows the attitude of our hearts and our intentions, good or bad. With this thought in mind, we should realize that God is *not* some kind of "cosmic vending machine." We cannot put in our "prayer request quarter," pull a lever, and expect Him to deliver the goodies. He alone is God, knowing what is best for us. His timing is perfect, even though it is often out of sync with *our* timing. During a recent prison session, one man seemed quite agitated as we engaged in a group Bible discussion about prayer. When I asked what was troubling him, he said, "I prayed for guidance regarding a family situation last night, and when I woke up this morning, God *still* hadn't answered my prayer!" His expectations for immediacy on his terms are quite normal. In this fast-paced age of technology, we expect—even demand—instant information and response. We enjoy high-speed internet, microwave popcorn, instant mashed potatoes, and fast food at restaurant drive-ins…why shouldn't God keep up with the rest of the world? In truth, God, being God, knows what we need—and what we're going to ask for—before we lift up any of our petitions to Him. Because He is omniscient, or all-knowing, His answer to us is "yes," "no," or sometimes "wait." But, even within the context of our quest for spiritual maturity, *are we willing to wait?* I was able to assure my impatient inmate-friend that God was not "asleep at the wheel." Describing, in the most general terms, a relational conflict within my own family, I explained how the answer to prayer might not be revealed for days, weeks, months, or even years. In my personal situation, a resolution began to be revealed after two decades had passed—twenty-plus years of prayer! And the answer did not present itself because the original circumstances of the conflict had changed; God's revealed insight came only after I had changed within the context of the situation! This was one of the greatest spiritual lessons of my life.

The devil is a liar and the father of all lies. A discredited angel, banished from heaven, he hates God. Because we, as God's prized possessions, are made in the image of God, the enemy hates us as well, seeking to destroy the human race by any means necessary. Through the death and resurrection of God's Son, Jesus Christ, as the only suitable substitute for the sins of mankind, the devil is a defeated foe. But even in defeat, Satan is like a rabid, snarling dog on a leash, with God pulling the choke-chain. For reasons far beyond our earthly understanding, the devil has been allowed a period of time to roam the Earth. Understanding this, we must "Be alert and of sober mind. Your enemy the devil prowls around like a roaring lion looking for someone to devour" (1 Peter 5:8).

Without prayerful protection and proper spiritual preparation, this defeated foe can still successfully plant seeds of doubt or inadequacy in our minds in an attempt to thwart our best efforts at living out our faith through ministry, or through life in general. In later chapters, I will reference prayer concepts modeled, within the *context* of ministry, as essential spiritual tools to bring hope to incarcerated men and women *inside* or *outside* the steely, confining penitentiary gates. In the meantime, you and I can rest in the knowledge that "The effective, fervent prayer of a righteous man avails much" (James 5:16). Prayerful application of the Word of God readies us for anything life may throw at us. It covers all eventualities. Prayer is the difference between you and me engaging in spiritual warfare fully-enveloped in a suit of protective armor (Ephesians 6:10-18) versus running headlong into the fray in nothing but our "birthday suits." Spiritual nakedness will inevitably lead to spiritual death, which is separation from God.

Even if we have not done so in the past, *now* is the time to run this race we call life wearing the proper "earthly attire."

In the next chapter, we will take a closer look at that segment of the population which *could* be—*should* be—included in our prayers: incarcerated men and women.

When studying regional trends for long-range prison expansion, developers rely on the time-worn statistic that boys without fathers are 300% more likely to experience incarceration.

Chapter Four

WHO ARE THESE PEOPLE? PRISON INMATES

"…I perceive that God is no respecter of persons."

(Acts 10:34)

Todd started life as a basically good kid in a challenging situation. A fair-skinned, baby-faced, lanky lad of Irish descent, he was known for the unruly mop of bright auburn hair that earned him the nickname *Mickey Red*. Growing up in the mean, blue-collar streets of South Philadelphia in a single-parent home was tough, but his mom was tougher. She kept Todd and his younger brother in line, holding down two jobs to make ends meet. Todd was a bright boy, a good student when he decided to attend school. But the lure of the perceived "good life" dulled his appetite for education. He dropped out of high school in his senior year. When he wasn't working a part-time job at the local pub, Todd spent much of his free time drinking cheap whiskey and getting high with the neighborhood Irish Mafia wannabes. When this bunch got together, trouble always seemed to follow. That trouble showed up as entries on Todd's lengthening rap sheet: drunk and disorderly, petty theft, drug possession.

It was a sweltering August evening and the city was restless. The stifling heat, compounded by inexorable boredom, was bringing out the crazy in people. Todd's boys were no exception. Low on cash and short on patience, a plan was quickly hatched to pull off a diversionary heist at a liquor store across town. Booze only, no stupid stuff, was the plan. Mickey Red, being the youngest in the gang of four, was the designated driver—the "getaway man."

Motoring slowly to their destination in a chopped and channeled '57 Chevy, they waited…and waited some more, as the last of several customers vacated the store. Ian, the undisputed leader, ordered his buddies to exit the vehicle and follow him inside. The plan was simple: The partners-in-crime would fan out, each taking an aisle. Ian would purchase a bottle of cheap wine, pay for it, and engage the clerk in casual conversation. His cohorts would hide several of the flatter, flask-type liquor bottles in the waistbands of their pants, under their shirts, and nonchalantly exit the store. But something went horribly wrong. As one of the men reached for the door handle, a smooth, slippery whiskey bottle squirted from beneath his belt, hit the linoleum floor, and exploded. The night clerk, not to be played for a fool, cursed the inept thieves and pulled a baseball bat from beneath the counter. In a panic, Ian produced *his* protection: a 45-special which he carried, but never used—until tonight. "Pop-pop-pop." Three slugs ripped into the chest of the liquor-store clerk. The force of the blasts propelled him backwards, blood spurting from the fatal wounds. He crashed to the floor in a lifeless heap. Pausing, but only for a second, Ian ran from the liquor store, joining the others in the waiting car. Todd jammed the Chevy into gear. With lake pipes roaring, and squealing tires scorching the asphalt, they careened out of the parking lot. Unfortunately, their hasty departure was seen in its entirety by a local beat cop on night patrol. He ran into the store, witnessed the carnage, and immediately issued an all-points bulletin, including a description of the vehicle. Three blocks later, the Irish Boys were pulled over, surrounded by an army of armed police officers, and taken into custody. The jig was up. Todd's sentence for accessory to murder was life in prison with no chance of parole.

Julie lived an exciting life. The pace was hectic, but she had learned to manage her time wisely. The future was nothing but bright. Blond-haired, blue-eyed and beautiful, she had been voted homecoming queen during her senior year and was voted *Most Likely to Succeed* in the class yearbook. She was an A-student, captain of the cheerleading squad, and excelled in track and field. She had just received word of her acceptance to a prestigious division-one university, which included a scholarship for both her academic prowess and her athletic abilities. Life was good indeed. And to celebrate, she invited her many friends to a graduation party which was touted as "the blow-out event of the year."

Julie's dad was a very successful architect. Her mother was a tenured English professor at the local community college. They lived in a suburban four-bedroom, three-bath, three-car garage, custom-built home, wonderfully secluded in the center of four forested acres. Since trust had always been a mainstay of Julie's relationship with her parents, she asked that her folks give her and her invited guests "some space" during the evening's festivities. They agreed. After all, these were A-list kids from good homes. Not riff-raff. No stoners or druggies. These were talented athletes and scholars, prepared to make their mark on the world.

With Julie's plans in place, the day of the graduation celebration was finally at hand. Musicians—and best friends—from her favorite local band came at about 5 p.m. to set up their equipment and check the sound. Catered food arrived. Word had spread through social media that this was a B.Y.O.B. affair. And so they came. First to arrive were Julie's inner circle, followed by dozens more classmates. As the party progressed, hundreds of young men and women celebrated, ate, drank, and danced. The sweet smell of weed permeated the air. Somebody brought ecstasy and soon a number of partygoers were experiencing the sights and sounds through an enhanced level of consciousness. And Julie had her own surprise—a pharmaceutical punchbowl of delights that she placed prominently on the serving table. She and some friends had pilfered medications and pills from medicine cabinets, family prescriptions, and the athletic training room at the high school. Xanax, Vicodin, Demerol, Hydrocodone, OxyContin, in splendid colors, shapes, and sizes, all arrayed in a clear plastic bowl. Several of the partygoers tentatively sampled a pill or two, until one bold young man—a college-bound all-state running back—tossed a handful into his mouth and washed them down with a beer chaser. The results were quick and deadly. As the toxic concoction short-circuited his heart and then his brain, he choked, shook violently, and with his eyes rolled back in his head, fell backwards—his skull sounding like a ripe melon as it struck full force onto the stone patio. A silvery, white foam bubbled from the corner of his mouth. As the star athlete twitched helplessly, the scene erupted into chaos. Julie freaked out, sobbing uncontrollably. Someone called 911. The police and paramedics arrived as kids ran for their vehicles or dashed off into the woods to avoid detection, or simply stood like statues in shock and disbelief.

Julie did not go to college that year. She began serving a sentence of two-to-four years for manslaughter in a state penitentiary for women.

Evil does not always look sinister. Just as you can't judge the proverbial book by its cover, neither can you judge a prison inmate by his or her appearance. Appearances can be very deceiving. If asked to create a composite image of an "evil" person in our mind's eye, chances are you and I would compose a similar picture. The visage of the undesirable man would have a drawn look; a swarthy complexion, sunken cheeks, weathered face adorned with an unkempt stubble of beard. Lips pursed and thin; nose narrow and slanted; dark, hollow eyes, no more than slits beneath bushy brows; and perhaps a tale-telling scar, slashing across the facescape for good measure. Shaggy, dirty locks, cascading to the shoulders, might complete our composite sketch. Certainly, this sinister image might represent *one* of the faces of evil, but it is by no means a complete personification.

Here is a case-in-point: Ted Bundy was a handsome, clean-cut, educated, articulate young man, with an ingratiating way that made it easy for him to meet and build relationships with members of the opposite sex. That is why, throughout the 1970s, he was able to contact, engage, rape, and murder at least thirty-six young women with some authorities believing that the number tortured and killed exceeded one hundred. The victims' sometimes decapitated or dismembered remains underscored a hellish pattern of carnage that crisscrossed the United States. Ted Bundy—the personification of evil with a "cherub's face"— was executed in Florida's electric chair in 1989. Evil does not always look sinister.

Expanding this idea to include a spiritual perspective, if you picture in your mind the most evil character throughout the ages, you might end up with a mental image of the devil, or Satan—whatever that fallen angel might look like to you. The devil is often comically portrayed as a fire-red nymph with cloven hooves, pointy ears, arched eyebrows, "Snidely Whiplash" mustache, and a hollow, dreadful laugh. Throw in some flames and the image is complete. This Hollywood-light portrayal of our deadly spiritual foe could lull the uninitiated into a false sense of security. So much so that we might relegate the devil to a simple annoyance, not even worthy of our awareness. Perhaps if you and I would picture this "harbinger of hate" as the most ghastly, monstrous, sulfur-spewing hell-hound our minds could imagine, we might better capture his truly sinister nature and intent. In the Bible, 1 Peter 5:8 states, "Be alert and of sober mind. Your enemy the devil prowls around like a roaring lion looking for someone to devour." Now that's evil *and* sinister!

But Satan, defeated foe that he may be, is also described in Scripture as a master of disguise, in keeping with his crafty, lying, destructive character. In Genesis 3:1, Satan disguises himself as a serpent—at that time, one of God's good and lovely creatures. Being pleasant to the eye, he is able to approach Eve, taking advantage of her innocence. Then he manipulates the situation so that she and Adam are led into rebellion in defiance of God's commands. Elsewhere in Scripture (2 Corinthians 11:14) Satan masquerades as an "angel of light"—a beautiful, luminous image—to carry out his dirty work.

So what on earth does all this have to do with prison inmates? Simply this: We can imagine the most horrid image of an evil *person* and totally miss the mark.

Incarcerated men and women represent a wide spectrum of humanity. As God has introduced me to imprisoned individuals within the context of ministry, it has become readily apparent to me that the stereotype of the down-and-out convict is but a small sample of the inmate population. Certainly, there are the habitual offenders—the career criminals who almost seem compelled to live life within the prison walls. But just as certainly as I have encountered the repeat offender, God has given me "divine appointments" with the white-collar professional businessman who, while driving drunk, was involved in an accident causing the serious injury of another; the jobless man who was caught stealing food from a grocery store; the young computer whiz who hacked into a financial system and transferred funds to his own account; the young wife and mother who, as a result of a prescription-drug dependency, stole medications and forged scripts at the local pharmacy, selling a portion to others and pocketing the proceeds.

A pastor friend of mine once said, "There are plenty of really intelligent people in prison." And such is the case.

Currently, within the prison system, there is another phenomenon that is increasingly more evident, even to the chronologically-older inmates (the "old heads") who inhabit our penal institutions. Younger, hard-hearted, unrepentant men and women continue to enter the system who seem not only disenfranchised from society-at-large, but appear mentally disconnected from the realities of the world around them. Examples might be the teenage boy who claims, "I *had* to shoot him; he looked at me wrong," or the girls charged with what society would traditionally consider "male crimes" such as aggravated assault, robbery, and murder. Far too many of the young people in prison today show the ravages of severely wounded spirits and a lack of spiritual foundation that manifests itself in a variety of ways, including bizarre and extremely antisocial behavior.

With the disintegration of the traditional family and the continual blurring of the lines between what is fundamentally right and wrong in society, "damaged goods" in the form of lost and needy people grows. To further compound the situation, mandated sentencing for certain categories of crime within the past several decades has resulted in an increased prison population that not only taxes the penal system's ability to adequately house offenders, but has increased the range of needed services (physical, mental, social, and spiritual), thus impeding the system's ability to rehabilitate incarcerated men and women.

That being said, the ministry to which God has called me—and may be calling you—can be a haven of hope to those behind bars. If the church is, in fact, a hospital for broken lives of all sorts, perhaps your concerns for others—translated into works of some sort—will be a catalyst to change the wounded hearts of those within your sphere of influence. As you continue to seek more information and knowledge regarding real life within the prison walls, you will find those who:

- are anywhere from eighteen to eighty years old.
- may be male or female or even in the midst of gender reassignment.
- are extremely intelligent and those who are mentally deficient.
- are highly educated and those who cannot read or write.
- are gifted in speech, music, or the arts and others who seemingly have little talent, focus, or initiative.

- have a genuine, heartfelt, personal relationship with God the Father, who are paying the price for their transgressions.
- can quote Scripture chapter and verse and engage in (sometimes exhaustive) spiritual conversations, having "head knowledge," but whose hearts are far from God.
- have never opened a Bible and have no concept of spiritual truths.

In other words, the prison population is a microcosm of the world around us! There is the good, the bad, and the ugly.

In the next chapter, we will begin to explore the darker side of the prison experience.

If the stress of life on the "outside"
becomes unbearable—or with the onset
of colder weather—certain habitual
offenders will violate parole or purposely
reoffend, so they may enjoy the "comforts"
of a prison environment.

Chapter Five

THE REALITY: PRISON IS A DANGEROUS PLACE

"Yea, though I walk through the valley of the shadow of death, I will fear no evil: for thou art with me..."

(Psalm 23:4)

The world around us is increasingly dangerous. International and domestic terrorism, school attacks, home invasions, robberies on the street in broad daylight, drive-by shootings, domestic violence, physical and sexual abuse—horrific crime is all around us. It has invaded our communities, we read about it in our daily papers, and we see the stories in living color on the nightly news. Chances are, within our own family or circle of acquaintances, we know people who have been victims of violent crime, as well as those who may have been perpetrators. Perhaps you, yourself, have been a victim.

Politicians and pundits may choose to debate the causes and effects of this precipitous upsurge in crime, but the reality is that the days of the *Leave It to Beaver* and *Father Knows Best* television-perfect families are, in most cases, long gone (although there are those who hold on to the belief that, in the spiritual scheme of things, our heavenly Father does, indeed, know what is best for His children). Within the past several decades, the disintegration of the traditional family, the breakdown of moral values and spiritual mores, the decline of world-leading nations, and the "dumbing-down" of America, in particular, have all contributed to an international societal erosion that will have repercussions on our country and the world-at-large for decades, if not centuries.

As a people, particularly within the United States, it would seem that our worldview is being rewritten. For those of us growing up in the post-World-War-II generation, more often than not, there existed a firm sense of right and wrong. As a child, when you did the "right thing" you were rewarded; when you chose to pursue the "wrong thing," you were punished. There were consequences for actions. Two-parent households were the rule, not the exception. And when a young boy or girl transgressed in some way outside the home, you could be fairly certain that word would reach his or her parents and appropriate action would be taken. There was community pride and a sense of belonging to something great. On a larger scale it might be labeled *patriotism*. On a more intimate scale, it might be defined as a security fostered by structured rules and regulations both in the home and within society. Respect was given to parents, teachers, police and law enforcement officials, and others in authority.

Just like the industrious ants in Proverbs 6:6–8, people worked hard for a living, judiciously spending, avoiding extraordinary debt, and saving for the hard times. Certainly inequities existed within society, but government handouts leading to a welfare mentality were the exception rather than the norm. People did *not* expect something for nothing. We were willing to labor and wait for the benefits that would result from our efforts.

A prevailing foundational belief in a creator fostered not only an appreciation for life but a sense that each unique, individual human being was made by God for a purpose: That every life was precious and had meaning. This belief produced a faith in things not seen and gave hope, even to those who struggled.

Fast forward to today. "Right" has become whatever is expedient to the individual for achieving a self-centered agenda. Notice I didn't use the word "goal" because that would connote a sense of purpose and planning, which are often lacking in today's immediate-gratification society. Microwave popcorn, instant mashed potatoes, endemic credit-card debt superseding frugal cash purchases. Principles and actions which would have been considered "wrong" in years gone by have been relegated to "fifty shades of grey." Our moral fiber is decaying, and with it our sense of purpose…and hope.

The sanctity of marriage is now too often replaced by co-habitation, with an increasing number of children being born out of wedlock. Divorce among all married couples consistently holds at 50%, resulting in a burgeoning proportion of single-parent homes, most with mothers holding down the fort and no father present. Abortion has become a "healthcare choice"—a convenience. And now, euthanasia—the legal killing of our elderly—is allowed in an increasing number of states. Suicide rates will continue to escalate as a result. Why? If a child's life can be terminated, if an elderly person can be disposed of when he or she is considered a burden, what message does this send to our young people about their self-worth?

Respect for authority in the home, in schools, in the workplace, and throughout the legal and political systems is at an all-time low. Too many children and young adults in our current culture have no proper esteem for themselves. This can breed confusion and anger in their own minds and hearts, as well as a lack of respect for others—particularly those perceived as authority figures. "Who am I and where do I fit into this world?" *"Do* I fit into this world?" In our high-tech society, where global connectivity can be achieved in seconds, we, as a people, are more disconnected than ever. The result: hopelessness, helplessness and a suicide rate among teens and young adults that is unprecedented in our history.

The events we see and hear about on the nightly news are simply symptoms of a far greater malaise—a *spiritual* battle for the hearts and souls of men and women around the world. A war that is being waged in the heavenly realm is manifesting itself on planet Earth. Good versus evil, right versus wrong, light versus darkness. And at the center of the struggle: hardened hearts of a people who are, too often, far from the heart of God. In our quest for autonomy, independence, and "freedom," many of us have lost our way. We approach life as best we can, in our own limited capacities, without *spiritual* strength, without hope of anything better than the day before. *"The heart is deceitful above all things and beyond cure. Who can understand it?"* And the answer: *"I the Lord search the heart and examine the mind, to reward each person according to their conduct, according to what their deeds deserve"* (Jeremiah 17:9-10).

The prison experience is a microcosm of society-at-large. Therefore, within the prison system we find a mirror society *within* society. Behind the concrete walls, there is a world replete with its own code of conduct, rules and regulations, and mores for social order. You and I can be armed with our God-given best intentions, the power of prayer, and the finest training available, but if we choose to enter *any* penal institution—as a visitor, as a volunteer, or even as a paid staff member—we must understand that we are entering a place where there is darkness on many levels. All prisons are populated, to some degree, with individuals who are manipulative, antisocial, impulsive, controlled by addictive behaviors, and who may be mentally or spiritually oppressed. Stressors within the prison environment may intensify any negative tendencies that an individual may have exhibited prior to incarceration. That being said, the hostile prison environment also makes for an intriguing backdrop against which God changes minds and hearts as only He can!

Picture the hottest, most humid, most uncomfortable day you have ever experienced. I guarantee you, this day was worse! It was a stifling, sweltering mid-August afternoon. Fran and I were visiting an institution which held a variety of criminals, including immigration violators and/or those who were to be deported after serving their sentences for any number of misdeeds. The prison chaplain met us at the entrance and informed us that our "concert/service" would take place in an open-air exercise yard. Now, the process of unloading our van and transporting the sound equipment into the prison got underway. The simple act of pushing an overloaded, wooden platform dolly left me soaked to the core. My short-sleeved, cotton-print Hawaiian shirt was drenched. Sweat trickled down my back and under the waistband of my khaki slacks. Fran, although dressed for a summer day, looked equally uncomfortable, very much like a colorful, wilted flower.

We were ushered into a razor-wire-enclosed courtyard where we set up our power unit, mixing board, and speakers for the service. The heat was magnified to an almost unbearable level by the midday sun, reflecting directly off the hard, concrete. The sweat that had been a trickle now was a river flowing beneath my clothing. The temperature was easily 110-degrees. Armed guards patrolled fifteen feet above us, traversing a maze of catwalks. Our host chaplain seemed uneasy, especially because a female (Fran) would be sitting behind the soundboard. He mentioned his concern several times. The soundboard was the only physical barrier between her and the "invited guests": the prisoners.

As approximately eighty men entered the enclosure I began to understand the chaplain's trepidation. It seemed that the inmates were grouped into gangs: the white skinheads, Caribbean blacks, Asian offenders, Puerto Ricans (not to be confused with the Mexican Hispanics). In they came dressed in sweaty, smelly prison garb—many adorned with ornate gang-related tattoos— segregating themselves, one faction from the other. Observing our motley-crew audience, Fran and I prepared to minister to what looked like a "United Nations of Mayhem!" I distinctly remember the officer-in-charge screaming a terse warning to the men to behave—or else. And then, in a much more conciliatory tone, he invited them to "enjoy the service." To escape the oppressive heat, many of the inmates clung close to a building wall, seeking comfort in the few shady areas beyond the sun's glare. I thought they were too far away from me to communicate effectively, but seeing the rag-tag group hugging the shadows, God brought such an appropriate verse to mind that I couldn't help but smile: *"This is the verdict: Light has come into the world, but people loved darkness instead of light because their deeds were evil"* (John 3:19).

Nothing seemed right about this whole scenario. There appeared to be absolutely no elements in our favor. And yet, in the midst of what might be considered chaos, I felt a surge of power and exaltation course through my being as God gave me a glimpse of His presence and a foretaste of things He had in store for the gathered assembly on that sizzling-hot and humid afternoon.

The chaplain was more uneasy than ever. But I was ready-to-roll! I informed those forgotten malcontents that Fran and I had a secret weapon that could change their lives forever. Through the shed blood, death, and resurrection of Jesus Christ, their sins were forgiven and they could find release from their captivity! I sang several songs to set the tone, and then unveiled the mystery of "new life" that was as much for *my* benefit as it was for the prisoners in the yard. That day, in a sweltering concrete pit, approximately twenty men gave their lives to Jesus Christ and were set free for eternity. Praise the Lord!

Another instance of God working in unexpected ways involved a young lady from a supporting church who asked us about the possibility of sampling prison ministry at the community level. We invited her to join us for two concert/services scheduled at the county jail. Her husband, who seemed less enthusiastic about the adventure than she was, agreed to accompany her for moral support. We obtained proper clearance for the couple and, on the appointed Saturday evening, entered the jail together, proceeding to the chapel area where we unpacked and set up our equipment. During the first session we ministered to the female inmates. The couple observed the dynamics of the service, seated with Fran at the back of the room behind the mixing-board table. As I sang and presented a message of hope, healing, and forgiveness, several ladies tearfully responded. As our friend's husband continued to adjust to the surroundings, I could see by her countenance that his wife was being impacted in a positive way by the emotional response of the incarcerated women to the Gospel message.

Soon after the women left the room we set up additional chairs to accommodate a larger group of male inmates who had been called for the second service. Things went off without a hitch until, about half-way through my message to the men, the "squawk box" in the chapel erupted with code-worded emergency warnings to the corrections officers. The inmates in the room buzzed with anticipation and wariness, as a CO opened the door and very succinctly informed **all of us** to remain in the room. The men were not to move from their seats. Through a series of plate glass windows, we could observe officers at the ready lining the hallway. (I found out later there had been a disruption involving prisoners in one of the cell blocks.) Seeing the faces of our guests from my chapel-pulpit vantage point, I thought, *they must be scared out of their minds.* But things settled down, the danger passed, the all-clear signal was given, and the inmates and I prayed over the situation. At the completion of the Gospel presentation, several men professed a new-found faith in the One who made them. It was, indeed, a fruitful evening!

As we packed up the equipment in preparation for being "released" from the prison, our female guest expressed her concern over the lockdown. To ease her mind, I replied, "Nothing to worry about, stuff like that happens all the time." It was not until months later, when we were reliving this adventure, that I confessed that the incident was a one-time occurrence that we had never experienced before or since. I shared this information with her because I *did* want my "county jail guest" to be cognizant of the reality that things sometimes do not go according to plan, but I did *not* want her to be fearful when looking back on her prison ministry experience. Rather, I wanted the young lady see how God—in His infinite grace and mercy—is able to work through the most unforeseen circumstances to accomplish His will.

Worshipping God one minute, flying fists and lunging bodies the next! That was the scene during a rather recent visit to a facility for adjudicated teens. As the service commenced, one young man in particular was being very demonstrative (and very attention-getting) during the praise-and-worship time. His actions were both distracting and annoying to those around him. Suddenly, one of the other attendees launched himself across the chapel pew, swinging wildly at the offending teenager. Thankfully, the counselors subdued the attacker before any real physical damage could be done. Both boys were removed from the room and it gave me an opportunity to explain to the rest how the enemy of our souls can and will use any means necessary to distract us from giving praise and honor to our Father in heaven. The incident definitely provided a "teachable moment," whereby those in attendance could see the consequences of unbridled emotions leading to a lack of self-control. The teens *also* experienced how the power of God could restore serenity and calm in the midst of a chaotic situation. Hopefully, these life-lessons will be remembered and translated in their world outside the facility upon release.

Whether you are engaged in active ministry or simply visiting an incarcerated person, when we step within the confines of a prison, we have entered into a very dangerous place. Both generic and clearance-specific materials issued by prison officials make that reality crystal clear. In many prisons, "ministry volunteers"—such as Fran and me—must sign a waiver stating that the facility is not responsible for our health and welfare. In the most extreme hostage situations, the rule-of-thumb is that prison administrators are limited as to what can be negotiated for, or promised to, inmates—even when staff or prison visitors' lives are at risk. Several examples of non-negotiable requests would be inmate amnesty or the delivery of drugs or other illegal substances into the prison.

Some prison layouts—particularly at the county level—are such that volunteers are not always in the immediate presence of a corrections officer while carrying out their duties. In such instances, particularly when the chaplain is not present, a "panic button" (personal security alarm) may be issued to the ministry volunteer to summon help if necessary. Once activated, this signal indicates an emergency response situation and immediately summons officers from that section of the facility. You may think that such a security device is a small comfort given how quickly an incident might escalate—and you are absolutely correct! That's why Fran and I specifically request that a corrections officer be present within the chapel or just outside the door during our services.

An active, operational faith that produces supernatural confidence and boldness beyond our own bravado is an essential tool for someone who wishes to be a Christ----like vessel behind prison bars. But, at the same time, the prison minister must know when to temper boldness with humility, meekness (which is extraordinary strength under the control of God), and even a sense of humor as he navigates his way through the ever-changing scenarios of institutional life.

In later chapters, a number of the how-to aspects of effective ministry will be examined in more detail. That being said, we must realize that those spiritual attributes which "work" behind the bars of penal institutions are the *same* principles readily available for you and me to use *outside* the prison walls—in the ever-darkening, dangerous world in which *we* live!

I am thoroughly convinced that God has provided all of us with a divinely-inspired handbook for living. I see the information, instruction, and illustrative teaching within the Bible as life-giving and people-changing when read, studied and *applied* to real-world situations. Wisdom and discernment, developed over time, can provide a firm foundation from which to operate with confidence and victory, whether we are navigating our way through the streets of a city or the corridors of a state penitentiary.

For those who choose to receive the Word of God as truth, He will continually reveal His sovereignty in circumstances which might seem totally out of our control. For Fran and me specifically, He has nurtured a spirit of expectancy—even in the midst of what might be considered uncertain or perilous situations—while cultivating a sense of flexibility and preparation for the unexpected. And, within the framework of ministry, God has given us the opportunity to deliver a life-changing message of redemption to those behind prison walls.

Prison ministry has fueled a clear and compelling purpose in our lives. We have seen God work miracles in the hearts of inmates who have now found a relationship with Him through faith in Jesus Christ. Perhaps, as I did so many years ago, you need an answer to the question, "There must be something more to life than this. How in the world can I fill this hole in *my* soul?" Or, having answered that question through a growing relationship with our heavenly Father, you may be wondering how God can use *you* to help change the lives of others who struggle to find meaning in an ever-darkening world. As you seek direction, remember this—bondage and imprisonment exist inside *and* outside the penitentiary walls. And know that you can make a difference as you allow yourself to be continually shaped by the Master Potter to become a vessel God can use to help provide spiritual nourishment to fellow human beings in need.

You have tasted a sample of what prison ministry can be and how it is able to impact the human heart. Now, if you're ready, let's make an even more intimate inspection of God's handiwork within the context of ministry to incarcerated men and women.

In El Salvador, the notorious gang Mara Salvatrucha (MS-13) run their own prison! Army and prison guards patrol the perimeter, to insure that no inmates breach the facility's outer gates.

Chapter Six

A MINISTRY SERVICE: A VIEW INSIDE THE PRISON WALLS

"Preach the Word; be prepared in season and out of season; correct, rebuke and encourage—with great patience and careful instruction."

(2 Timothy 4:2)

*I*magine for a moment, as Shakespeare so eloquently expressed in the play *As You Like It,* that "All the world's a stage, and all the men and women merely players. They have their exits and their entrances…" This intriguing idea can apply to all of us in our lives, and it is no different within the prison system. Incarcerated men and women, living life each day as best they can, all have their part to play on a world-wide stage.

Setting the scene…the actor has totally captured the essence of his character. His wardrobe transports the audience to a unique place and time. The voice, strong and bold, rises and falls in flawless dialect, providing color and nuance to the spoken words. Prowling the stage with authority, the thespian breathes life into the backdrops and scenery, ushering the expectant audience into a world far beyond their cushioned theater seats. His eyes scan the crowd, drawing the viewers irrevocably into his world. The audience is enchanted…enthralled. They are witnessing a masterpiece performance.

Soft, lilting notes from an unseen orchestra cue the stage, as a pin dot of light pierces the darkness, revealing the solitary chanteuse. As she opens her mouth, a delicate, breathy, almost plaintive cry fills the room—alerting the audience that something very special is about to unfold. The songstress weaves her story in a tapestry of lyrics and melody. The music accompanies her every move, ebbing and flowing like waves crashing onto a rock jetty, then spilling over sparkling sand. Emotion increases…the sonic flood escalates as a wash of color reveals singers in a background chorus, emerging from the shadows, swaying, from side to side, as if in a trance. In climactic sound and fury, the artist completes her musical journey. The crowd—unable to remain seated—erupts in a return chorus of adulation and applause, their very souls touched by what they have just seen and heard.

Think back to a few of those special moments in your life when, after seeing a silver-screen hero rescue the native villagers from the lava-spewing destruction of an erupting volcano, you burst from the theater, determined to do something equally as great in your life. Beyond saving a village, you were determined to—somehow, some way—save the world! Or, after the concert of a lifetime, as you remained glued to your seat, long after most of the crowd had gone, trying to sort out the tangle of emotions that left you totally undone. Crying one moment, laughing the next, you marveled at how one simple performance could so profoundly impact and energize your soul.

Music and the spoken word, presented with excellence, honesty, and passion, have the power to touch and affect the human heart in ways that are beyond our imagination. Within the context of ministry, these performance elements—humanly enacted, while under divine direction—create an even more potent catalyst for positive, and eternal, change. When the topic turns to building relationships and connecting with prison inmates, the power of the spoken word in ministering to minds and hearts seeking something more in life, is the key to reaching men and women at their deepest level of need.

Ministry, when used as an action verb, means many things to many different people. In the broadest sense, according to the *Random House Dictionary,* the word *ministry* refers to "the service, functions, or profession of a minister of religion." This definition certainly provides a great amount of latitude in both the conceptualization *and* application of this category of service to humankind. For some, ministry may present itself as a form of functional, hands-on service. Such activities might include, but certainly would not be limited to, providing food for the hungry, counseling to the oppressed, shelter for the homeless, or job-skills training for the disadvantaged. In these illustrations, the minister would exemplify the mandate that you and I should be "the hands and feet of (Jesus) Christ"—one body composed of many working parts, each divinely arranged to be of use to the Kingdom of God (See 1 Corinthians 12).

In later chapters we will discuss different modes of ministry but, for the time being, we will concentrate our thoughts on the idea of religious services as it affects the spiritual hearts and lives of the incarcerated. The incarcerated—those who have transgressed the laws of society and are now paying the price of restricted freedom—are not "losers," but may be lost for the moment in a world beyond their control.

Within the realm of such services, those of us willing to embrace the title of *minister* certainly are not without outstanding material with which to carry out our mission. You and I have been provided with an otherworldly manuscript, authored by the One who created all things—every word, every note and melody. His is the "breath of life," which activates all things He has created. God is the author and ruler, or governor, of this world and all it contains—all peoples, all nations, all social and political entities. "To whom will you compare me? Or who is my equal?" says the Holy One (Isaiah 40:25). His Word, as contained in the Bible—and by whatever means it is presented—illustrates and illuminates the greatest story ever told. For those of us actively engaged on the front line of ministry, as well as those of us serving in an ancillary or supporting role, this should be all the inspiration we need to respond in obedience to God's call in our lives. And if more motivation to minister, in some way, *is* needed, it is encouraging to know that the truth of God's Word can create a divine connection *inside* or *outside* prison walls. That truly should be a life-giving realization because, if you think about it, we are *all* held captive, in some kind of prison, in one way or another.

The sacrifice of God's only-begotten Son, Jesus Christ provides a backdrop and current storyline for every human being who has spiritual eyes to see, ears to hear, and a heart to receive the Gospel message. The words describing the power of Jesus Christ's death and resurrection over the "sin that so easily besets us" are akin to the colors on an artist's palette before he or she begins creating a new work on a blank canvas. Jesus is the propitiation for our sin; He is the atonement ("At-One-Ment") for sin; God's Son is the only suitable substitute for our sinful state—the only one qualified, if you will, to stand in the gap between carnal man and a holy God.

Conveying this good news to incarcerated men and women is vital. When a spiritual awakening or renewal within an individual prisoner takes place, not only are there eternal rewards, there are earthly dividends as well. Inmates can experience a personal sense of peace and well-being that allows for greater mental stability and emotional health within the stressful prison environment. Another serendipitous benefit of even one prisoner's transformed life is the ripple effect that a new Christian's behavior can have on other inmates. Fellow prisoners will notice the changed inmate's non-traditional, Christlike reactions to the circumstances, situations and stressors of prison life. These ripples can even extend to the prison's corrections officers, staff, and administration. And the even *greater* good news for you and me is that this creative, flowing spiritual renewal process works just as effectively in the world *outside* the prison as it does for the *Inmate Within*. So there *is* hope…for *all* of us!

Just as an artist strives to captivate his audience intellectually and emotionally, so we, as spiritual ambassadors—desiring to be God's most excellent representatives—should be intent and intentional in our efforts to capture *our* audience within the context of prison ministry. *Do you see the irony in this mission?* You and I may be called upon to speak new life into the hearts of men and women who are hurting, hopeless, hapless, and helpless to change without the guidance of God's Holy Spirit. And within the county jail or state and federal penitentiaries, we who minister do so—literally and figuratively—to a "captive audience," encouraging men and women to choose freedom for eternity, even while they are residing in iron cages! By rising to this challenge, you and I accept the responsibility to be agents of change. Through word or deed, God's divine direction, combined with our own perspiration, can provide the *inspiration* for incarcerated men and women to alter the spiritual topography of their world and the *entire* world—one heart at a time.

So what *does* a typical prison ministry service really look like? The answer may surprise you, because the celebration may be very similar to a praise-and-worship gathering at your local church. The tone and personality of any given religious service or volunteer session within the prison system is really determined by the spirit, talents, and preferences—coupled with God-given discernment—of the service provider. Simply put, the message and methodology of the ministry and ministers should complement the occasion.

For some, a ministry service might comprise several hymns sung by the guest volunteers and/or the inmates, a capella or accompanied by a guitar, piano, or electronic keyboard. The songs, "setting the table" for the Word of God, might be followed by an evangelical or lifestyle teaching message. In some instances, a choir of inmates who are part of a ministry team assisting the chaplain, might provide the music, followed by the visiting minister's sermon. Or a volunteer organization might enter a given facility with a full-blown band or drama team to execute the service from start to finish. Although man-made restrictions limit, to some degree, what can transpire behind penitentiary walls, God's creative sparks are constantly ignited within the context of prison ministry.

To give you a more organic, nitty-gritty example of what an actual prison event might look like, may I invite you to join us for a day-in-the-life of SonPower Ministries, as Pete and Fran Einstein prepare for and administer a "concert/service" at a state penitentiary.

(Advance preparation, such as providing proper paperwork and clearance material, will not be covered here, but will be addressed in greater detail within the How-To section of this book.)

A Day in the Life of SonPower's Prison Ministry

Condominium living is efficient and convenient, but is not conducive to storing much of *anything*—particularly several hundred pounds of bulky sound equipment. That's why virtually every ministry opportunity begins with a trip to our local storage facility where the loading exercise is a fairly well-established procedure. After allowing the slightly stale air to escape through the opened doorway, I push aside a few filmy cobwebs, squish several creepy-crawlers, and move other stored items aside, allowing access to the sound system components. Then the equipment is extracted and loaded, following a tried-and-true routine, into our Toyota Sienna van.

Throughout the year, the process remains the same—in the broiling heat of summer, to the bone-chilling frigidness of winter—loading (and consequently *unloading)* speaker cabinets and stands, mixing board, power head, multiple-CD player, and a sizable container jam-packed with seventy-five pounds of stuff needed to make the system work. This heavy-duty plastic tub contains sound-reinforcement cables, heavy-duty extension cords, back-up microphone and connector cord, a multi-input "snake" which enables several microphones and/or instruments to be plugged into a single power source, and the most important item of all: duct tape! My personal microphone, in a protective cloth case, and our performance-track CDs are kept in the climate-controlled environment of our home, escaping the confines of the dank, dark storage unit.

Back at the condo, Fran is busy packing a small canvas suitcase with whatever apparel and toiletries our journey requires. Upon my return, I take the carry-all, plus hanging clothes, from our third-floor abode to the van. Some ministry trips may include a small cooler filled with bottled water, healthy snacks, and other edibles. On the way out of town, we stop for gas and my obligatory traveling mug of coffee, before heading three hours upstate, where a modestly-priced motel room awaits. Prior to pulling out of our assigned condominium parking space, we always take a moment to pray for a mantle of God's protection over our lives, the van, the equipment, and those people He puts in our path. And our prayer is *never* complete without the following: "…and Lord, please, *no deer on the road!*"

Because this particular Sunday service is more than three hours from home, Fran and I begin our journey late Saturday afternoon. Although we may contend with heavier traffic or the setting sun in our eyes as we travel, I prefer to arrive at our destination before dark. It is also easier to maneuver past those aforementioned deer in the light of day as opposed to dodging them at dusk.

Once we have registered and settled into our motel room, we leave our unpacked suitcase on the extra bed, vacate the premises, and seek out a local restaurant for dinner. We take this mealtime to decompress and discuss our plans for the following day. I also check in with Fran to see how she feels and the condition of *her* spirit—even as I prepare my heart to minister to the spirits of others.

As you have undoubtedly discovered through your own work and travel schedules, I find that a good night's sleep prior to a full day of activity enables me to be more mentally alert, more emotionally even-keeled, and more effective in completing whatever task lies ahead.

With that thought in mind, evening time is spent going over Sunday's scripture lesson, creating a song list if I have not already done so, and snuggling up with my bride to watch something of interest on one of the many cable channels we don't get at home before retiring for the night.

Five-thirty a.m. is *not* a normal time for me to wake up, but my body tends to be particularly energized—even at this hour—on ministry days. It is early May and the air is cool and crisp, but the early sun provides warm relief. Within the hour, we have showered, dressed, and eaten some fresh fruit and an energy bar before driving the short distance to the state penitentiary. As we journey, I enjoy a courtesy cup of coffee from the motel, while Fran sips hot tea with honey. From a somewhat metropolitan area, we meander into the countryside, through a hardscrabble town and end up pretty much in the middle of nowhere.

We reach our destination—an extraordinarily foreboding place, to be sure. In days gone by, this particular prison was a mental institution and it continues to look the part. An immense building of reddish-brown native stone fills the hillside. Bounded by heavily wooded and mountainous terrain, the draconian edifice obliterates the landscape, the building serving as the centerpiece for a complex of similar but much smaller structures, all surrounded by concertina wire in front of, behind, and on top of seemingly mile-high electrified metal fences.

The only access to this penitentiary is across an exceptionally long, ancient, "whistle bridge"—so named by my wife, because of the high-pitched whine your tires make as you drive over the open-grate metal deck. The bridge spans a wide section of a swift-flowing creek, connecting the highway exit to the prison grounds. Crossing that span, while staring straight ahead at the "dungeon on the hill" makes the final leg of our journey seem even more ominous. I can only imagine what thoughts must go through a prisoner's mind as he rides, shackled, in a penitentiary bus across that creek toward his new home.

Arriving on time—at 7:15 a.m. for an 8:30 service—I pull our equipment-laden van past the many designated parking spaces into the visitor's lot. The parking area is dusty and dirty, littered with trash. Fran and I leave our cell phones and all personal belongings in the van, carefully placed out of sight. Stepping out of our vehicle, I experience a collision of the senses, as the fresh air of the woodlands and the fragrance of honeysuckle mixes with the grit and fossil-fuel aroma of the prison. Armed with our photo IDs, we proceed on foot to the front gate, where unseen eyes, through a swiveling spyglass, scrutinize our arrival. A harsh buzz tells us the heavy metal gate has been unlocked, allowing access to an inner fortified holding area known as a *sally port*. Once inside, we cross a narrow paved courtyard, where another gate opens to the steep concrete stairs leading to the visitors' entrance. I wonder how some visitors are able to physically overcome this final obstacle to spend time with incarcerated loved ones.

At the top of the stairs, we are once again buzzed in by the guard. The facilities' chaplain is there to greet us and we exchange handshakes and pleasantries as the friends we have become. Catch-up conversation, as well as any official information, will unfold as we travel together throughout the facility. Now at the guard station, we show our IDs and sign in as volunteers/visitors. Fran and I, separately, write and print our names, provide home addresses, briefly state the purpose of our visit ("chapel service"), and list the make, model, and license number of our vehicle. This signing-in sequence is standard operating procedure, at virtually every facility we visit.

For those not familiar with prison protocol, the next procedure is akin to what you may have experienced while traveling through the nation's airports. Fran and I remove our jewelry, belts, and shoes, and empty the contents of our pockets into a wooden tray. Then we walk through an arbor-like, full-body metal detector. Initially, this requirement was intimidating and intrusive, but now it is simply an expected part of our clearance process, one designed to keep everyone safe. It is only after completing all these procedures that we receive the visitors' badges or wrist bands that must be displayed at all times while we are within the confines of the prison.

The chaplain, a former musician/evangelist himself—and fully understanding our ministry needs—has secured a large wooden platform dolly from the kitchen to transport our sound system. As I retrace my steps from the guard station to the parking area to retrieve the van, Fran, the chaplain, and a second corrections officer wait for me at the sally port. The CO is armed with a master list of all of our items. As we unload, each piece of equipment is opened and inspected prior to being loaded onto the dolly. With the chaplain's assistance, we begin our pilgrimage to the chapel building, one of the most distant locations within the prison complex. Unlike past visits, where we have utilized a freight elevator to transport our cargo inside the prison, on this morning we follow a cement path which winds through a razor-wire-enclosed corridor along the outside perimeter of the administration building. Entering the prison commons area, our ministry caravan is joined by two inmate trustees—chaplain's assistants—who take over the cart-pushing duties, as they engage us in pleasant conversation. Fran and I are encouraged by the warm welcome and the positive confessions of the men as they praise God for the beautiful morning, our willingness to visit the prison, and the service to come. Other inmates smile and extend salutations to the chaplain as we pass by, confirming what I have already surmised—that he is a good-hearted man, well-liked by many of the prisoners within this all-male bastion of captivity. The air is filled with fumes that catch in my throat, as many of the passersby grab a quick smoke while moving from place to place. I am particularly thankful for the inmates' help in moving the equipment because, after pushing the platform dolly loaded with three hundred pounds of gear up and down inclines for several hundred yards, I truly have been "warmed up" for this morning's concert event!

A free-standing, multi-purpose aluminum-sided structure serves as the center for all religious activities including, Protestant, Catholic, Islamic, Buddhist, Native American, and Rastafarian services. Under Fran's direction, equipment set-up proceeds rather quickly.

The many willing hands of the chaplain's inmate staff make short work of the process, assisting Fran with mounting speakers, running cords, and the like. During this set-up period, I take time to discuss service logistics with the chaplain and the prison praise-and-worship team. It provides a sweet time of fellowship where I am able to engage in easygoing conversation with the inmates, breaking down barriers to communication even prior to the service itself.

At the appointed time, eighty to one hundred men from the various cell blocks converge upon the building, accompanied by corrections officers, each prisoner signing in at a long table near the chapel entranceway. On cue, the praise and worship band plays several up-tempo songs to set the stage for the upcoming activities. After the chaplain welcomes the men and dispenses several housekeeping announcements, Fran and I are introduced as the special "guest ministers" for the morning. As Fran monitors the sound, I approach the front of the room, quietly instructing the praise team to repeat the song they had just finished prior to the chaplain's welcome. And, completely unrehearsed, led by the Holy Spirit, I begin to sing to their musical accompaniment. The men in the crowd love the spontaneity and begin to cheer and applaud. They are seeking something out of the ordinary during this service, something beyond the mundane routine of prison life. And they experience it on this particular Sunday. Heartfelt music, combined with a woven tapestry of spiritual stories between songs— often my own history and testimony—creates an ebb and flow, relaxing the minds and spirits of the listeners and allowing God's Holy Spirit to have His way. Fran and I have seen it before and we see it this day: disinterest turning into inquisitiveness, the softening of piercing eyes and time-worn faces, joy and laughter replacing tension and stress, tears shed by men not used to showing—let alone sharing—emotions.

These captives are searching for—and finding—hope in a hopeless place. These "rejects of society" are understanding that they have value, infinite worth, and that they are truly heirs to a kingdom—not only outside the prison walls, but beyond this Earth! And after several other songs of encouragement, followed by a simple, relevant, and practical message on the grace and love of God, a half-dozen lost souls are ushered into a personal relationship with the King of Kings, while others recommit their lives to the Lord of Lords.

Following the facility's strict ninety-minute timetable, the service concludes with a song. A group of inmates scurries to assist Fran in tearing down the sound system and preparing the equipment, once again, for transport to the outside world. Other prisoners come forward to shake hands and to thank us for spending the morning with them. Several of the men offer words of praise and encouragement for us and SonPower Ministries. Some seek clarification on a point made during the message or ask a quick question. Still others relate spiritual needs and request prayer. There is a sense of peace throughout the room. Just as the men are thankful for our ministry, so Fran and I are blessed to have been a part of the service. And the chaplain is smiling and relaxed, because we have blessed *him* by sharing his burden and relieving some of the stress that characterizes *his* position within the over-taxed penal system!

So what does a prison service look like? Very often, it looks like a distinct and unique work in progress, limited only by the obedience of the men and women called upon to minister, and the personalized touch of an all-powerful God. It is a phenomenon for which we can prepare, but often are not prepared. Because the moment we believe we have things under control, that's when we are presented with twists and turns we could never expect. Scripture reminds us that, in this world, "…we see through a glass darkly…" (1 Corinthians 13:12). Whether we are on the dispensing or the receiving end of the Gospel message, we are not *supposed* to have all the insight or all the answers. It's as if God is smiling down at you and me and saying, "Just remember, I am God…*and you are not.*"

And so we continue to present our bodies as a living sacrifice (Romans 12:1) and we prepare for the unexpected during each and every prison ministry service.

As evangelists, Fran and I have been given many opportunities to come alongside incarcerated men and women as they navigate the personal spiritual journeys God has set before them. Over time, we have developed kinship and fellowship with some of those the Lord has placed in our sphere of influence. But, with inmates in particular, when does a developing relationship become *too* close? When does "going the extra mile" on behalf of someone signify that, perhaps, we have gone *too* far? Find out in the next chapter.

> Through continuing education, or simply by modeling the "religious services" they have experienced, a number of men and women, upon release from prison, embark upon their own ministry careers, often returning to serve their home communities.

Chapter Seven

EVANGELISM VERSUS ADVOCACY

"Be on your guard; stand firm in the faith; be courageous; be strong."

(1 Corinthians 16:13)

A county prison inmate cautiously approached me after our group discipleship session. Glancing surreptitiously over his shoulder to assure himself that he was not being overheard, he came close enough that I instinctively took a step backward, seeking "social distance." Marcus had been a periodic attendee at the weekly "Pre-Sentencing/Pre-Release" classes I facilitate at the local county jail, so I had some previous contact with him. "Brother Einstein, I got a court hearing next week and I wonder if you could put in a good word with the judge." Months later, in the casual setting of that same multipurpose room—this time shouted boldly for all to hear—a similar request came from another prisoner named George: "Yo, Pete—I'm supposed to get out in a few days. I need a 'Home Plan.' Can you hook me up with a place to live?"

Both of these cries for help emanated from the troubled hearts of two men, as they do from many other prisoners in similar situations, seeking easy solutions to seemingly insurmountable problems in their lives—problems they ultimately have created for themselves. The two inmates were requesting last-minute help from someone perceived to be better-equipped or more capable of influencing the system than they were. Both pleas for assistance underscore the conundrum which can surface at any time during the course of prison ministry—evangelism versus advocacy. *Evangelism*—preaching the gospel message of salvation to incarcerated men and women, versus *advocacy*—petitioning for the personal or legal rights of one or more inmates.

In today's prison environment, there is often a fine line between what administrators within the system would consider *relational ministry* versus what might be seen as *advocacy.* In our previous chapter, we examined the essence of ministry within the prison experience—how one's service to God, presented to the glory of God, can be an innovative process, limited only by the rules and regulations of the institution and the creativity of the individuals providing the ministry.

Let's shift perspective a bit: How might the waters of spiritual guidance be muddied by the reality—or the *perception*—that an inmate is receiving advice or aid, legal or otherwise, from a ministry volunteer? Whether through written words, the strains of a sonnet, or the lyrics of a love song, many of us are familiar with the notion that "there's a thin line between love and hate." And regarding the topic of ministering to "the inmate within," there is also a thin line between *ministry* and *advocacy.* For the sake of this writing, we might define the idea of advocacy as supporting or espousing the cause of another person, often associated with representing a particular viewpoint in a court of law. And therein lies the rub. When Marcus and George posed their requests to me at the spur of the moment, what would be—*could be*—the ramifications of my response? My response, coupled with the degree or type of assistance offered, could blur the lines of providing spiritual advice or counsel to a prisoner *inside* the facility, versus pleading the case or cause of an individual *outside* the prison—particularly if this "help" was associated with an inmate's judicial or legal affairs. The perception that I, or *you,* or *anyone* signing on as a "Public Visitor for Religious Ministry" would take on the mantle of advocate for prisoners' rights could have serious consequences. At the least the offending volunteer could be reprimanded and reminded of the reason that they were granted admittance. Or the individual could be barred from entering the institution to conduct or facilitate religious services. The worst-case scenario would involve a state-wide penitentiary ban!

In the broadest sense, when an individual enters a penal facility to deliver the good news of the Gospel of Jesus Christ, he is, in fact, advocating that the life, sacrificial death, and resurrection of the Savior paved the way for all people to be forgiven of their sins. With salvation comes the indwelling supernatural power of the Holy Spirit, opportunity for changed, even transformed, lives here on Earth and eternity with God in heaven. Most chaplains or those in charge of religious services understand that inmates who **voluntarily** attend evangelical, Christian services will, hopefully, be exposed to a scripturally-based message along this line of thinking.

Nationwide, throughout the prison system, spiritual transformation *is* taking place among a growing segment of the inmate population. Despite their isolation and desolation, the Word of God continues to resonate and find its place in the hungry hearts of men and women behind prison walls. The joy of salvation transcends *any* length of sentence an inmate might serve. And, at least for me, there is special cause for celebration when someone who has been sentenced to life in prison with no chance of parole accepts Jesus as their Savior. In the eyes of the world, these individuals are cell-bound for life. But in the eyes of God—and in their own hearts—these "new creations" are free for eternity!

Incarcerated men and women are human beings with real spiritual needs. Because most prison chaplains are terribly overburdened— having far too many souls to serve in a timely or efficient manner—they *and* the inmates truly appreciate the "outsiders" who come bearing spiritual nourishment to feed a multitude of hungry hearts. And, over time, relationships, *within* certain boundaries, are bound to develop between the civilian ministry service providers and the prisoners. The fine line of advocacy is crossed, however, when it is deemed that an individual who has been cleared to conduct religious services *within* the confines of a prison is acting as an agent or representative for the cause of a group of inmates or an individual prisoner *outside* the prison. This could include defending an inmate's position or cause before a corrections officer or an administrator; inserting oneself into an inmate's case and lobbying on his behalf before prison officials or within the court system; disseminating information about an inmate or his or her case publicly outside the prison walls (to garner public support), among many other situations which might develop during the course of relationship-building between a religious volunteer and an inmate.

Another factor added to the mix is that a certain percentage of inmates—intentionally or unintentionally—will use relationships as bargaining chips to manipulate or "play the system," or an individual, to their best advantage. Half-truths, errors of omission, exaggerations, or outright lies may be employed to better position an inmate's effort for leniency, better treatment, or more freedom within the facility, even the possibility of earning a "get out of jail free" card.

Some prisoners who are desperate or are in what I call "survival mode" will abandon moral and ethical conduct to ease the pain or distress of the moment. Other convicts are more cunning and intentional, utilizing accumulated street smarts and ingrained destructive habits to disarm, placate, or impress their needs upon others, with no regard for truth—and unconcerned about relational fallout as a result of their actions. These individuals exhibit an almost pathological intent to use whatever means necessary to achieve an end they believe will benefit their own well-being. Using high-pressure tactics, guilt, pity, or conciliatory tones to achieve their goals, these individuals show no regard for others' feelings, no remorse when the tables are turned against their ploys, and no responsibility for the consequences of their schemes. The lurid stories behind these aberrant relationships (i.e. jailbreaks, sex, or smuggling behind prison bars) are too often played out for the world-at-large through sensational television news features or titillating newspaper articles or even made-for-TV movies, providing the public with a skewed view of prison life.

Can you see the potential for problems and the need for relationship monitoring and awareness by prison administrators *and* those who volunteer their services within the penal system? It is for these reasons and more that the prison minister must take to heart God's admonition in Matthew 10:16 which states, "I am sending you out like sheep among wolves. Therefore be as shrewd as snakes and as innocent as doves."

The prison system reacts quickly to situations and stressors which upset the delicate balance of structure, order, and procedure. If pressed, officials will err on the side of caution. Can you blame them? Therefore, it is imperative that you and I, or *anyone* who desires to minister to incarcerated men and women, adhere to the rules and boundaries set forth by the institution in which we serve. And please understand that these rules and regulations can and do change from place to place and without notice. The bottom line is that—as was mentioned earlier in this chapter—individuals who are deemed to have transgressed, within the context of prison ministry, face the possibility of losing their credentials to minister at **any** facility within the state wherein alleged infractions have occurred.

This is a very real situation. Several years ago, I received word that a friend and fellow prison minister had lost his volunteer/visitor ministry credentials and was banned from entering the given state's penitentiary system. Knowing this man's heart and his compassion for inmates, it was difficult for me to comprehend that what I was hearing through the grapevine was true. Here was a man who had a track record of service to prisoners that spanned more than three decades. Truly, his reputation preceded him. He was the founder and driving force behind an evangelistic ministry that had grown and expanded through the years to include prisoner aftercare upon release and re-integration of ex-offenders into society. So what had transpired to lead to such harsh consequences? What nefarious deed led to his downfall? In reaction to some un-named problem within the system, prison administrators began to check the telephone call sheets of state penitentiary inmates. During the course of their investigation, it was determined that prisoners had been calling this particular pastor's cell phone with a frequency that merited further attention. Not being privy to all the details—but having spoken to my pastor friend after-the-fact—I could corroborate what I had heard. Without any specifics of wrongdoing, but simply as a response to some stressor within the prison system, my friend was determined to be persona non grata within the state's penitentiaries. He was unable to minister for more than a year. As of this writing, he has been reinstated and continues to serve lost people behind the prison walls. Praise the Lord! Even when our most noble intentions and best-laid plans are thwarted by circumstances beyond our ability to direct or regulate, God can make a way where there seems to be no way, as was illustrated in this scenario with my pastor friend.

What a great lesson this pastor's temporary prison exile is for you and me—and him—about the sovereignty of God. Despite my friend's previous good work and best intentions, he was removed from prison ministry for a period of time. However, God is omniscient—knowing all things. *Nothing* surprises Him! When things seem totally out of our control, we can take comfort in knowing that *He* is in control, creating order out of chaos and structure from seemingly discombobulated events and situations. You know as well as I that, in this life, many things are beyond our full comprehension or our ability to navigate or fix. Prison ministry simply represents a microcosm of the world-at-large in that we sometimes have to "go with the flow," realizing that there is a Creator who controls it all, but Who also gives us authority and decision-making power in the midst of both the pleasant sunny days and, more importantly, during the turbulent storms of life.

So when it comes to the sometimes uncertain terrain of evangelism and discipleship to male and female offenders, the best advice for the person ministering within the prison system might be this: Keep the preaching of the Gospel of Jesus Christ as your main intent, and let the Holy Spirit of God handle the details.

Now get ready as we prepare to tackle some of the "how-to" aspects of ministering to the *inmate within* as we enter Part Two: Prison Ministry Guidelines.

Although the numbers may vary, the average case load of a current-day Public Defender ranges from 60 to 80+ men or women awaiting trial or sentencing.

PART TWO

PRISON MINISTRY GUIDELINES

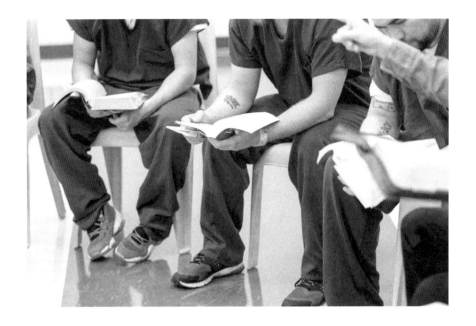

Chapter Eight

THE FACE AND STYLE OF YOUR MINISTRY

"…Let nothing move you. Always give yourselves fully to the work of the Lord, because you know that your labor in the Lord is not in vain."

(1 Corinthians 15:58)

"*I have decided…to follow Jesus…no turning back,*" sang the choir with more enthusiasm than harmonic perfection—a rag-tag group of men earnestly seeking the correct notes to the familiar gospel song. The light-blue clad choral assembly, composed of newly-arrived prisoners, was being musically whipped into shape by a tall, gangly, dark-skinned praise-and-worship leader outfitted in a medium brown jumpsuit, replete with a black "DOC" (Department of Corrections) stenciled across the back. His team of talented musicians, consisting of a keyboard player, drummer, bassist and electric guitarist, were identically attired in brown.

In the corner of the room, a grizzled, salt-and-pepper-bearded black man, well into his seventies, provided melodic fills to the musical arrangement, producing sweet notes which he tenderly caressed from a tarnished and battered alto saxophone. In contrast to the ever-changing cast of vocalists, the praise-and-worship musicians performed with confidence and excellence, having honed their craft over years—even decades—of playing.

Each had a story to tell. The saxophonist had traveled the world with some of the greatest jazz players on the planet; the guitarist was one of the most sought-after studio musicians "back in the day," recording with Philly-soul and Motown greats. The keyboardist had a doctorate in musical composition and had owned his own music school and recording studio. And now they were convicts, outcasts in the eyes of many, praising God through their love of music on a Sunday morning behind the turreted walls of a maximum-security prison.

These were the sights and sounds that surrounded me as I sat on a metal folding chair in the back of the prison chapel. The vaulted wood-beamed ceiling enriched the musical tones that reverberated throughout the space. Hints of fresh air were ushered into the chapel through the old opaque windows with their hand-cranked louvers. Ceiling fans, dangling from the rafters, spun lazily, coaxing the rising air downward toward the waiting church pews below.

And then they entered. A multitude of worshippers, dressed in blue, filing in one cell block at a time, each group accompanied by at least one corrections officer. As the inmates approached a series of long sign-in tables, some of the congregation seemed distant or distracted—as if they were mentally adjusting to their new chapel sanctuary which offered a sense of relief from the cramped confines of their prison cells. Others appeared more at ease, singing along with the choir and clapping their hands to the music as they signed one of the endless sheets of white paper covering the tables before being guided to their assigned section by one of the guards. Familiar faces from past services beamed a smile in my direction or gave a quick wave. A few men approached quickly to extend a hand of fellowship or to speak words of welcome. One or two of the men had studied with me during my weekly sessions at the local county jail. Several more inmates I recognized from drug and alcohol rehab facilities Fran and I had visited within the past year or so. However, the majority of the incoming audience were strangers to me. These were the "blues"—men sentenced to state time who were being evaluated and classified according to their categories of crime, psychological demeanor, and medical needs before being reassigned to one of the many other penal institutions across the state. The process was this: After a short stay at this "classification facility," most of the blues would be parceled out to minimum, medium, or maximum-security state penitentiaries, based upon the seriousness of their crimes and the level of violence associated with their transgressions. Others might be sent to institutions with more specialized approaches to rehabilitating sex offenders or treating those with drug and alcohol dependencies. Because the window of opportunity to impact the hearts of these prisoners is so narrow, it was important that God's Word break through any clutter and confusion in their minds and hearts and make a spiritual connection on this particular morning.

Two hundred men now filled the chapel. Most stood and moved to the music, appearing to enjoy the opportunity to "relax in the Lord," leaving the cares of this world and life on the cell blocks behind for a short time. I felt a light tap on my shoulder. A prison trustee was beckoning me to accompany him. It was time to go, so we began the journey from the back of the room, down the aisle, toward the staging area in the front of the chapel. During our trek amidst a sea of blue, I began to settle in to the moment, sensing a peace but also a prompting, an urgency in my spirit. Several men extended hands for a brief fist-bump or touch. The air around me was filled not only with anticipation, but also a hint of sweaty bodies and the pungent aroma of clothes in need of washing. As we approached the choir they parted like the Red Sea, allowing us to mount the platform steps to our destination.

It felt like home to me.

Seated on a functional but uncomfortable wooden bench during the service announcements and Scripture reading, I marveled at the diversity in that sea of faces before me. It was always an interesting exercise to attempt to put myself in the minds of the attendees and to determine what they might be thinking. I had seen the entire gamut of "looks" in previous prison services: the hollowed eyes of hopelessness and helplessness; the defiant stare of the one wondering, "What does that skinny, middle-aged white guy got for *me?*" On many faces, however, were the warm smiles of gratitude, shown by men who appreciated the fact that Fran and I had dedicated our Sunday to be with them at this hour, in this house of worship, in the midst of their incarceration.

On this particular day, God presented me with a glimpse of something so peculiar, something so seemingly out of place, that it instantly elicited a smile of amazement. Among the black and brown visages, the burnished Hispanic or olive-skinned Italian and ochre Asian faces, there sat a diminutive man with the bowl-cut hairdo and long flowing beard of the Amish and Mennonites. As it is written, "There is no one righteous, not even one" (Romans 3:10).

Now it was time. The stage was set with a microphone, a music stand, and a wooden chair upon which I laid my Bible and a glass of water. "My brothers," intoned the chaplain's assistant, "it is my pleasure to welcome this morning, our friend, Minister Pete Einstein."

I gave an imperceptible nod to Fran, manning the mixing board, along with an inmate sound technician and an ever-present CO in her distant balcony perch at the far end of the chapel.

Instantly, a wall of sound cascaded from the speakers, the bass response pumping and thumping with a metronome-like cadence. Several of the men in the audience exchanged glances, as if to say,

"What is going on here?" Time to usher in the presence of the Holy Spirit with song. I opened my mouth and the high tenor of rhythm and blues began to fill the room with a message of hope and salvation. The guys in blue and brown jumpsuits erupted in applause and shouts of encouragement. "Sing it brother!" "Tell it!" "Hallelujah!" They knew this would be no ordinary church service.

Today, the prisoners were enjoying what I like to describe as a "SonPower Ministries concert/service," but on the next Sunday they might be blessed with a totally different worship experience.

What *does* prison ministry look like? There is no singular answer to this question.

Prison facilities are simply locations where ministry takes place. The elements of praise, worship, and teaching can be as varied as those individuals performing the service and/or the needs of the recipients of the message being delivered. Through the years—inside or outside prison walls—I have experienced ministry performed in a myriad of ways, including musical concerts, lectures centered on theology, evangelistic preaching, instruction in spiritual principles, and interactive Bible studies. And, specifically *within* the prison system, there is no right or wrong form of ministry, as long as the theological underpinnings are sound. Over time, however, I have observed and experienced that certain *methodologies* may be more effective than others when it comes to ministering to the incarcerated.

Think about your *own* life for a moment. What are your likes and dislikes or personal preferences when it comes to worship? Are you the type of person who enjoys upbeat, contemporary music presented by a praise-and-worship band? Do you prefer the more traditional approach of gospel music standards sung from a hymnal with organ accompaniment? Perhaps you are a more reserved worshipper, more prone to silent, reverent prayer, as opposed to some—perhaps even within your own congregation—who opt for a more vocal, demonstrative worship style. When it comes to the message, do you appreciate a pastor who presents the Word of God in a low-key, thoughtful, contemplative manner? Perhaps you are moved spiritually and emotionally by a lively "fire-and-brimstone" preacher, or you gravitate toward a more modern expository style of teaching, complete with a PowerPoint presentation.

It may be that such thoughts and comparisons regarding personal worship experiences have never entered your mind, or such contemplation has been stored on the shelf of your life, only to be dusted off and employed during spiritual emergencies. If such is the case, trust me, you are not alone. I've been there too.

For those who *do* regularly attend a house of worship, whatever your likes and desires, whatever your choices or preferences, please understand that the same holds true for incarcerated men and women throughout the nation and around the world. The major difference is that this particular assembly of worshippers is confined and more constrained in their choices. That is why it is incumbent that parachurch organizations such as SonPower Ministries remain persistent and consistent as they take the transformational message of the Gospel of Jesus Christ to those in bondage behind prison walls.

Before we proceed any further, if you have ever wondered how *your* ministry to lost souls in prison might present itself, now would be the opportune time to pause and ask a simple question: "Lord, what is the vision you have for *me* regarding this thing called 'prison ministry'?" We serve a personal God. Therefore, what He may have in store for one person could be entirely different than His plans for another. Each of us is uniquely "spiritually wired" by the Creator and, therefore, we possess distinct traits that affect the way we think, speak, and act. God-given personal attributes impact every facet of our lives, so it should come as no surprise that we would exhibit these qualities as we seek to minister to others. For example, some people tend to be extroverted and demonstrative in their behavior, which translates into a more dynamic, even theatrical, approach toward ministry; others tend to exhibit a teacher's spirit, turning spiritual principles into life lessons to impart wisdom and guidance; still others tend to be somewhat introspective and more deeply thoughtful in their approach to ascertaining the meaning and application of scriptural truths.

What better place to discover illustrations of spiritual gifting within individuals called to serve God and others than in His handbook, the Bible? God's Word is replete with colorful characters and personalities, the face of whose ministries were molded and shaped by *His* hand, so that seemingly ordinary folks could be made fit to be ambassadors of the highest calling. From Exodus through Deuteronomy, the Old Testament chronicles the journey of Moses, a reluctant messenger to whom God revealed Himself in the midst of a flaming bush that did not burn. In Exodus chapters three and four, Moses offers what he considers five valid excuses as to why he should not be the one considered for the responsibility of delivering the Israelites from Egyptian tyranny and bondage: "…Who am I that I should go to Pharaoh and bring the Israelites out of Egypt?" (Exodus 3:11); "… Suppose I should go to the Israelites and say to them, 'The God of your fathers has sent me to you,' and they ask me, 'what is His name?' Then what shall I tell them?" (Exodus 3:13). Moses continued minimizing his credentials, citing a lack of authority, his inability to speak eloquently and—the truly heartfelt objection—that he had no real desire for the task, until "the anger of the Lord was kindled against Moses." Before he could consider his role in freeing the imprisoned Israelites in Egypt (a journey which included forty years of meandering in the wilderness), Moses had to realize in his mind and heart that God, working through him, was more than enough for the undertaking. Perhaps you see some of yourself in the insecurity and lack of confidence or motivation that Moses exhibited, as he dialogued with the Creator of the universe about his inadequacies and concerns.

Talk about flamboyant! Here is another excellent example of God accomplishing His will through a rather unorthodox minister. In the cavalcade of personalities God enlisted to bring forth the gospel message on earth, John the Baptist made quite the impression. He might best be described as the "rock star" of his day. His striking physical appearance as a man dressed in clothing made of camel's hair, adorned with a wide leather belt…his thick, flowing, unkempt hair blowing in the desert wind as he preached…all this and more captured the attention of the populace, who hung on his every word. His message, proclaimed throughout the wilderness of Judea, urging listeners to "Repent, for the kingdom of heaven has come near" resonated with the common folks who were searching for something more meaningful—a more "noble" component—in the midst of their humdrum lives. As people throughout the region observed this wild man dining on locusts and honey, as they felt his strong hands submerging them in the baptismal waters, as they heard him challenging the Pharisees, Sadducees, and teachers of the day, calling them out for their anemic spiritual condition, what must they have thought? But John the Baptist—an ordinary man under the authority of an extraordinary God—was quick to defuse any elements of the spectacular, drawing attention away from himself and instead proclaiming the power of the One who was to come. "He came as a witness…so that through Him (Jesus Christ) all might believe. He himself was not the light, he came only as a witness to the light" (John 1:7, 8). God used John to baptize His Son, ushering in the three-year adult ministry of Jesus Christ on Earth. And then, like a shooting star, the high-profile, meteoric ministry of John the Baptist was gone, having served its God-given purpose. The only other reference we have concerning this extravagant servant was of his beheading in Matthew 14:1-12.

One of the most extraordinary examples of the changing face of ministry is the biblical account of Saul's transformation to the apostle known as Paul. Saul was a zealot, intent on harassing, imprisoning, and even killing Christ-followers…*in the name of God!* Truly a man on a mission, the havoc surrounding Saul's persecution of Christians was only thwarted when God Himself intervened—striking Saul blind as he traveled on the road to Damascus. As he lay stunned on the ground, God posed a life-changing question to the man: "…Saul, Saul, why do you persecute me?" (Acts 9:4). In his blindness, this misguided "bull in a china shop" was able to "see" God for who He was or who He could be in his *own* life. And, sight restored, as the apostle Paul, he changed the landscape of ministry, preaching salvation through relationship with Jesus Christ, not only to the Jews, but to Gentiles throughout the world. Ironically, much of Paul's writing in his New-Testament letters to the churches—expressing freedom and hope—was penned from the dark, damp dungeon of a Roman prison, where he was executed after his second incarceration.

The three-year, adult ministry of the Son of God revolutionized the world. Conceived by the Holy Spirit of God, in the womb of a common, teenaged virgin girl named Mary, to be fatherly-nurtured by a carpenter and tradesman, Joseph, this baby came with an angelic directive and mission statement: "She will give birth to a son, and you are to give him the name Jesus, because he will save his people from their sins" (Matthew 1:21). God, in an "earth suit" of flesh, was born in the most humble of circumstances—laid in a feeding trough for cattle, in a stable for animals—on the outskirts of Bethlehem. In one of endless Godly ironies, the One who would be referred to as "The Bread of Life," was born in a place also known as "The City of Bread."

As the only suitable substitute—the propitiation—for the utterly fallen state of humanity, Jesus Christ's mission was not simple, but it was succinct: He would shed His blood and die for the sins of all mankind…*including you and me.* Exhibiting all the perfect characteristics of God, Jesus came, not as a conquering king to free Israel from the suppression and oppression of Roman rule, but as the Prince of Peace, to take away the sins of the world. According to scripture, even in prophesies foretold hundreds of years before His coming, "He was despised and rejected by mankind, a man of suffering and familiar with pain. Like one from whom people hide their faces he was despised, and we held him in low esteem" (Isaiah 53:3).

Truly, Jesus Christ was "a man of sorrows." But, as recounted time and again, He laughed, shed tears, shared humor, and offered encouragement—with an especially-intentional interest toward the young children who clamored for His attention. In the midst of the most trying circumstances, Jesus exhibited the characteristics of "…love, joy, peace, forbearance, kindness, goodness, faithfulness, gentleness and self-control…" (Galatians 5:22-23) which we know to be the fruit of the Spirit of God. But when the name of His Father in heaven was compromised, Jesus could exhibit more forceful emotions, including righteous anger. In Matthew 21:12, we read the account of Jesus entering the temple courts, overturning the tables of the money changers and those buying and selling in the temple, and driving the offenders from the house of prayer. To emphasize an important lesson to those who were "hard of hearing," Jesus' language could, indeed, be strong. He saved His harshest words for the Pharisees and Sadducees knowing that, although they considered themselves wise through adherence to legalistic ritual, their hearts were far from God. He proclaimed these teachers of the law to be "white-washed sepulchers filled with dead men's bones," and wondered aloud, "You snakes! You brood of vipers! How will you escape being condemned to hell?" (Matthew 23:33).

Jesus Christ spoke truth…or reality, as God sees it. He could do nothing else, because He *is* God. Just as easily as He could disarm foolish men with divine revelation, when it came time for Him to fulfill His mission on earth—to die for our sins—He reluctantly relinquished His supernatural authority, and was led "like a lamb to the slaughter." As the very people He created presented false testimony against Him, as they mocked Him, as they spat upon Him and beat Him to the point that He was barely recognizable as a man, the Bible tells us, "…as a sheep before its shearers is silent, so he did not open his mouth" (Isaiah 53:7). As Jesus Christ hung, dying, on the cross, He looked down upon His creation and—once more exhibiting the unconditional love of God—uttered these words: "Father forgive them, for they do not know what they are doing" (Luke 23:34).

You and I need look no further than the biblical accounts of Jesus Christ and countless other men and women throughout Scripture to glean spiritual insight and truths, useful information, or even tried-and-true techniques that could assist us in any and all of our ministry endeavors…and improve every aspect of our lives, as well.

Now, with a bit more history and understanding, let's return once again to the specific question as to what ministry to incarcerated men and women might look like. Without trivializing the topic, if we could settle upon one phrase to summarize the multiplicity of spiritually-ordained human traits that help to shape, mold and therefore characterize our presentation of the gospel message, might we use the phrase *personal style?* "Style" is a great descriptor which can encompass a variety of attributes, including a person's physical appearance, dress, his or her method of communicating, and to some degree the manner in which biblical instruction is translated into present-day applications. Growing up, I remember derivations of a phrase that certainly still applies to *all* manner of presenting the Word of God: "Be true to yourself," or, in a more formal vernacular, "To thine own self be true." Different phrasing; same relevance and meaning. Let's explore how this premise would play out in real-life prison ministry situations.

If you are the "buttoned-down" type—conservative hairstyle, suit and tie, horn-rimmed glasses, thoughtful and slightly introverted—that's *your* style. With that style, you can portray an air of authority and a no-nonsense approach to the matters-at-hand. How foolish would it be to create a new persona whereby you would appear to be the cool, street-wise preacher in baggy jeans and a hoodie, preaching the message of salvation and healing to the accompaniment of a hip-hop beat? Not only would inmates see through your masquerade, but I can't imagine that you, in the role of minister, would feel comfortable—or capable—in your newly-created identity. Likewise, there are those ministers who, because of their spiritual gifting and life experiences, prefer more casual dress and a less-formal vocabulary to break down God's Word into bite-sized tidbits that are more easily digested by the audience. There are many other ministry styles that we could describe.

For example, I might appear before a group of male inmates in a weekly Bible-study session, decked out in a dress shirt and fashion-cut jeans. Calling upon my past personal experiences, during the course of study and conversation involving spiritual principles as applied to current lifestyle issues, I might use *myself* as my own "best worst example" when discussing alcohol or drug abuse, inappropriate sex, selfishness and self-centeredness, or other matters of the heart. You, the reader, might find such an admission hard to believe. But I have discovered that being transparent and vulnerable in this way allows me to establish a closer rapport and bond of fellowship with this unique audience.

My language would tend to be more pointed—but *always* appropriate and God-honoring—and some colloquial or "street" phrases could punctuate the conversation. To ascertain whether or not the attendees understand a point being made, I might say, in the style with which God has gifted me, "Do you feel me on this?" Another minister, appearing before the same group of inmates, dressed in a sport jacket, white shirt and tie, with a more traditional approach to ministry, would simply ask, "Do you understand what is being said regarding this matter?"

Those who are gifted in the area of teaching might find it advantageous to employ visual aids creating more of a classroom environment. As rules and regulations permit, those who are technologically savvy may wish to utilize such resources as PowerPoint presentations or videos to enhance presentation and retention of information. Other ministers may be content to use a particular book, a printed article, and/or study materials to guide discussion. Still others may find the Bible to be the sufficient stand–alone text from which to minister in a variety of ways.

No style is better or worse than another. If it is a *God* thing, it is a *good* thing. If what is said and done during the course of ministry is heavenly-directed, God can and will use it for earthly good. But the question remains…how best can we seek and *verify* this direction? How do you and I know if the thoughts and emotions entering our minds and hearts are God-inspired or figments of our own imaginations?

Stay tuned, because we will address this question and more within the next chapter: *Totally Accountable or "Wild Ducking" It?*

"If you look at the one factor that
most closely correlates with crime,
it's not poverty, it's not unemployment,
it's not education; it's the absence
of a father in the family."

(Former U.S. Attorney General William Barr)

Chapter Nine

TOTALLY ACCOUNTABLE OR "WILD DUCKING" IT?

THE BIRTH OF SONPOWER MINISTRIES

"Plans fail for lack of counsel. but with many advisers they succeed."

(Proverbs 15:22)

"*P*ete, SonPower Ministries generates such a small amount of income that you could *never* mishandle your finances," joked one of my trusted friends, an advisor to what was then a fledgling ministry. Many years have passed and we still enjoy a hearty laugh over that statement.

But there is a solid moral and *spiritual* truth underlining my friend's comment. Whether we have much or little, God demands that we be good and faithful stewards of His resources. "Wait a minute," you might say, "What's mine is mine. I work hard for all I earn and I should be able to do whatever I want with my money and my possessions." You may, in fact, labor diligently, utilizing extraordinary gifts, talents, and knowledge to accomplish great things. You may have reached the pinnacle of success in the eyes of your family, your business associates, your peers, and the world around you. That can be a good thing...*if* you realize and recognize the source of it all. God's Word declares, "The earth is the Lord's, and everything in it, the world and all who live in it" (Psalm 24:1).

Whether we choose to believe it or not, our money, houses, vehicles, creature comforts, children—our very lives—are on loan from God. He is Author, Creator, and Ruler of all things, all peoples, all nations, and all governments. *He* owns it; we don't. Are you beginning to get the picture? Because, at times, I *still* need to be reminded of this foundational principle. Too often, my life and all my "stuff" revolves around me, as opposed to Him. Over time, that could be a recipe for disaster or, at the very least, less than God's best for me...and for you. The bottom line is that you and I are accountable to somebody for almost everything! Under law, we are obligated to turn over what seems like an ever-increasing amount of our income to various levels of government in the form of taxes. If we don't we are held accountable in the form of late fees, garnished wages, or worse. In the workplace, depending upon our position in the hierarchy of a corporation or business, we answer to an owner, a boss, or a supervisor as we fulfill the duties and requirements of our jobs. If married, husbands and wives should be accountable to each other. And so it goes. This concept of accountability affects every aspect of our lives, including business, finances, religious or spiritual life, education, recreation, and interpersonal relationships.

Have you ever had a *brainstorm*—a really great idea that simply would not go away? When you woke up in the morning...when you laid your head on the pillow at night...in the middle of a busy day...this revolutionary thought, this potentially life-changing notion, this conceptual nugget of brilliance literally commandeered your mind. Try as you might, you couldn't shake it. *"It"*—whatever "it" was—refused to be denied. If you have experienced such a stimulating, captivating, yet sometimes exasperating state of mind, join the club. I've been there too. Often. I firmly believe that God, having endowed us with intelligence and decision-making capabilities, will continually introduce us to opportunities through which we are able to utilize a multitude of gifts. In this way God enables us to exercise and to develop our "intellectual muscles." But at a much deeper level, He allows us to contemplate the *spiritual* question: "Are you going to develop this thought, pursue this idea, or realize this dream *with* Me or *without* Me?"

Many who are far away from any sort of personal relationship with God act upon the visions cast in their minds, pursuing them to seemingly successful conclusions. The world is forever honoring men and women for their accomplishments in business, economics, finance, health and medicine, athletics, and entertainment. These individuals dream dreams and respond extraordinarily, often working tirelessly toward the goal of excellence. The end result of their efforts often places them on a pedestal of success in the eyes of an adoring public. The fact is that scriptural principles *do* work within the framework of a secular society. Through their own efforts—using God-given abilities—individuals can experience fame, fortune, and a modicum of comfort in life. However, these "successful people" can attain all the world has to offer and miss out entirely on far greater rewards. As it is written, "Do not store up for yourselves treasures on earth, where moths and vermin destroy, and where thieves break in and steal. But store up for yourselves treasures in heaven…For where your treasure is, there your heart will be also" (Matthew 6:19-21). I found myself on this rollercoaster ride of life for several decades, dreaming big dreams; working hard, if not smart; believing that anything I achieved would come as a result of my own blood, sweat and tears…because I did not have a heart for God. Perhaps even today you find yourself on that same long, winding, seemingly endless road that often leads nowhere.

For those who profess a personal relationship with God, the idea of being answerable to someone greater than ourselves not only enables us to better handle the trials, tribulations, and temptations of life during our earthly sojourn, but provides us with a mantle of protection along the way. I don't know about you, but I have discovered that, too often, this protective "hedge" best serves to shield me from—me! That is to say, God's power, fortifying my spirit, provides me, time and again, with the opportunity to subjugate or to control my carnal nature (the "flesh"), so that my thoughts, words, and actions reflect more and more His will for my life versus my own selfish desires. Over time, the diligent application of God-directed principles can produce sweet results in the spiritual journey of the believer, as opposed to the bitter fruit that manifests itself when we try to "wild duck" it…simply living life on our own terms and by our own strength or intellect.

After His crucifixion, but prior to His ascension to sit at the right hand of the Father in Heaven, Jesus Christ made one last appearance to the disciples. During His final discourse to these faithful but all-too-human followers, Jesus made it clear that He was *not* forsaking them. He would never abandon them to fend for themselves during their time of fear, confusion, and spiritual need. He said this to His timid and troubled tribe: "…I am going to send to you what my Father has promised, but stay in the city until you have been clothed with power from on high" (Luke 24:49). The "power" to which Jesus Christ referred was the indwelling of God's Holy Spirit. It fortified these mortal men with a supernatural strength to better understand the mysteries of God, while empowering them to do—paraphrasing Jesus' words—"…even greater things than I have done." Fear and doubt were replaced by boundless faith and a missional sense of purpose which enabled the disciples to gather themselves in preparation for continuing the "good fight"…spreading the Gospel Message to the ends of the earth.

I needed to be supercharged in that way. Lord knows, I had tried for years to tackle virtually everything in life on my own terms and in my own strength. If the trade-off for obedience was my best God-directed effort at accountability, then so be it.

Armed with a bit more information, let's return to the reality that God can and does put specific dreams and visions in our minds to motivate and direct us toward the accomplishment of something great on this Earth. In the eyes of the world, the connotation of "something great" is most often equated with "something big." But such is not always the case. In God's economy, "something great" could be *anything*—large *or* small—which brings Him glory! An individual reaching millions of people through a world-wide platform of evangelism is held in no higher esteem than the person working behind the scenes in a small-town soup kitchen, feeding the homeless and disadvantaged…or the man or woman taking time to conduct a weekly Bible study for a small group of inmates in the multipurpose room of a county jail. To quote a current, popular expression, "It's all good," if it's ordained by God.

Having a somewhat visionary inclination, I could see God working in my life—even in the years prior to my becoming a Christ-follower—preparing me for some sort of foray into the music-and-ministry field. I remember the day in 1992 when I walked into the kitchen, interrupting Fran's meal preparations, and announced that I was going to work part-time versus full-time at the advertising and marketing firm where I had been employed for a number of years. Why? "God," I proclaimed, "has called me to pursue a vision for ministry." Now this "vision for ministry" was something new to my wife, as the topic had not been discussed at length—or in any specific way—around the dining room table, or anywhere else for that matter. In fact, two weeks prior to my announcement, Fran had left her job at the local YMCA where she had taught swimming and aquatic fitness for more than thirteen years. If Fran had desired to dispute my rather impulsive-seeming decision, it was an argument she could never win. Remember, *God* had called me to forsake full-time employment to begin this new adventure in ministry…*and who is going to argue with God?* I can imagine a rueful smile on the visage of the Creator as he watched an impetuous, not-so-young man charging into the unknown, presumably in His honor. My self-confident declaration might have sounded something like this: "Come on, God…follow me…I've got this ministry-thing covered!" And so it was that SonPower Ministries was born.

"…(God) provides for those who grieve in Zion—to bestow on them a crown of beauty instead of ashes, the oil of joy instead of mourning, and a garment of praise instead of a spirit of despair…" (Isaiah 61:3).

Lest you believe that, due to my impulsive nature, SonPower Ministries was doomed to failure from its inception, we can *all* take heart in knowing that God—through divine direction that is His alone—can take the *worst-conceived* plans of men and women and create things of beauty; transforming less-than-stellar ideas into fruitful realities that will bring Him glory, honor, and praise. He did just that during the formative months and years of the ministry He so graciously bequeathed to Fran and me. I like to joke that, every once in a while, I mess up and do something right! Looking back on your life, perhaps you can identify with this rather self-deprecating notion. Even though my timetable for "success" continually seemed to precede God's *perfect* timing for my plans, I constantly felt the Lord's presence in my mind and heart…continually molding and shaping me to conform, more and more, to *His* image and *His* will regarding the matters-at-hand. This guidance led me to understand, in short order, that I needed a "band of brothers" to help provide spiritual, financial, moral, and ethical oversight to my efforts. Thus, the SonPower Ministries' board of advisors came into being.

When you were growing up, didn't you enjoy the company of friends? I don't know about you, but I liked the idea that, in my younger years, there were several trusted companions that I could rely on through thick and thin, amid the ups and downs of adolescence, exploring mysteries of the universe or the even greater mysteries of the opposite sex! These were my best buddies, the ones with whom I shared my closest secrets and my most extravagant dreams. Without realizing it, many years ago in my childhood, I was being introduced to the concept of an "accountability group," because, even as young boys, we tended to keep each other in line. If you said something mean-spirited, if you acted in a way that was off-putting to others, you heard about it! That was the nexus leading to the formation of the initial SonPower board of advisors. The group was composed of men who had hearts for God—seeking what was best, not only for their own lives, but for my life, Fran's life, and the life of the ministry. They knew me well, taking on the role of what God's Word refers to as a "multitude of counsellors." These friends understood the vision God had given me for music and ministry. (Notice, at this point, I did not say "us," to include Fran, in the formative years of this adventure.) These friends came alongside me willingly, to share their talents, skills, expertise, and experience, to assist in the evolution and growth of SonPower Ministries, and to help insure that the ministry functioned in the most efficient and *effective* manner possible.

In the early days of the ministry, I must admit that my board members tended to be "yes men," more content to let me run with the latest idea than to thoroughly scrutinize my thoughts and actions. Far too often, board consensus might sound something like, "That sounds like a good idea, Pete…go for it!" Over time, however, board members became more insightful, noting that, although I could easily grasp the "big picture" or the grand scheme of an idea, I was not as adept or disciplined when it came to mastering the details that would allow me—or the ministry—to arrive at the desired destination. My advisors understood that my visionary tendencies did not make me the best delegator. Having keen foresight, I would work hard to achieve an end result, but could easily become distracted and overburdened with disciplines and details that I was not well-suited to address. That is when my accountability partners began to take on the yoke of ministry, utilizing *their* unique talents and expertise to provide assistance, to lighten the load, and to prevent me from exhausting myself. In ministry, burnout can be a very real consequence of "wild ducking" it, but delegation of duties among many counsellors can allow a ministry—or *any* endeavor—to flourish, while providing more joy in the journey for all the participants. Jesus Christ taught and modeled this truth and other sound business principles throughout scripture. In John 15:14, 15, He discussed the disciples' role in God's mission and ministry for Him: "You are my friends…I no longer call you servants, because a servant does not know his master's business. Everything I have learned from my Father I have made known to you. Go and bear fruit—fruit that will last…Love each other."

Through the years, SonPower Ministries' board of advisors—ranging from three to nine in number—have come and gone. Many have served for a dozen years or more. To illustrate the diversity within the Body of Christ—and within this ministry—our current board members include an evangelical pastor with excellent technology and media skills; a computer-aided design (CAD) engineer and long-time ministry supporter who is empathetic, pro-active, and assists with financial accountability; a lawyer and state legislator who takes an unwavering stand on biblical truths—doing the right things for the right reasons; a credentialed minister with prison ministry and aftercare background currently working with mentally-disadvantaged adults; a young man in corporate sales, with a distinguished background in athletics, who brings enthusiasm and a fearless approach to befriending and evangelizing needy people; and an elder from a supporting church who describes himself as a "good old boy"—a man of simplicity who contemplates issues deeply and will contact me to offer a word of prayer or to check on my well-being. Perhaps one of these descriptions reminds you of *yourself.* After all, an advisor is simply an ordinary person allowing himself or herself to be used by an extraordinary God. Whether it is in a secular or sacred environment, trusted advisors are akin to nuggets of silver or gold—studying issues; recommending courses of action; providing wise counsel, and developing deeper personal relationships with those around them in the midst of this journey called life.

In addition to a structured board of advisors, experience and study of Scripture have convinced me that every person, and therefore all ministers, should hold themselves accountable to church fellowship within a body of believers in Jesus Christ. To that end, SonPower Ministries, although not directly affiliated with our home church (or a particular denomination), is conceptually and financially supported by our pastor and home-church congregation as a "stateside missions" outreach. My pastor—and friend—is a former long-time SonPower Ministries board member. We communicate on a regular basis regarding the state of the ministry, church and family affairs, and our personal walks with God. It is a sweet relationship that provides another intimate layer of accountability and trust. Our local church body becomes a welcome home base when Fran and I are not traveling throughout the region within the context of SonPower Ministries. This fellowship provides revitalization and refreshment, helping us to reconnect with the Body of Christ at a local level.

If you are married, God has provided you with a built-in accountability partner. I didn't always realize or accept that premise. In fact, being a headstrong, self- motivated, extremely self-centered man, I was content to expect Fran to respond to my decisions regarding life and living and then to follow obediently in my footsteps. (A note to men: What I just conveyed is *not* the biblical description of a "spiritual leader!") As a thirty-year-old bachelor/musician/advertising executive, I was used to calling my own shots, doing what I thought needed to be done, often on my own time schedule. I carried this philosophy into my married life. The problems created by my insistent, independent thinking were magnified through the covenant of marriage. Intellectually, I may have understood the "two-becoming-one," "flesh-of-one-flesh" principles, but until I studied God's Word, examined my own heart, and *inquired of Fran* what the marriage covenant looked like from *her* perspective, I tended to minimize her potential contributions to *my* ministry. What foolishness and arrogance on my part! After years of spiritual examination and growth, which included participating in and then briefly helping to facilitate a marriage-mentoring curriculum, God continued to reveal to me the incredible talents and attributes Fran brought to our marriage and to SonPower Ministries.

Today, Fran still participates in ministry activities as she always has—including her role as "sound person" behind the mixing board when I am singing or preaching. The ongoing challenge for me is to foster, in Fran, a more intimate connection to our ministry efforts by continuing to develop that intimacy in our own marriage relationship. God faithfully unveils qualities in Fran that enable me to receive her wisdom, counsel, and advice as my helpmeet and life-long ministry partner. Please understand that the spiritual ramifications for the word *helpmeet,* within the covenant of marriage, go far deeper than the more modern concept of *helpmate.* In the original Greek and Aramaic biblical text, the sacred bond between a husband and wife best described the woman's role not only as a "completer" of the man, but as a "helper suitable" for him. This is how I view Fran in my life. No person on this earth is invested in my life or our marriage more than she. Nobody knows me—my strengths, my weaknesses, my inclinations—better than Fran. In our travels, we continuously observe ministries in which the wife is not seen or heard, but I cannot fathom God's continuing to bless SonPower Ministries without her input and support. She was designed by God to speak truth into my life. If she perceives I am once again falling into a pattern of self-centeredness, or if she sees my carnal nature rearing its ugly head, Fran can completely disarm me by simply asking, "Is that your Christlike attitude or are you in your flesh? Is what you're proposing a 'Pete-thing' or is it from God?" Truly, Fran is my all-important "emeritus" board member and advisor!

Addressing our accountability to almighty God is, without question, saving the best for last! In a believer's vertical relationship of authority, obedience to the Author and sovereign Ruler over all peoples, nations, and governments should be the preeminent motivation in our lives. The reason is simple: If we do not allow God to speak truth and minister into our *own* lives, how in the world could we be expected to minister effectively to others? Calling God "the Creator" acknowledges that He is, indeed, creative, using various innovative means to catch our attention and then direct our minds to stay on Him…relying on *His* wisdom, and not our own…*His* grace and mercy, and not our constant striving for things that do not satisfy. The following examples illustrate some of the ways in which God can work in our lives, as part of His heavenly "tutorial" for spiritual growth: God's Word throughout the scriptures is Truth, instructing us in righteousness or "right living;" the lyrics of a hymn or a modern Christian song can illuminate our minds and hearts, providing comfort and solace; the testimony of a friend who was lost-then-found can give us hope; or the passionate message delivered from the pulpit during a Sunday service can stir our spirits to action. God never runs out of ways to call us to Himself, and the accountability only He can provide. Isaiah 55:6 declares, "Seek ye the LORD while he may be found, call ye upon him while he is near." There is great hope in this verse, because God is *always* around…He is *always* near. It is only our own pride and rebellion which cause us to forsake His leadership, His lordship over our lives. To paraphrase an old television sitcom title, instead of *Father Knows Best,* we convince ourselves that, in fact, we know the best course of action to pursue in life. In our natural state, apart from God, *we* determine the best thing to say or do without first checking with the One who *made* us and everything in our world. To further illustrate how we can overtly shun or imperceptibly drift away from accountability with God, here is a thumbnail sketch of a story with which many of you should be somewhat familiar.

David, a lowly shepherd boy of humble origin, was chosen by the prophet Samuel to serve God as king over all the tribes of Israel (1 Samuel 16:13). Prior to his incarnation, David entered into the service of King Saul as his armor bearer. He comforted Saul's tormented soul, helping the king to relax by playing soothing sounds of music on his lyre. When the Philistine forces assembled for war against the Israelites, the heathen enemies sent their champion warrior, Goliath, into a valley separating the warring armies. Goliath was a giant of a man, approaching ten feet in height! He issued a "winner-take-all" challenge to Saul's army: "Choose a man and have him come down to me. If he is able to fight and kill me, we will become your subjects; but if I overcome him and kill him, you will become our subjects and serve us" (1 Samuel 17:8, 9). This demonstration went on for forty days with no combatant emerging from among the terrified Israelites. Finally David, undoubtedly motivated by the reward of a large sum of money and the king's daughter in marriage, stepped onto the field of battle and slew the armor-clad giant with a sling and one well-placed smooth stone to the middle of his forehead, declaring prior to the deed: "This day the Lord will deliver you into my hands, and I'll strike you down...and the whole world will know that there is a God in Israel" (1 Samuel 17:46).

David rose to power and, as king, became a mighty ruler. While his military forces were off conquering the Ammonites, David stayed in Jerusalem. One evening, while relaxing on his rooftop retreat, the king spied a beautiful woman bathing. A messenger informed King David that the woman's name was Bathsheba, and that she was the wife of one of his loyal soldiers, Uriah the Hittite. In spite of the fact that both he and she were married, David sent for her, had sexual relations with her and later, to his dismay, found that she was pregnant (2 Samuel 11:2-5). In a calculated effort to undo his transgression, the king devised a plan to bring Uriah home from battle so that he might enjoy a conjugal visit with his wife. When the loyal soldier arrived, he refused to go to his home, instead pledging his allegiance to King David and his compatriots on the front lines. David, now exasperated, sent him back into battle with orders that he should not return, but die in the fighting. After Uriah's death, King David called for Bathsheba. "…she became his wife and bore him a son. But the thing David had done displeased the Lord" (2 Samuel 11:27). As recompense for his sin, the infant boy died.

David not only abused his God-given power, he abdicated the mantle of protection and blessing his accountability to God had provided. From his hillside abode as a shepherd boy, to the throne room as king, David had lived for God and served Him. In spite of his divine ordination, he strayed from his personal relationship with the Creator, committing fornication, adultery, and murder. He lied, cheated, and stole what was not his to own. Nevertheless, after a time of silence which almost destroyed David physically and mentally, the chosen one who had so precipitously fallen from grace relented, repented, and, completely disarmed, declared that, first and foremost, *he had sinned against God*…the most grievous thing any man could do. David returned and recommitted his total being to his first love—God. As a result, despite a multitude of sins, David's epitaph refers to him as "a man after God's own heart." I trust you'll agree that this story about the rise and fall of a king provides hope for us all…within and outside prison walls.

The concept of accountability is more than simply a preparatory mechanism for various forms of ministry. Being responsible to a higher authority is a learned character trait which should permeate every aspect of our lives, enabling us to create more harmonious relationships, whether we are worshipping in a church service, strategizing within a corporate office setting, or carrying out the plan of action on a football field or basketball court.

Specifically, regarding ministry to incarcerated men and women, the aforementioned levels of accountability can equip you, me, or *anyone* entering the confines of a prison environment, preparing us to receive an institution's rules, regulations, and instructions with a resolute mind and a properly humbled heart. As we will explore in greater detail within upcoming chapters, prison inmates will more readily receive your message and hold themselves accountable to *you* if they perceive, through your words and actions, that you are willing to defer to the divine authority of God first, and the authority of Godly mentors on Earth as well. There is **nothing** more problematic than a well-meaning minister flying blind in a caged fortress inhabited by birds of prey!

The bottom line is this—humble, accountable men and women, endowed with servants' hearts, can produce a bountiful harvest in God's Kingdom whether they are engaged in secular or sacred pursuits. We will continue to put accountability—and other attributes—to the test in our next chapter, as we prepare to physically enter the prison environment.

U.S. Sentencing Commission figures show that illegal immigrants are three times more likely to be convicted of murder as the general population.

Chapter Ten

SUBJECT TO SEARCH: ENTERING THE PRISON ENVIRONMENT

*"Enter his gates with thanksgiving
and his courts with praise…"*

(Psalm 100:4)

Fran and I were rather new to the prison scene. Having traveled for the better part of a year with a fellow evangelist who had introduced us to ministry within the penitentiary system, we were now flying solo under the banner of SonPower Ministries, providing music and expository preaching to state-prison inmates. On this particular Sunday, Fran and I were paying a first-time visit to an ancient, castle-like fortress, very much unlike the more modern "cookie-cutter" penitentiaries throughout the region. Accompanied by the facility's chaplain, we were winding our way through a maze of linoleum-clad hallways, headed toward the chapel in which we would minister to approximately a hundred men. This assembly of inmates would, hopefully, enjoy their first taste of what we refer to as a SonPower concert/service.

The chaplain and I were engaged in casual conversation when, rather abruptly, he stopped talking and looked quizzically at my wife. "Fran," he asked, "Are you chewing gum?" Somewhat taken aback, Fran acknowledged that she did have a small piece of gum in her mouth. "Follow me," he beckoned to both of us. Detouring 180-degrees from our original destination, the chaplain led us down still another hallway to his office, where he retrieved a paper towel from the washroom. He asked Fran to deposit her chewing gum onto the towel and then, wrapping the gum securely in the paper toweling, he tossed the wad of paper into a grey metal wastebasket. After double checking to make sure that the office door was securely locked, the three of us proceeded once again toward the prison chapel. This time there was no small talk. Instead, the chaplain spent the next several minutes explaining how a simple piece of chewing gum in the wrong hands could jam a lock, be a mold to fabricate a makeshift key, or in some other way be responsible for mayhem within the facility.

That was our welcome—our initiation—to prison ministry. I remember that event and the ensuing conversation as if it had occurred yesterday. The lesson was, and still *is,* both humbling and convicting.

Fast forward twenty-some years to the present.

"Feet apart," the corrections officer ordered, as he slowly scanned my torso with a handheld, electronically-sensitive paddle, also referred to as a *wand*. Fran and I were standing in the cramped visitors' entrance to a maximum-security state penitentiary in Pennsylvania, on an unseasonably frigid early-November morning. Normally, we would walk through an imposing full-body metal detector prior to being admitted to the facility, but on this day that machine was not working, so an alternative security device was needed. The paddle emitted a high-pitched squeal as the officer paused at my waistline. "Metal in your belt buckle," the CO exclaimed tersely. I removed my belt, silencing the device, and he continued the process. When the device reached my shoes, that same irritating sound filled the cubicle-sized area. I removed both shoes and immediately felt a jolt, as my stocking-feet met the cold, concrete floor. Upon further examination of my footwear, the officer determined that the shoes had a metal support strut embedded in the molded-rubber soles. Having passed the CO's screening, I gathered some personal items and the contents of my pockets—a necklace, my wedding band, a rumpled cloth handkerchief, and a folded dollar bill—from a circular aluminum bowl—and waited as Fran was treated to the same scrutiny. Through it all, we remained pleasant and upbeat, determined to be shining lights in what might be an otherwise dreary day for this corrections officer and his compatriots.

When entering any prison environment, a modicum of wisdom and common sense, combined with a humble heart, can go a long way toward starting your ministry experience on the right foot. Particularly, in this unique setting, an even-keeled and gracious demeanor can enable you to avoid trials and tribulations of your own making. The aforementioned search scenario illustrates what might happen once any person, outside a prison, has been buzzed in and admitted to the guard shack via a thick, fortified, electronically-controlled steel door. But in reality, the security process for any visitor, to any state or federal facility, begins as guests approach the institution. In Chapter Two, to better introduce readers to the sights and sounds of the total prison experience, I gave a detailed description of our entering a state penitentiary, from our initial approach to the parking area to the front door. In this chapter, in an effort to more readily equip those contemplating service of some sort within the prison system, or for those engaged in ministry, or even for those who are simply interested in this process, I would like to provide more practical commentary.

In our travels, Fran and I frequent a number of state penitentiaries. Although the physical lay-outs of some institutions may be similar, each facility has its own anomalies. That being said, entering and parking in the properly designated area is not always guaranteed. Even traveling at a mandated, much-reduced speed, and in spite of a plethora of directional signs, I can still find myself searching for that proper place to park and disembark before Fran and I make our way, on foot, toward the administration building. If you, as a visitor or volunteer, find yourself in a similar situation, fear not! Chances are, before you travel a significant distance on *any* penitentiary property—especially if your vehicle appears to be meandering through the complex—you will be approached by an officer or prison staffer in a clearly identified truck or utility vehicle. In all probability, you will be asked to explain who you are and what business you have at the facility. This interaction can afford you the first of many opportunities to smile, to answer all questions courteously, and to follow instructions explicitly.

It is a given that, upon entering the prison proper, your person, clothing, and belongings will be scrutinized. Therefore, there are certain items that should not be taken inside prison walls. But did you know that the vehicles of visitors, volunteers—and in some cases, even prison staffers—are subject to search as well? Random searches, of any and all vehicles, may be performed at the request of corrections officers or administrators. Signage on the prison grounds (and verbiage within written rules and regulations) indicates that unannounced inspections of all vehicles parked on prison property are *not* beyond the realm of possibility. Understanding this, I make it a point to have as little as possible in my vehicle. Clothing headed for the dry cleaners is left at home. Boxes filled with old china earmarked for our storage locker are removed from the SonPower Ministries van. Last week's newspapers are dropped off at a recycling bin prior to our arrival at the facility. If you are scheduled to visit an SCI (State Correctional Institution) in some capacity, you might consider following the same course of action. Although not an everyday occurrence, in addition to unscheduled random searches, some facilities may employ the services of specially trained drug or contraband-sniffing dogs who "hit" on certain vehicles, which then target them for closer inspection. Truly, prison security begins *outside* the walls and progresses inward! It never ceases to amaze me when I read a local paper report that "'So-and-so' was arrested while visiting the local prison after a search of her vehicle uncovered two ounces of cocaine hidden in a storage compartment on the driver-side door." Or, "A loaded gun was recovered during a random search in the parking lot of the state penitentiary Saturday morning. The weapon was determined to have been stolen more than a year ago during a home invasion robbery. The owner has been charged with firearms not to be carried without a license and receiving stolen property. Additional charges are pending." Really? In this fallen world, there is enough trouble to be found without inviting it into your life. "For the foolishness of God is wiser than human wisdom, and the weakness of God is stronger than human strength" (1 Corinthians 1:25).

For those volunteering to minister, to teach reading or academic skills, to provide substance-abuse counseling, or to serve in some other way within a penal institution, it would not be expected that entering prison grounds with illegal drugs, alcohol, or a weapon of some sort would be an issue. Prescription medications, on the other hand, without proper clearance, *could* present a problem within the penal system. Unless absolutely necessary, it would be wise to leave such medicines at home. Fortunately, Fran and I have been blessed with excellent health. We are not prone to take prescription meds of any sort, so this issue has not affected us directly during our prison ministry stays. However, experience with a SonPower Ministries' board member who traveled with us on several occasions, plus conversations with wardens and administrators at the county and state prison levels, has shown me that— in most cases—items such as a medically prescribed inhaler would be permitted to be carried by a volunteer during his or her prison visit. Nevertheless, medications of *any* sort should be declared and shown to authorities during the prison clearance and sign-in process.

It's now time to go inside the facility. Why don't you join us as we relive the "sign-in and search" process at a state penitentiary?

We've parked in the designated visitors' section of the parking lot and locked our vehicle. All wallets and personal items have been concealed within the van, including Fran's small pocketbook. While standing in the parking lot, you instinctively check your cell phone for the reply to that last text message. Now we are going to unlock our vehicle once more. Why? Because we must deposit that phone—and any other mobile devices—inside the car, hidden out of sight of prying eyes, including the gaze of other visitors to the facility, whose motives may be less than honorable. You are, in some cases, allowed to take a cell phone as far as the lobby of your local county jail, but you are *not* permitted to carry a cellular device inside the entrance to a penal facility at the state or federal level. Such items top the list of contraband and will be confiscated if not returned voluntarily to visitors' vehicles. Much like the piece of gum in the opening paragraph of this chapter, a cell phone in the hands of an inmate poses an enormous problem within any prison. Imagine the power possessed by a convict who has the ability to communicate clandestinely with the outside world! Prohibited information could be exchanged; escape plans could be conceived and carried out; criminal enterprises or conspiracies could be overseen; even contract killings could be orchestrated. Make no mistake—your cell phone remains locked in the car!

Ready to proceed once again, we cross the dusty, gritty parking lot—our footsteps stirring up bits of decaying cigarette filters and tiny scraps of litter—toward the paved walkway leading to the stark but clearly marked visitors' entrance. It always amuses me that, no matter how nondescript the building entrances are, most prisons have gaily colored seasonal flowers lining the paths, much like rays of light leading to a dark, hopeless place. Fran and I are prepared for what's next…but you flinch and take a step backward, as the harsh, metallic buzz emanating from the lock on the secure steel door announces our arrival. We immediately find ourselves in the visitor's area which, although it may differ from facility to facility, has a sterile sameness about it. We are greeted by the desk-duty officer who asks to examine our photo IDs. Current driver's licenses are the identification cards of choice. (Note: Depending upon the prison, IDs may be returned to the visitors or volunteers, or they may be kept at the front desk until time of departure.) Satisfied, the CO invites Fran to fill in pertinent information on the sign-in sheet. She prints her name and designates "SonPower Ministries, Carlisle, PA" as the visiting group or organization represented. Next, Fran indicates the purpose of our visit—"Chapel Service"—followed by a brief description of our vehicle, including the make, model, color, and the Pennsylvania license plate number. At this point some penitentiaries might request that she sign her name in cursive, others may require a signature when leaving. Now it is my turn. I follow the exact same process. No short-cuts… no "same as above"…no "ditto" marks. Now it is *your* turn…once again, you follow the process exactly as Fran and I did. The officer waits and watches. He instructs us to remove our coats, checking the pockets and linings for contraband. Satisfied, he gathers our apparel on the countertop for us to take into the prison with us now that we are at the end of the sign-in process.

"Empty your pockets and place the contents in a tray, prior to walking through the metal detector," we are advised. I produce a small amount of paper currency, a white cotton handkerchief, my car keys and two cough drops. I mention to the officer that, because I will be singing and speaking over an extended period of time, I would appreciate him allowing me to take the lozenges inside the facility with me. He grants permission for me to do so. On another day, in another prison, with a different officer overseeing this process, I may be denied the privilege of keeping the cough drops on my person. I place the items in one of several shallow wooden trays, much like you would expect to see as an "out box" for papers atop an old-fashioned metal desk. The CO informs me that I can pick up the car keys from him at the front desk when we depart the facility. Fran has nothing in the pockets of her long-sleeved white blouse or the black, tailored dress slacks she is wearing. Purposefully, she left a tube of lip balm and her fingernail clippers in our vehicle, knowing those items would be questionable for clearance. Once again, it is *your* turn. Put all personal belongings in the wooden box…good; now we can proceed.

The full-body, metal detector reminds me of an arched wooden arbor which you might see in a gentrified garden or vineyard decorated with fruited grape vines or flowers. But *this* arbor is a stark, powder-coated, industrial metal apparatus, devoid of any semblance of beauty. Under the metallic arch is a subtly humped "bridge," with granular anti-skid appliqués over a steel frame. This device has one purpose— to detect metal. It does its job as I proceed slowly through the arch. "Buzzzz," loud and clear, as if to say "I got you." First I removed my belt and buckle, followed by my comfortable leather dress shoes (with metal supports in the soles). The third time being the charm, I pass the metal-detection test. Fran, on the other hand, sails through the machine on her first attempt, having nothing on her person to antagonize the steel beast. Now it's *your* turn. "Buzzzz." Gotcha!

Some prison visitors may have to alert the on-duty officer about metal or other objects *within* their bodies which may trigger the detection alarm, including metal or titanium plates, other surgical implants, pacemakers, shrapnel fragments, etc.

As future reference for *all* readers, allow me to list, in no specific order, other items which you should *not* consider taking with you during prison visitation: excessive amounts of paper currency or coins; fingernail clippers or other manicuring devices; pocket knives; "bobby" pins or other types of hair pins; large hair combs or picks; paperclips; any tobacco products; chewing gum; or any liquid in containers, such as hand sanitizer. An exception to this rule may be baby formula if an infant child has been granted clearance

Some penal institutions include, within entrance protocol, procedures that are unique unto themselves. At times, after sign-in, visitors or volunteers may be instructed to listen to penitentiary rules and regulations as they are read aloud by a corrections officer or shift commander. In several instances, Fran and I have been photographed to provide facial recognition during our prison stay. We have been fingerprinted…even though, I'm sure, both sets of our prints are on file in a national database. And on one occasion, my wife was escorted to a private room, where she was patted down by a female corrections officer. I believe that God is constantly providing real-life opportunities for each of us to learn spiritual lessons from the physical events which surround us. In addition to such character traits as patience, humility, and accountability, experience has shown me that the Master Planner can and will use everyday occurrences—even seemingly mundane experiences such as prison admission procedures—to open our eyes and hearts, enabling us to gain new or different perspectives on the extremely serious endeavor of safety—for the inmates, the staff, *and* the visitors.

In the lobbies of many facilities you may discover one-foot square metal cubicles or larger lockers much like those in an elementary or high school. These small units are for storing hats, coats, gloves, wallets, purses, pocketbooks, keys, or other approved paraphernalia during your visit. Safeguarding possessions under lock and key can occur in one of several ways: the visitor or volunteer may be able to sign out a locker key at no charge from the duty officer, a token for a coin-operated storage space may be obtained at the front desk for free, or the guest may be required to pay a small fee for safeguarding items during his or her stay.

Prison volunteers, depending upon the purpose of their visit, may wish to enter a facility with materials such as a Bible, workbooks, or study guides. In theory, any instructional or teaching aids should have approval by the chaplain or another administrative authority prior to transporting them into a prison environment. You can be assured that these materials, in addition to the aforementioned personal items, will be subject to scrutiny. Boxes will be opened and pages of individual books, and other printed materials, will be riffled through in search of anything not in compliance with established regulations. For this reason, Fran and I try to keep loose pages to a minimum, as on any given day a CO, responding to some stressor totally out of our control, may determine that those "freestanding" papers may not be taken into the prison. In some extreme instances, CDs or DVDs may be required to be sent prior to a visit, so that the institution's IT (Information Technology) team can screen such media in advance of its use. The purpose of such cautionary measures is to prevent viruses or malicious malware from being introduced into the penitentiary's computer systems.

After reading the blow-by-blow account of the procedures—and the *variables*—when entering the county or state prison system, you may think, "Could this process possibly get any more complicated?" And the answer would be…"Yes!" Fran and I encounter an even higher level of security when we are required to truck in our sound system and additional equipment for prison ministry music and concert events. That exciting adventure in patience and perseverance will have to wait, however, until a later chapter.

Although this detailed description of the prison-admittance process may seem burdensome and somewhat overwhelming, fear not. After several visits, all these procedures will flow more smoothly and will fall into place as you begin to comprehend the whys and wherefores that surround your entry into a penal facility. Through the years—even with the intangibles and unexpected changes we have encountered in our own prison ministry adventures—Fran and I have remained patient and flexible to the extent that we have been able to cultivate casual friendships with chaplains, corrections officers and staffers during our travels. The rules and regulations which seemed so ponderous to us initially are now received with considerably more grace and understanding, being seen as steps in our spiritual journey to bring the light of the Gospel to imprisoned men and women.

Now as we stand on the threshold of entering the cellblock area, the community room, or the open campus of the prison yard, are you ready to begin setting the stage for relationship and ministry—a "close encounter"—with incarcerated men and women? It's time to get "down and dirty." This is where the real work—and the eternal rewards—begin.

Approximately one-half of all imprisoned
adults are parents of minor children.

Discussing ground rules with
the deputy warden.

View from the sally port,
separating the lobby from the
holding area.

Praising God in the chapel.

Inmate registration for SonPower
Ministries' weekly "chapel service."

Making a point during the
study session.

Distributing the Our Daily
Bread study booklets.

Intense concentration from men
earnestly seeking solutions.

Reading and studying
"The Handbook."

Contemplating the
day's lesson.

A "band of brothers" prepares for battle.

Pete responds to an
inquiry.

"Are you going to live with Him or without Him?"

Pocket Bibles, ready for use.

Question and answer time.

Ending the weekly get together
in prayer.

Inmates make their way
back to the block.

Sign in and sign out...always.

Exiting county prison after
an afternoon of ministry.

Heavy lifting prior to a
concert/service.

Walking the seemingly endless
corridor to "freedom."

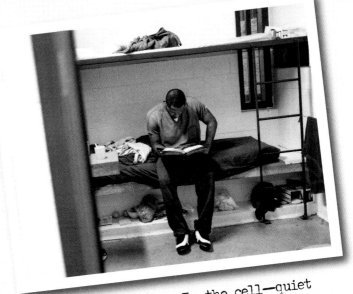

In the cell—quiet
time with God.

Rebel without a cause. "Captivity" personified.

Intentionality amid the steel
fencing and razor wire.

Looking to the future—
more work to do.

Chapter Eleven

SHAKING UP
THE BIG HOUSE

"There is no one who calls on Your name,
who arouses himself to take hold of You;
You have…delivered us into the power of our iniquities."

(Isaiah 64:7)

Six in the morning. Time to rise and shine. Breakfast is delivered to your door: eggs, toast, a piece of fruit. Is this the dawning of a new day during your relaxing vacation at a five-star resort, with concierge service delivering a delectable continental repast? Far from it! This is the beginning of still another day as an inmate at your local county jail or state penitentiary…aka "The Big House." The breakfast tray is delivered unceremoniously by an inmate to your *cell* door. The eggs are powdered, the toast is just warm enough to disturb the smear of butter-substitute on top, and the fruit-of-the-day, a banana, just misses the mark on ripeness. Day after day. Six in the morning. "Breakfast in bed." Part of the convict's lifestyle trifecta of "three hots and a cot."

Breakfast is followed by lunch at 11 a.m.: a questionable veal patty, beans and rice, a cookie, and a flavored-water concoction. Dinner is around 4:30 p.m. Today's menu might include spaghetti with meat sauce, color-faded peas and carrots, a slice of whole-wheat bread, and another powdered fruit drink. Each meal is designed to meet certain required dietary standards. In most prisons, the menu selections are prepared with an eye on caloric intake. The higher the number of calories, the more costly the meal. The prison diet absolutely affects the facility's bottom line and is, therefore, kept under constant surveillance, much like the prisoners themselves. Each mealtime is accompanied by a period of lockdown, when inmates are prohibited from moving about the jail or penitentiary. This affords the corrections staff the time and opportunity to engage in what must seem like a never-ending series of head counts. Morning, noon, and night, "the count" is an utmost priority. Much like the biblical story in Matthew chapter 18 when the shepherd leaves his flock of ninety-nine to search for that solitary sheep that has wandered away, so it is within a prison if an inmate is reported missing from among the general population. Everything stops. *Everything.* The facility is locked down until the lost individual has been accounted for. Through the years, God has shown me how this vitally important physical routine, which keeps inmates from straying, can illustrate a profound spiritual lesson as well. Perhaps you too will see that connection as we continue our travels inside the Big House.

In an effort to maintain constant security and order, corrections officers make their rounds, walking a prescribed path throughout the facility. In doing so, they, too, become a part of the routine—or the distraction—of prison life. Each patrol officer carries in his or her pocket a metal disc called a *chit.* Activated throughout the course of their journey within the prison, the chit identifies the individual performing security checks at any given hour of any given day. The CO carries a metal device referred to as a *pipe.* Imagine a thick, metallic

Oscar Mayer Wiener, and you will have a fairly accurate description of the pipe. At checkpoints throughout the facility, the officer inserts this object into a receptacle mounted in the wall which transfers time, location, and other pertinent information to the pipe. This collected data is downloaded to a computer where it is stored for future access. For example, if trouble of some sort was reported on a given block somewhere around 2 a.m., the computerized data could be examined to determine the officer on duty, the exact time of the security check at that location, and other relevant information that might be useful in clarifying the situation. For an inmate, security rounds can be seen as an unwanted distraction, especially if he or she is engaged in an activity which might be frowned upon by the CO or in violation of prison policy. Examples might include using an unauthorized heat source to prepare a snack in one's cell, engaging in illicit drug use, etc. Late at night or early in the morning, the audible "beep," as the security officer inserts the pipe into the wall-mounted receptacle, may also serve as a source of annoyance for the sleeping prisoner.

If it is true that mealtimes, to some extent, dispel the monotony which can so easily beset many incarcerated men and women, there are additional activities—some mandated, some voluntary—which can also help alleviate boredom, provide structure, and offer positive assistance to the residents behind the electrified fences and the impenetrable stone walls. Mandatory activities are scheduled for certain inmates, several times per week, throughout the day and evening hours. Examples of such appointments include drug and alcohol counseling, anger management sessions, educational classes—including the opportunity for men and women to attain their GEDs while serving their sentences. In addition to attending basic educational classes, which may be a requirement of an inmate's sentence, there are, in some instances, voluntary opportunities for men and women to receive specialized teaching and/or vocational training, including college-level academics. Through the years, numerous studies have shown that the recidivism rate among prison inmates drops extraordinarily for those engaged in attaining higher-education degrees. To round out our examples of mandated instruction, prisoners involved in sexually-related crimes are often required to complete programs specifically designed for sex offenders.

Still other mandated distractions which break up the mundane prison routine revolve around inmates' medical needs. Whether welcome or not, cell visits or authorized trips to the nurse's station become part of the regimen for inmates in need of health-related care. Medications are usually administered twice a day for the growing number of inmates suffering from physical or mental maladies. Diabetics depend upon daily monitoring of blood-sugar levels. Heart patients need specific medications, as do those who require periodic testing for high blood pressure. Antibiotics and various prescription drugs are professionally dispensed to inmates with conditions ranging from depression, to bipolar disorder, to HIV, to tuberculosis and cancer, to name a few.

"Sheets and towels," echoes the cry throughout the prison block. Another inmate on the job dispenses these items during any given week…usually alternating the "sheet" days with the "towel" days. To the men and women in their "huts," it's another break in the routine— and a welcome relief in the effort to provide a modicum of cleanliness and personal hygiene as the days…the weeks…the months…or the years pass.

In addition to fresh linens, prisoners are able to receive laundry service, in most institutions, once or twice a week. Upon commitment to a jail or penitentiary, offenders receive a "property box" with an assigned number, which serves as an identifier for personal items. Throughout their incarceration, this property box number is written on the inmates' laundry bags. Each week, approved personal clothing items worn into the facility, as well as socks, underwear, and other apparel purchased from the prison commissary, are laundered. The pick-up, washing, and drying of soiled clothing and delivery of fresh laundry is usually the function of work-release inmates or "out-mate trustees." As part of paying their debt to society, approved prisoners perform tasks such as laundry duty for the handsome salary of approximately $2.50 per day!

Although closely monitored, as part of ongoing security measures, there are opportunities for social interaction among the prison population. Community areas, or "day rooms," provide tables and seating for such activities as checkers, chess, card games, and spirited exercises in Scrabble…where the absence of a dictionary to verify made-up words sometimes leads to less-than-friendly disagreements. Wall-mounted televisions in the common area broadcast video images constantly throughout the daylight and evening hours, until the call for "lights out"—usually around 11 p.m. For the population on a given cell block, any cell within view of a television is truly a "penthouse suite." Power and influence among the inmate hierarchy often determines which channels, special programs, or sporting events are watched. Notice I mentioned video images only when referring to the TVs. More on that topic in a moment.

Without a doubt, the event relished by most institutionalized men and women is the one day each week when inmates have an opportunity to purchase, with their own money, basic and creature-comfort items from the prison commissary. Goods-for-sale range from soap, deodorant, and toothpaste, much sought-after candies and snack foods, to the most prized possession for some convicts—coffee! Throughout the prison system, in response to budget cutbacks, efforts to control caffeine intake or "get tough" policies, coffee is no longer a menu item for mealtimes. The caffeinated beverage made available to the inmates is packaged instant coffee. Bags of coffee are bought, sold, bartered, and shared among the prison population, usually brewed in "hotpots" or small, single-burner heating units, found in the day rooms or common areas.

Still another sought-after item allows prisoners to solve the dilemma of "video-only" television viewing. Through the commissary, prison-issued portable radios can be purchased. These radios synchronize audio to the TV video images throughout the facility, allowing inmates to complete the television-viewing experience. In addition, those possessing the device have a workable radio with the capability of receiving a limited number of local stations.★ Television viewing, radio listening and, if permitted, visits from family and friends create opportunities for convicts to keep abreast of current events in the outside world, as well as providing relief from the everyday prison routine.

Commissary purchases are made utilizing monies deposited in an inmate's account by family members or friends. In addition, money can be credited to an account as the result of work performed by an inmate inside or, in the case of county jail work release, outside the facility. The bottom line for each prisoner is this: no money, no commissary. For those without money, deals are struck and favors are extended, creating a form of "jailhouse usury" which might even border on indentured servitude. Commissary items can be parleyed to create "in-house enterprises," to pay off gambling debts, to provide an enjoyable after-dinner snack, or to extend an individual's power and influence in this society-within-a-society. And the aforementioned bags of coffee tend to be the primo bargaining chip of choice.

"Hello—Mom?"

A vital cog in the wheel of inmate communication with the outside world revolves around access to the prison telephone system. From the elation of talking to an infant son, daughter, or grandchild, to the intense, gut-wrenching drama of working through relational or personal situations with a spouse or other family member, to the inevitably frustrating back-and-forth dialogue with attorneys and parole

★Note: In some institutions, enterprises have been discovered where ambitious inmates or dishonest guards have established illegal sales of sanctioned, or unsanctioned, electronics—including televisions, radios, computers, or cell phones—which were discreetly smuggled into the prison or were left by inmates upon their release. Such items are sometimes referred to as "hot trash."

or probation officers, the telephone provides a lifeline to those who often cannot see the light of day. Under the watchful eyes of COs, inmates place calls from among banks of wall-mounted telephones, often located in the prison common areas. In many institutions, you might find one telephone for every ten inmates, but the inmate-to-phone ratio could easily be higher. Calling hours are available throughout a given day, with the exception of "overnight" (from approximately 11 p.m. to 6 a.m.) and during meals, when facilities go on lockdown. For decades, prison telecommunication has been limited to *outgoing, collect calls only.* Now, with the advent of new technology, debit-based telephone charges can allow monies to be subtracted from an inmate's prison account to pay for calls. To avoid issues with excessively long conversations and the problems which might arise, standard prison policy is to limit all telephone calls to twenty minutes. Audio prompts inform an inmate as to the amount of time remaining until the system automatically shuts off at the twenty-minute mark.

"Love you—bye!"

When you drive by a state or federal penitentiary, chances are you are struck by the enormity of the interconnected stone and concrete structures and the ominous presence of glinting razor or concertina wire draped over the entire complex, much like the ribbon on a poorly wrapped Christmas gift. Given a second glance, you may notice a series of expansive exercise areas, some complete with basketball courts, soccer fields, or weightlifting stations. These amenities provide prisoners with the opportunity to enjoy fresh air, to expend energy and aggression through participation in physical activities, as well as to engage in social interaction with fellow inmates, particularly those housed on other blocks or in a different section of the facility. In some quarters, debates still rage as to whether or not it is prudent to allow men to "pump iron" and, as a result, to become bigger, stronger, and to cultivate more massive physiques while serving their time in a correctional institution. Be that as it may, this component of physical exercise and socialization among incarcerated men and women remains part of the delicate balance of maintaining order and discipline in the never-ending push-pull relationship between the administration, the corrections officers, and the prison population.

In smaller facilities, particularly county jails, the more expansive prison exercise area may be replaced by a smaller space known as the "urban yard." The urban yard, which is open to the elements, tends to be enclosed with a security grill and overhead roofing to provide some semblance of protection during inclement weather. This space gives inmates the opportunity to enjoy a fresh-air environment while also providing periodic opportunities for limited exercise and movement.

Monotony and lack of freedom: they can seem like a death sentence, even to the inmate who's only doing sixty days for drunk driving. Why? Because even with all the distractions I described—unwanted or not—there still exists a sameness behind prison bars that can suck the life from the human soul, dulling the mind and draining the prisoner of spiritual vitality and the hope of a better tomorrow…

Unless there is something more…

This is where **you** come in. ***Why don't you—and God—become the distraction that shakes things up in the Big House?***

Have you ever wanted to make a difference? I'm not referring to causing a few ripples in a lake, but about creating a *tsunami* with towering, thunderous waves that even the most skilled surfer would fear to ride! In this lifetime, you can quietly play your part in bringing about imperceptible changes, or you can come onto the scene with guns a'blazing—ready to break down walls and to "shake things up!" It's your choice. The first option is like a lazy-river attraction at the local amusement park, where you drift along easily, in a sea of like-minded people, toward a predetermined destination. The second opportunity is much more like a crazy, careening roller-coaster adventure, which takes your breath away as you rise to meteoric heights, only to plunge a second later into the great unknown. Take it from me: Serving incarcerated men and women—even in the quietest of moments—can be that great adventure you have always craved but, for one reason or another, have never pursued.

Do you know what makes prison ministry so exhilarating to me? It is experiencing the supernatural elements that only God can inject into any given situation. It is knowing that, even in my weakest, most human moments, there is a creative authority at my disposal that nobody but the Author of the Universe can give. This wonder-working power provides the difference between timidly knocking on the door of unresolved sin, of spiritual ignorance, stagnation, malaise, or apathy, and blasting that door off its hinges, bringing honor and glory to the One who deserves it all. There will be more than a few challenges along the way, but God's Word encourages you and me to "Trust in the Lord with all your heart and lean not on your own understanding; in all your ways submit to him, and he will make your paths straight" (Proverbs 3:5, 6). We can add to this truth the realization that *all* of God's ways are higher, wider, deeper and nobler than our ways, and that He knows what's best for us and those we endeavor to serve. Now *that's* power! And fully equipped with that sort of spiritual armor—to quote the words to an old soul song—"You can't lose with the stuff you use…"—as long as we're using God's "stuff" and not relying on ourselves too much.

In spite of limited monies for chaplains and materials and no budgets available for outside providers, religious services are continually sought after by imprisoned men and women. They are truly needy people seeking to break through the spiritual clutter in their minds and hearts to arrive at a better place in their lives. I believe that God has put these desperate offenders in jail to keep them from utterly destroying themselves in a lost and dying world outside the prison walls. And so, for you or for me, I see the opportunities to serve within the prison system—to engage with seeking-souls or struggling believers face-to-face—as "divine appointments," not simply happenstance or the luck of the draw. Whether you are involved in presenting a film series, facilitating a Bible study, preaching the Gospel, or performing uplifting music, your presence can and will affect the lives of lost people in this unique environment.

God has endowed in me—as He has in everyone—certain spiritual characteristics which affect the way we respond to the world around us. As a result of this spiritual gifting, one of my tendencies is that I want people to like me. Growing up, I achieved that end by cultivating a sharp wit and a sometimes irreverent sense of humor. Throughout my junior and senior high school years, I relished my role as the class clown who *still* wanted to be taken seriously. As a young man, and well into adulthood, I found acceptance and accolades through vocal and musical performance. I took it personally when people didn't want to hear—or failed to agree with—what I had to say. Through a successful career in advertising and marketing, leading into the call to ministry, I sensed a maturation process taking place regarding my desire to want to be accepted and appreciated. However, God, in His unique manner of teaching me His ways, employed a bunch of criminals to show me, in no uncertain terms, that not only is the Gospel of Jesus Christ often offensive to the hardened heart, but that the inability to articulate one's faith succinctly and boldly or to stand up for what you say you believe is truth, will make the mission of changing hearts for eternity an even more dicey endeavor than it normally may be within the hostile environment of a penal institution.

During the early years of SonPower Ministries' prison evangelism efforts, when Fran and I were invited to state penitentiaries to perform our brand of contemporary Christian music and preaching, I failed to realize that certain members of my audience were simply using this occasion to break up the monotony of their day. Prison religious services provide welcome relief for a man★ to get out of his "hut," off the cell block, and to move about the facility. Also, such occasions may

★Note: The majority of SonPower Ministries' state penitentiary concert/services take place in male facilities, simply because—from state-to-state—for every prison dedicated to females, there may be a dozen such facilities for male offenders.

provide an opportunity to communicate or to "take care of business" with other inmates with whom the prisoner may not have contact on a regular basis.

The aspect of "taking care of business" during time spent in the prison chapel might include catching up with a *homie* about what's happening in the old neighborhood; it could involve the exchange of contraband, commissary items, or weapons; or it might revolve around the consummation of a drug deal. In Matthew 21:12, the Bible teaches us that, "Jesus entered the temple courts and drove out all who were buying and selling there. He overturned the tables of the money changers…" In this short Scripture passage we see evidence that Jesus Christ Himself demonstrated righteous anger when he observed the oblations to His heavenly Father being blasphemed and God's house of worship being prostituted for the carnal and self-centered pleasures of humanity. In my position as God's representative among the prisoners, I may not be able to run around the chapel overturning tables, but I *can* and *do* pray that God, in His sovereign majesty, will thwart the plans of the enemy (Satan) and the evil minds of men, to provide order, attentiveness, and hearts seeking truth during the service time…with as few diversions as possible.

Because *I* can rather easily be distracted, I believe God has equipped me to be cognizant of that tendency among the inmates. In our early concert services, before larger audiences (as opposed to smaller Bible studies), if the chaplain on duty did not issue such a statement, I found myself, kindly but firmly reminding the men that the chapel service was not the time for catching up with friends or for idle chatter. I endeavored to impress upon those in attendance that *their own interruptive actions could provide the distraction which might prohibit another inmate from gaining greater spiritual understanding or—even more disastrous— might cause him to miss the opportunity to change his life for eternity!* On one or two occasions, when situations with crosstalk and discourteous behavior threatened to spiral things out of control, God *did* empower me to respond with a righteous ferocity that caught even the most callous inmates off guard—letting them know in the most demonstrative way that God, His Word, and His ambassador were not to be disrespected! In case you're wondering how *that* approach worked, all I can say is this: if the inmates—or anyone else, for that matter—understand that you are sincere and serious about the time you spend with them and the message you bring, they will respect you and will "back you up" if and when distractions occur. I'll talk about real-life examples as we explore in greater detail the "rubber" of ministry concepts meeting the "road" of life.

Empathy…trust…respect. These represent important building blocks as we begin personal interaction and relationship-building with incarcerated men and women. You'll find this out in our next chapter as we begin face-to-face ministry with men and women behind the steel bars in the Big House.

An encouraging alternative to incarceration
within a typical prison facility is secure
"boot camps"—offering structured military-
type training—to strengthen the body,
mind and spirit of the inmate.

Chapter Twelve

FACE-TO-FACE: INITIAL INMATE INTERACTION

"When did we see you sick or in prison and go to visit you?…Whatever you did for the least of these…you did for me."

(Matthew 25:39, 40)

*I*t was a Wednesday afternoon and I was doing what I seemed compelled to do every week at this time: I was conducting what I like to call a "pre-sentencing/pre-release" class at the local county jail.

Ten molded plastic chairs were arranged in a compact circle in the new multipurpose room, a large rectangular space with a high acoustical-tiled ceiling, off-white cinderblock walls punctuated with several horizontal rows of safety glass "picture windows" looking out onto two perpendicular hallways which met at the front corner of our meeting place. At each end of the multipurpose room was a heavy, metal door. Inside the front door, open to the incoming inmates, was a literature table with magazines, print articles, and assorted materials rearranged to provide room for my "discipleship class" sign-in sheet. A mobile lectern and audio-video cart were pushed up against the block wall. Across the room, additional columns of beige plastic chairs were stacked in what had been an empty space flanked by the plate glass windows. Although the room was off the main corridor of the prison and, therefore, provided less line-of-sight security for me personally, it was preferable to the original chapel area which was used by male and female inmates and provided many more opportunities for distraction. Besides, I had the comfort of knowing that, at all times, one of the many all-seeing eyes of the jail-wide security system was monitoring our goings-on in the room. A quick smile darted across my face as a motley crew of scoffers, seekers, and believers entered the hallway leading to the entrance door, passing in front of an expanse of windows as they did so. Thirteen men. These were the souls God had chosen to be with me on this day.

The sign-in process had bogged down, as two inmates who were first-time attendees to my weekly get-together engaged in small talk as they riffled through the numerous publications which covered the table. "Gentlemen," I encouraged, "Let's save the catch-up conversations for after class." The two new guys grudgingly complied. Several of the regulars behind them nodded understandingly as they waited in line. The "newbies" grabbed chairs, placing them behind the boundary of the circle. "Expand the circle please…no back row." Chair legs scraped across the shiny linoleum-tiled floor as additional spaces were filled and the session members seated themselves—nine familiar faces and four first-timers. I stated, as I had many times before, that we were seated in a circle because that was the strongest form ever created. I went on to explain that a circular form has no beginning, no end and, therefore—even though I was facilitating this particular session—a circle has no head.

Inmates need to know that they are not going to be judged, minimized, or made examples of within the context of religious services—no matter in what form this ministry takes place. In a prison environment, if we are going to develop any sort of meaningful relationships, we must understand that, in reality, we are guests in the prisoners' home. That idea may sound a bit strange, but think about it for a moment. Within the penitentiary walls is a society within a society. Rules and regulations are set by the administration, but they are also instituted by the inmates. Penal facilities tend to be high-stress environments, where individuals may be burdened with **guilt, denial, depression, various forms of mental illness, underdeveloped communications and social skills, poor coping mechanisms, spiritual oppression, and addictive behaviors.**

To better understand the nature of our mission field—and factors that drive the thinking and behavior of prisoners—let's briefly touch on some of these overriding burdens which weigh down the minds and spirits of incarcerated men and women. Addictions to alcohol, hard drugs, prescription medications, sex, etc.—can and often do affect every aspect of a prisoner's existence. Through the years, various studies have shown that unresolved addictions factor directly or indirectly in approximately 80% of prison sentences across the nation. These physical dependencies are often accompanied by coping mechanisms such as lying, deception, and manipulation as affected individuals try to maintain some semblance of order in lives that have been turned upside down and inside out. The "con," or "running game," becomes a way of life, to get by and to "get over" on society-at-large. Deception becomes a mechanism for survival.

In time, individuals living in denial—even some professing to have a personal relationship with Jesus Christ—tend to exhibit hardened hearts, far from God. Generally, in order to exonerate themselves from the moral and spiritual edicts of everyday life, people in denial are more prone to receive deception as truth and to incorporate lies from the pit of hell into a lifestyle built on a lack of responsibility and accountability…content to blame others for their personal failures, but never themselves. Tragically, within the penal system, there *are* men and women who have been falsely accused and imprisoned for crimes they did not commit. Accepting that fact, as you venture into the unknown waters of prison ministry, you may be surprised by the number of inmates who resolutely maintain their innocence despite overwhelming evidence of their guilt. As if to fulfill the adage that "If you repeat a lie long enough it will become truth," over time, circumstances surrounding a particular transgression may morph, in the mind of the convicted felons, to accommodate their skewed rationale for outright denial of the offense. To further complicate matters, some inmates have taken a cue from the current legal system utilizing law libraries within the prisons to craft defenses based on judicial errors, additions or omissions of evidence, or the claim of inadequate representation— which can be a reality—to circumnavigate the spirit of the law in their own criminal cases. These are the imprisoned individuals with whom God is equipping you and me to build relationships. Through the twists and turns of interpersonal connections, fledgling minister/inmate relationships must be based on foundational principles of *spiritual* truth above all else. This can be a difficult assignment in a world where self is king…where too many people—far beyond the prison population— demand rights to which they are not entitled or privileges which hold no value in the eternal scheme of life.

A variety of factors may impede the ability of some inmates to process information and to arrive at sound, sensible solutions to successfully cope with the problems which surround them. Some of these impediments include dysfunctional family histories (in spiritual terms, "generational curses"); physical, verbal, or emotional abuse; a lack of educational or job skills, which can affect clarity of thinking and the ability to communicate thoughts effectively; and mental illness or the ravages of various addictions. As a result of these and other stressors, male and female inmates may magnify the downside of given situations and expect worst-case outcomes. As mentioned earlier, throughout the lives of many individuals—inside *and* outside prison walls—crisis situations have become the normal way of surviving, but not *thriving,* here on planet Earth. God's Word is very clear that such a "settle-for" existence is *not* the plan He has for His people. God's desire is that you and I, and every incarcerated man and woman as well, would enjoy an abundant life. "The thief comes to steal and destroy; I have come that they may have life, and have it to the full" (John 10:10). Ironically, some inmates exhibit not only a fear of failure but a *fear of success*—going so far as to subconsciously sabotage a good effort or outcome to ensure a less-than-desirable result. You may know people who do the same— friends or acquaintances, living free in the eyes of society, but locked in prisons of their own design. Perhaps you, yourself, have fallen into this trap at one time or another. I believe that I have.

Incarcerated men and women have copious amounts of time to sit and think, even in the most structured prison setting. Without a proper focus or spiritual direction, thoughts can easily degenerate to the lowest standard the world has to offer. This process can result in the inmate's inability to let go of a legacy of past failures, to be unstable and unsure in the present, or to be anxious or fearful about what the future holds. In spite of God's Word of encouragement, "Do not be anxious about anything, but in every situation, by prayer and petition, with thanksgiving, present your requests to God" (Philippians 4:6), the task of maintaining some semblance of hope remains daunting for the man or woman who has no answers to the questions of life and whose relationship history reflects abuse, disorder, manipulation, or the shallowness of symbiotic "street-level" alliances. The high-stress surroundings within a penal institution tend to magnify guilt, depression, frustration, anger…even hatred. When allowed to fester and remain unresolved, these emotions can manifest themselves in violent outbursts with seemingly little provocation. A one-on-one visit…a weekly Bible study…a concert…you and I can be that haven of hope for men and women struggling with hopelessness. When you and I choose to *make* the time, and when we *take* the time to minister, in some way, to prisoners, we become "good medicine." How so? By allowing ourselves to be used by God to sow spiritual seeds into another's life we can be a catalyst for change, enabling offenders to take their minds off the here-and-now of their current circumstances and, instead, focus their attention on the eternal promises of God's Word. The objective—to transform the condition of the human heart from a dire, dismal, *hopeless* worldview to that of the life-giving, *hopeful* perspective of Kingdom wisdom and works.

You and I should realize and take ownership of the fact that hopelessness extends far beyond prison walls. It is a worldwide "dis-order." Hopelessness, without alleviation, is a universal "dis-ease." It wearies the mother who home-schools her three children; it discourages the husband who toils in a corporate office setting; it destroys the high-paid—and even higher-esteemed—professional athlete or entertainer; it renders less-than-effective the ministry of a priest or pastor in the pulpit. After more than thirty years of restless wandering and searching for "the answer," I was left with the realization that I had a spiritual "hole in my soul." The good news of the Gospel filled that void because mine was a God-shaped hole. The result: a "new birth," a fresh start in life…fortified by the belief—the *hope*—in something greater than myself. All this was accomplished because someone made an *intentional* commitment, to speak the truth in love, to present an age-old message that I had heard many times before, so that I might choose the gift of everlasting life at the exact moment I was prepared to receive it.

You and I can allow ourselves to be used by God to speak life and hope into the hearts of needy individuals—in the classroom, at the office, on the softball field, in the foyer of a church, at the grocery store, or within the bowels of a county jail or a state penitentiary. *Or,* we can go about our lives focusing solely on our own needs and desires and never even consider taking such a bold, vulnerable step of faith. The choice is yours and mine to make. "But if serving the LORD seems undesirable to you, then choose for yourselves this day whom you will

serve…But as for me and my household, we will serve the LORD."
(Joshua 24:15).

From a practical point of view, prison is a place where what might seem like insignificant problems are blown out of proportion becoming major obstacles or impediments to living life with any sense of victory. Examples might include a lack of basic toiletry items, harassment by another prisoner, or release paperwork that is three weeks past the expected due date. Existing in these surroundings, day in and day out, crises too easily *can* become the norm. You and I are visitors invited into this world for a specific spiritual purpose. We may come with a modicum of authority, but we are visitors nonetheless. As we proceed with whatever it is that God has prepared for us to do, we can arm ourselves with the power of His Word, as illustrated in Matthew 10:16, when Jesus spiritually fortified His disciples with the following admonition: "I am sending you out like sheep among wolves. Therefore be as shrewd as snakes and as innocent as doves." This statement should remind us that, in *any* environment, we should be cautious and aware of our surroundings, as well as our calling. But, to me, it is also a reminder that incarcerated men and women are people much like ourselves. God made them, He loves them, and we are called upon to do the same.

Within the state penitentiary system, the larger concert/preaching-type services in which Fran and I participate are highly regulated, time-sensitive events. A predetermined order-of-service provides structure, as do the presence of a cadre of corrections officers who maintain absolute continuity and order throughout the proceedings. Admittedly, there is a bit more creative freedom in the small-group settings, especially at the county-prison level. But with that freedom comes responsibility. Why? Because the onus for establishing structure and order within the context of ministry falls on the shoulders of the outside/volunteer service providers: you and me.

Back to our current session: Here we sit, in a slightly out-of-round circle. Our study time, reflection, and discussion begins with prayer. Then I request that the men volunteer their first names. Some do so loudly and clearly, others offer little more than a mumbled whisper. I read their faces. Given proper time, there is a story to be told—and heard—behind each visage. Some of my students have been attending these sessions for a year or more, having opportunity to serve sentences of up to two years at the county level, as opposed to doing time "upstate," or in a federal penitentiary. (The decision as to whether a man or woman serves county or state time is affected by any number of variables including standard sentencing guidelines, the prisoner's criminal history, or the extenuating circumstances surrounding a particular offense.) I remember several of the inmates from weeks, months, or even years gone by. They have violated parole or have reoffended and now find themselves back in the place to which they had vowed never to return. One young man in his early twenties sits quietly. He has gained quite a bit of unwanted notoriety—his mug shot plastered throughout the region in newspapers and featured on television newscasts—as he awaits transportation to a state facility for a first-degree murder conviction. His penalty will be life without the possibility of parole. Through our months together, I have watched God transform him from a braggadocious, argumentative, vile-tempered street thug to a more humble servant, willing to come alongside and assist other struggling convicts with a kind word or a good deed, expecting nothing in return. For him, the state penitentiary will either become his mission field or his undoing. Whichever path he chooses, this heir to the Kingdom of God will remain in prison for the rest of his earthly life.

Roughly one-half of today's participants have brought their own Bibles with them from the cellblock. I offer several used Bibles to the remaining cast of characters. Three inmates take me up on my offer. As I do at every meeting, I remind the prisoners that the chaplain has

124

new or slightly used "handbooks," as I like to refer to them, to use while they are in the jail and to take with them when they leave.

The companion source of scripture study which God put on my heart many years ago to use as a practical teaching aid is the three-month edition of the *Our Daily Bread* booklets. I have found these to be simple, effective tools, utilizing short stories and vignettes to more-clearly illustrate the daily Scripture verses. The inmates never know which *Our Daily Bread* reading of any given week God will put on my heart to pursue. But over time they *do* realize that during each class session, if they approach His Word with the proper heart-attitude, God will never fail to reveal some sort of useful, uplifting, and empowering truth to them. Not some mysterious, deep theological clap-trap that they must struggle to understand, but real-life information bursting with an unconditional, abiding love which transcends any worldly alternatives.

I begin to engage the eclectic "band of brothers" whom God has presented to me on this particular day with the selected Scripture lesson. My language vacillates from formal to casual, as the situation demands or as the Spirit leads. "Remember gentlemen, there is no such thing as a dumb question." The men are also reminded that this is a sacred time…an opportunity for them to show respect to God, to His representative (me), and to each other through appropriate language and actions. And, last but not least, I inform the inmates that the lessons presented on this particular day, to them, are equally important for me to learn from and employ in my life as well.

And so we begin, first reading the pre-selected daily scripture reference from the *Our Daily Bread* devotional lesson, then moving immediately to the corresponding passage in the Bible, where we will spend the majority of our time. By design, I request that each inmate read one verse of the chosen lesson, until the Scripture-of-the-day is read in its entirety. "Those of you with Bibles…as we proceed around the circle, if you don't care to read, simply say 'Pass,' and the next guy will pick up the verse that needs to be read." Some of the offenders render the words and meaning eloquently; others struggle to interpret the jumble of letters and syllables in front of them, reading at a first or second-grade level. They are assisted by their fellow inmates who seem to sense that this is a special time in their day—perhaps in their lives—during which they have been given a chance to lift up and support another brother in the midst of his struggles as opposed to putting him down or subjecting him to ridicule.

With our first read-through complete, we now return, again, to the initial verse. Word after word, line upon line, the inmates and I explore the Scripture lesson for greater understanding—to better determine how the *practical* application of God's Word can affect each man's life in real and meaningful ways. In our weekly discussions, one or two of the participants will inevitably be more vocal than the others, sometimes to the point that I may be forced to gently short-circuit their "contributions." Today is no exception. One of the first-time attendees, a middle-aged black man, seems determined to "teach" all of us the facts of life as he knows them to be from his experiences on the street. After more than a few minutes of interruptions followed by rambling dialogue, several of the inmates begin to shake their heads in frustration. One rises from his chair and quietly exits the room. He has had enough. Sensing that the class session could be in danger of being hijacked by the newcomer's constant commentary, I request politely that we allow others equal opportunity to speak and that statements be directed to the subject-at-hand…no "bunny trails." The gentleman receives my admonition with grace and the dialogue proceeds, with those inmates who choose to do so expressing heartfelt concerns, fears, hopes, and desires, providing examples from their own lives to support the discussion topics.

Another newcomer to the session is a short, stocky, pale-complexioned, young white man—perhaps in his mid-twenties—with his right arm sleeved in elaborate, vibrant tattoos. A particularly noticeable "tat," snaking from beneath his shirt collar onto his neck, disappears beneath scraggly, unkempt, jet-black hair that cascades down upon his shoulders. His face mirrors defeat; his dark, sunken eyes dart back and forth, as if signaling "Someone help me...*please.*" From a Bible I had given him he haltingly reads a scripture verse, and as the session unfolds, the first-timer poses several questions. There is a desperation in his voice. To me, it reveals a mind and human spirit that has no answers. After class, as I bid farewell to several of the inmates on their way out of the multipurpose room, I catch the young man's attention, beckoning him to stay for a moment. "Thanks for joining us," I smile, shaking his hand. "Could you teach me your first name again?"

"David," he replies, his eyes looking up to meet mine.

Sensing the Holy Spirit's leading, I dive into the waters of evangelism head first. "I really appreciated your willingness to ask questions..." Pausing for an instant, I continue, "Would I be correct in believing that, God forbid, if you were to die today, you might not be sure if you would spend eternity in a place called 'heaven'?"

Shuffling his feet uneasily, David's gaze wavers slightly. "My parents took me to church as a kid...but I haven't been there in, like, forever," he explains, perhaps thinking that he has produced the correct answer.

Undeterred, I query him about whether or not he understood the portion of the day's lesson explaining how Jesus Christ died and shed His blood, so that *our* sins might be forgiven...so that we could receive the gift of everlasting life with Him in heaven. He nods. "Any reason why you wouldn't want to receive that gift of personal relationship with Christ today?" I ask.

"No," comes the reply, expressed quickly and with hope. Standing in the middle of the now-empty room, my hands resting on David's shoulders, we bow our heads, pray together, and another soul is ushered into the Kingdom of God.

David immediately starts beaming and begins to relay to me how crazy the last two hours of his life have been. Lying on his cot in the cell, he heard the call for "SonPower Ministries in the multipurpose room," and immediately thought about catching some more shuteye. "But something told me to get up and come down to 'church,'" he explains. I laugh, encourage him to continue reading his Bible and tell him I look forward to seeing him at next week's session. David shakes his head. "You don't understand, Mr. Einstein—I'm being released tomorrow!"

I laugh all the more proclaiming, "Brother, this was no coincidence that you showed up in class today. This was a divine appointment!"

Another vibrant victory over spiritual death, creatively orchestrated by the Savior of our souls. Another opportunity for the light of Jesus Christ to pierce the darkness of a human heart.

But what if that darkness is just too dark…too pervasive… seemingly too oppressive to endure? Let's continue our journey.

Some prison systems have pioneered programs whereby selected inmates earn the right to help train and socialize rescue canines, to prepare the dogs for adoption—thus adding to the quality of life of the animal and the offender.

Chapter Thirteen

A WORD ABOUT MENTAL AND SPIRITUAL OPPRESSION

"For our struggle is not against flesh and blood,
but against…the powers of this dark world and…
spiritual forces of evil in the heavenly realms."

(Ephesians 6:12)

Seated at the T-intersection of a central hallway within the prison facility, behind a table in an open-ended cubicle, I waited uneasily for my appointment with a stranger.

I derived some comfort from the knowledge that I was within spitting distance of the guard shack, where uniformed duty officers were available at a moment's notice. But bad things sometimes need only seconds to materialize. This mid-day rendezvous—this possibly "unholy alliance"—was the result of my agreeing to get together one-on-one with a troubled prisoner at the request of his parents. A pastor friend, familiar with the family dynamics and the current situation, had forewarned me that the young man with whom I would be meeting had been both verbally and physically abusive to his parents and others attempting to help him. He was in a state of rebellion in his spirit and

129

currently was refusing to take prescribed medication for a mental disorder. Thus, he was prone to unpredictable, violent, psychotic episodes. So, here I sat…all five-foot-nine, 145 pounds of me…waiting.

My back was to the wall so that, hopefully, when my guest was seated across the table, he would have *his* back to the prison surroundings and thus would be more attentive during our conversation. Also, my positioning allowed me to have line-of-sight with the COs on duty, just in case something unforeseen occurred. From a distance, I observed a solitary figure moving down what seemed like an endless hallway toward the visitation cubicle. He didn't walk so much as he lumbered, shuffling his feet slightly with each step. A large man in his late twenties to early thirties, I presumed; he was not particularly tall, but broad and thick, much like an enormous brown-clad tree trunk wearing scuffed, off-white tennis shoes—an imposing, frightening man-child of a figure. As he approached the meeting table, I rose from my chair, smiled and extended my hand in welcome. The inmate simply stood before me and stared, his eyes bulging from beneath a shaggy mane of thick, unruly, dark hair. Then he squinted his eyes tightly, as if to clear his mind to better focus on my presence. I sat down; he did as well, facing me with a vacant, confused look. Observing the tortured countenance before me, I remember thinking, "Dear Lord, there's nobody home." In spite of prayerful preparation for this event, I felt an ominous darkness fill our space. Nevertheless, I introduced myself and began to explain the reason for my visit. He interrupted, asking over and over again, "Who *are* you? Why are you here?" Inserting bits of information as best I could, I related that I was acquainted with his parents and facilitated a weekly class session at the prison. Deep-set eyes in hollow sockets seemed to bore right through me, as this troubled soul sought to connect, in some way, with what was right in front of his face. Repeated attempts to engage the man in any sort of fruitful dialogue were met with confusion, indifference, and eventually a sense of building irritation. Our visit concluded with the young prisoner rejecting any offers of relationship or spiritual counsel. He slowly pulled himself to his feet, turned his back, and lumbered once again down the long hallway, finally disappearing behind a series of sliding, iron-barred gates.

Preparing to leave the facility, I began to sort through the variety of emotions bombarding me as the result of our strange encounter. I was discouraged because the offer of relationship and the light of the Gospel message had fallen on seemingly barren ground; I was distressed by the fact that I had witnessed the power of demonic oppression—or worse—within the spirit of a man; but I was hopeful, knowing that God was (and is) still sovereign and in control in every moment of life and that He works all things for our good and His Glory in *His* perfect time…which often is not according to our *own* timetable.

That evening, reliving the incident with Fran, when I marveled at the man's constant state of confusion, she exclaimed, "Why should you be surprised?" I immediately understood where she was taking the conversation. You see, as part of my preparation for ministry—particularly within the prison system—I lift up a "customized" prayer for empowerment and protection. Among other requests, I invoke the name and the shed blood of Jesus Christ, asking that the enemy or his demonic minions would not be able to recognize me in human form, but instead, when seeking me, would only see a gleaming wall of polished granite through which their sight could not penetrate. For Fran, her spiritual armor is manifested in the form of a blinding white light upon which anything that is not of God is unable to gaze. When I acknowledged that I had prayed "my" prayer of protection prior to entering the prison, Fran reminded me that the demonic presence within the inmate had only been able to see me as a "wall of granite" which his gaze could not pierce. This was, in fact, the source of his confusion during our time together. If God's Word is "yes and amen," Fran's line of thinking sure made sense to me.

Spiritual oppression—or even demonic possession—is a biblical reality, even though the topic may engender lively debate—or, more often, silence—throughout the Body of Christ. Scriptural passages are replete with detailed accounts of ungodly manifestations in the minds, spirits, and physical bodies of tormented men and women, creating bondage, imprisonment, and a sort of living hell in the lives of those afflicted. In the Gospel of Mark, Jesus restores a sound mind and body to a demon-possessed man. "This man lived in the tombs...no one could bind him...he had been chained hand and foot, but he tore the chains apart...no one was strong enough to subdue him. Night and day...he would cry out and cut himself with stones. When he saw Jesus...he shouted...'What do you want with me, Son of the Most High God?'...Jesus had said to him, 'Come out of this man, you impure spirit!' Then Jesus asked him, 'What is your name?' 'My name is Legion,' he replied, 'for we are many' (Mark 5:3-13). The demons within the tortured man, who seemed to have complete control over their host, begged Jesus not to cast them into the abyss. Instead, they requested to inhabit a herd of swine feeding on a nearby hillside. Jesus granted their wish and sent them to dwell within the animals. Immediately, the pigs went crazy, hurtling themselves over a cliff and perishing in the sea. Even today, far beyond the latest *Star Wars* fantasy, you and I should understand that there *is* power on the "dark side."

Infinitely more common than the full-blown possession of an individual, are the vexing *oppressive* influences and characteristics exhibited in struggling men and women both within and outside of prisons made of iron and stone. The Old and New Testaments of the Bible offer the reader numerous examples of non-Christlike unclean spirits which affect the lives of nonbelievers and believers alike. In the fifth chapter of the book of Acts, when Satan "filled their hearts" with greed and deceit, Ananias and Sapphira withheld a portion of the proceeds from the sale of some property which they owned. What might seem like a minor indiscretion, in today's economic and moral climate, resulted in death for the offending couple. In Ephesians 6:11, even *believers* are warned, "Put on the full armor of God, so that you can take your stand against the devil's schemes." Satan is a defeated foe as a result of the shed blood, death, and resurrection of Jesus Christ, but make no mistake about it: he is real. "Be alert and sober of mind. Your enemy the devil prowls around like a roaring lion looking for someone to devour" (1 Peter 5:8). Satan is not looking for people to annoy. He is not searching for individuals to irritate or trouble. No, our adversary is seeking spiritually unprotected sinners *and* saints whom he can, literally or figuratively, devour. The devil senses his time is short; he is doing his worst to those he hates—you and I—human beings created in the image of a loving and infinitely powerful God.

Today, at a time when mental health facilities offering qualified treatment and care are sorely lacking throughout the United States, it would be naïve to not recognize that, throughout our prison system, there are a growing number of men and women who suffer from mental or spiritual illness. Through the study of Scripture and more than twenty years of ministry in county jails, state penitentiaries, and federal facilities, God continues to show and teach me that spiritual oppression—and demonic possession—is alive and *unwell* within the prison community, just as it is in the world-at-large outside prison walls. For a number of years, in my young adulthood, I was intimately involved in New Age occultism. During that period of time, I saw and experienced spiritual oppression first-hand, including "supernatural" power which can be harnessed by an individual plugged into the "wrong socket." In my misguided quest for truth as I thought it to be, I studied aberrant theologies and cults, have been a student of reincarnation and "past-life regression," have communicated with discarnate spirits through the Ouija Board, have flown over Los Angeles—without benefit of an airplane—in a trance state called astral projection, and been completely healed of a torn hamstring muscle—

within two days—by a psychic witch. Quite an impressive resume for disaster, wouldn't you say?

More recently, God has turned the ashes of my life into something useful and beautiful, enabling me to use my self-destructive spiritual adventures, within a different context, to proclaim the soul-satisfying and abiding truth of *His* Word. Calling upon my experiences with New Age occultism, alcohol and drug use, and a seemingly never-ending love affair with music, God has used my past history as current testimony, providing a relatable backdrop with which many prison inmates—as well as a sizable percentage of worshippers in church pews throughout the nation—can relate. On a number of occasions I have been able to counsel prisoners regarding the dangers of mind-expansion techniques which promise insight and enlightenment to the practitioner but, instead, lead to mental disturbance, stifling bondage, and a hellish legacy. In one particular instance, at the conclusion of a state penitentiary concert/service, I was able to dissuade an inmate from continuing his experimentation with astral projection, where the mind (spirit) separates itself from the human body while the participant is in a self-induced trance and travels through time and space. The experience is much like flying at low altitude and viewing the world around you in motion and living color. Seeking "freedom in captivity," the young man confessed that, at one point, he was looking down upon his flesh-and-blood form lying on the cell floor, but was unable to reenter his physical body. It had scared the daylights out of him, but the ungodly experimentation still seemed to hold a morbid fascination in his mind and heart. Because the prisoner had heard me relate similar experiences during the message that day, he was willing to receive my admonition that there are psych wards populated with individuals who never "returned" from such ill-advised journeys. During our conversation, I was able to reiterate to him the true freedom that only a personal relationship with Jesus Christ can give!

At a state penitentiary for women, located in the countryside on the outskirts of a quaint, blue-collar community, God gave me still another opportunity to witness the darker side of the human spirit. Fran and I had just finished an exuberant Sunday-afternoon worship service. On this particular day, the "joint had been jumping," as the ladies responded enthusiastically to the music, setting the stage for a powerful evangelistic message. As is customary during our concert/services, I had given the women opportunity, after prayerful consideration, to signify—by the raising of hands—first-time professions of faith in Jesus Christ, followed by those signifying recommitments of faith, desiring Jesus to be Lord of their everyday lives. The inmates' response to the altar call had been significant.

As we prepared to dismantle our sound equipment, several ladies approached Fran and me to exchange a kind word, request prayer, or simply to thank us for spending that past hour or so ministering to their needs. One woman waited until the other inmates had left before approaching me. Petite in stature, she gazed somewhat shyly up at me, a slight smile playing across her face. She spoke in a whisper, as if sharing a deep, dark secret. "I raised my hand," she said. "But they got really angry when I did that." Thinking that perhaps several of the female inmates sitting near her may have been harassing her, I inquired as to who "they" might be. "The voices in my head," she responded. "They tell me what to do. Sometimes they make me think and do very bad things." Alarmed, I asked whether or not she wanted to rid herself of those voices. When she replied in the affirmative, "all hell broke loose"…literally. Her body began to twitch and lurch. Her eyelids fluttered and her eyeballs rolled back in her head, leaving only round, white spheres. The soft, delicate whisper became a snarling, guttural growl which shook me to the core. I responded, rebuking Satan and *anything* that was not of God, calling out the demons within her in the name and through the shed blood of Jesus Christ. Her face contorted grotesquely, hoarse curses were uttered through clenched teeth, convulsive movements wrenched her from head to toe. I watched a battle rage as the forces of darkness fought to control her spirit. Unrelenting, I continued in prayer, commanding the evil horde to vacate their prize, summoning those unclean spirits into the lake of fire, never to be seen or heard from again. After what seemed like an eternity, but was, in fact, only several minutes, the woman's breathing eased, her countenance softened, and a sense of peaceful relief enveloped her. Thanking me demurely, she turned and slowly proceeded down the aisle, exiting through the open chapel doors. The blood of Christ had triumphed—for now.

I say this not because the power of God is insufficient to withstand the test of time, not because the precious blood Jesus Christ shed for our sins cannot cleanse us for life, but because, as human beings, *all of us* have decision-making capabilities which can and do affect or alter our destiny. Carnal desires, aberrant needs or behaviors, and outright rebellion can serve as a portal or re-entry point for ungodly manifestations, habits, and traditions in our lives. Case in point: after the unsettling incident in the prison sanctuary, I relayed what had occurred to the chaplain. Remarkably, she was not overly surprised. She confirmed that the inmate in question had exhibited similar behavior, albeit to a lesser degree, in the past. The prison administrator went on to explain to me that the inmate seemed hesitant to completely release herself from the influence of the demonic manifestations. It was as if, in the prisoner's troubled mind, the possession by these "unholy visitors" gave her a unique sense of identity, and therefore a semblance of status, within the prison population.

Dear Lord, protect us from ourselves!

"Whoever dwells in the shelter of the Most High will rest in the shadow of the Almighty. I will say of the Lord, 'He is my refuge and my fortress, my God, in whom I trust.' Surely he will save you from the fowler's snare and from the deadly pestilence. He will cover you with his feathers, and under his wings you will find refuge" (Psalm 91:1-4).

A Word About Mental and Spiritual Oppression

Over time, as we gain experience in prison ministry, God will build in us discernment and understanding about facets of mental and/or spiritual oppression. Maladies of the mind or spirit may demonstrably affect the behavior of certain inmates, compelling them to act out or to respond inappropriately—in rare instances, even violently—to Bible discussion and teaching or to the presentation of the Gospel message itself. Inappropriate behavior may be evidenced during times when an inmate may feel convicted by God's Holy Spirit of the poor choices, the shortcomings, or past failures he or she has experienced. The idea of something eternally better, in addition to breaking the bondage of sin and experiencing a new life in Christ here and now on this Earth, may stir and release powerful, pent-up emotions. These feelings may range from joy and elation to frustration, doubt, and anger. At the darker end of the spectrum, the prison minister may see those emotions expressed as "talk-back" in the form of challenging and argumentative statements, or sullen non-participation by the inmates undergoing cataclysmic changes within their human spirits. Also, it is important to note that, in addition to direct attacks from the enemy of mankind, certain medications given to inmates-in-need may elicit behavior which can masquerade as spiritually rooted oppression.

As religious volunteers in the prison system, or as everyday citizens trying to make this chaotic world a better place in which to live, you and I must recognize the impact of mental—and spiritual—illness and the role it plays in our society. Understanding this reality, however, does not gives us license, particularly within the context of prison ministry, to become amateur psychologists…even if we have studied or received training in that area. You and I, as ministers, are called to *represent* and to *present* the Gospel of Jesus Christ to a lost and dying generation. Specifically, we are to be the hands and feet of Christ to a needy population of incarcerated men and women…not another shrink in whom the inmate must confide. As relationships develop over time we as *spiritual* ambassadors may be better able to ascertain the degree to which such illnesses may or may not color the thoughts and actions of particular individuals within the prison system. It is then—relying on the foundational principles of our Christian faith—that we can seek God for *His* answers to the questions which may arise.

Armed with this additional information, are you ready to continue the journey of relationship-building with people in pain—the "inmates"—within and around each of us?

Seventy percent of juveniles incarcerated in long-term correctional facilities grew up without a father's presence; approximately 80% of these inmates wrestle with minor to major psychiatric issues.

Chapter Fourteen

GETTING TO KNOW YOU: BUILDING RELATIONSHIPS

"Do nothing out of selfish ambition or vain conceit.
Rather, in humility value others above yourselves."

(Philippians 2:3)

*V*aluing others before ourselves: Easy to say; a bit more difficult to live up to—especially if we have preconceived notions or learned history regarding the individuals involved. This can be particularly true if those in the relationship-equation are prisoners, convicts, the "least of these" in society.

To God, sin is sin. Black or white, right or wrong, no shades of gray. We, as people tend to do, often wish to add elements to God's simple, spiritual truths. Left to our own designs and desires, we prefer to categorize or prioritize sin. In our imaginations, we can create a sort of pyramid, much like the modern-day nutritional chart showing the relational value of various foods in our daily diets. But *this* pyramid illustrates an unhealthy diet of sin, beginning with the rather innocuous *little white lie,* then building and rising to much more heinous acts such as rape and murder. When sins are represented in the form of crimes committed in violation of set standards within our society, we readily categorize some as more egregious than others. After all, there must be appropriate penalties meted out for various trespasses against humanity. There has to be a standardized process through which the courts can operate to impose fines, restitution, prison, or even death sentences when society's rules are broken.

Human bias is a very real, very subjective, very personal thing. For a judge—or a member of a jury for that matter—the preferred rule of thumb would be to remain unbiased and neutral. To resurrect the iconic quote from Detective Joe Friday in the old *Dragnet* television series, we want: "Just the facts, ma'am—just the facts." Yes, the legal process does indeed rely strongly upon the "letter of the law" in reaching decisions regarding the guilt or innocence of those transgressing the standards of legal behavior. To those seeking to minister spiritually "good medicine" to incarcerated men and women there is *another* aspect of the law which demands serious attention. That is the *spirit* of the law. To best serve prisoners in this manner, it would be wise for us to distill our thinking to the simplest of terms: God hates sin, but He exhibits a supernatural, unconditional love for the sinner. Common sense tells us that, in most circumstances, the criminal who murders another human being will spend a much longer period of time in prison than the wayward soul who steals a pack of cigarettes from the local convenience store. In reality, there could be exceptions to this rule in states which uphold a three-strike policy. The "three-strikes" ruling subjects persons convicted of the same category of criminal offense on three separate occasions to the harshest penalties allowed by law—penalties which might far exceed the normal range of sentencing. Therefore, a lifecycle of petty crime could condemn an individual to seemingly uneven-handed punishment resulting in further degradation of a life which may already be devoid of hope.

As much as you and I might desire to be used by God to impact the lives of prisoners—or *any* spiritually needy individuals—we should realize that the Christlike attitude we develop and cultivate must initially be within our *own* spirit. The condition of our own heart directly impacts our relational effectiveness with those around us, whether they be spouses, family members, friends, business associates, or the man or woman serving twenty to thirty years in a state penitentiary for robbing banks. First and foremost, you and I must develop what we will refer to as "the mind of Christ." This means our thinking must transcend the worldly concepts of people, places, and events and all the entanglements those affinities inspire. Instead, we must embrace a "Kingdom perspective," where eternal values such as love, kindness, patience, and self-control have uppermost priority in governing the way we think, speak, and act toward *ourselves* first, then toward *others* whom God puts in our path. Some examples to illustrate "the mind of Christ" in real-life situations might look something like these: When assaulted by an attention-getting story on the TV news most people tend to get caught up in the titillating, surface details of the event. Our reaction would include horror as the news anchor recounts the tragic story (complete with bloody crime-scene images) of the "monster" who butchered a sales clerk with a machete during the commission of a convenience-store robbery. We could express utter disgust about the twenty-eight-year-old "pervert" who engaged in an illicit sex act with a five-year-old child. Or we might laugh derisively and scratch our heads in wonderment as the early-morning host jokes about the middle-aged woman being caught red-handed—for the third time—attempting to exit the local grocery store without paying for food and personal-care items she had surreptitiously concealed beneath her clothing.

As a concerned citizen of the Kingdom of God, with a former career in advertising and marketing that spanned three decades, perhaps I am overly sensitive to the constant barrage of spectacular—even lurid—headlines, ladled liberally to an ever-eager, awaiting public by an insatiable media intent on building ratings and, therefore, increasing advertising revenues. I find it both fascinating and disturbing that our society seems content to feast upon a diet of mass communication which degrades and minimizes human life and the human condition, seeing no correlation between our nation's current state of affairs and the lack of accountability, responsibility, or personal and spiritual relatability. This does *not* mean that I believe we, as a people, should be "soft" on crime and/or criminals. What it *does* mean is that I have to continue to seek a transformative process in my *own* mind and heart which will allow me to see all those "annoying, disturbing, disgusting, destructive, hateful people, who clutter the landscape of my life" as God sees them: They are just like me. "For God does not show favoritism" (Romans 2:11). If you and I are comfortable labeling individuals who fail to measure up to our *own* perceived standards of acceptance as losers, what sort of heart-attitude will that engender within us? Will we not tend to view such people as lesser, unworthy of love or compassion, burdensome and as unwanted intrusions in our lives? Now place these so-called losers behind prison bars and observe how you and I—or society in general—might exponentially magnify our negative attitudes toward them. This "naming and shaming" process may take place consciously or at the subconscious level. But within a heart controlled by its carnal nature—the flesh—formation of such nefarious perceptions seems inevitable without the counter-balancing attributes that only the Spirit of God can provide.

Jesus Christ didn't view the sinners—the liars, adulterers, prostitutes, tax collectors, and murderers around Him—as losers. He saw them as "lost people." This frame of reference enabled the Son of God to extend unconditional love, compassion, patience, and understanding upon sin-filled human beings—men and women on their spiritual deathbeds. Poignantly played out in Matthew 25:34-40, Jesus Christ, as the Good Shepherd and Coming King, encourages believers who are intent on following His teachings, to: "…take your inheritance, the kingdom prepared for you since the creation of the world. For I was hungry and you gave me something to eat, I was thirsty and you gave me something to drink, I was a stranger and you invited me in, I needed clothes and you clothed me, I was sick and you looked after me, **I was**

in prison and you came to visit me. Then the righteous will answer him, 'Lord, when did we see you hungry…thirsty…a stranger… needing clothes…sick or in prison…?' The King will reply…whatever you did for one of the least of these…you did for me." You and I cannot minister to *anyone* in such heartfelt and practical ways if we, in our pride and arrogance, see them as losers.

Many of us have heard or have actually uttered the phrase, *"There, but for the grace of God, go I."* For me, these words suggest that, without God's grace and mercy—His unmerited favor toward those who love Him—I would continue to march in a solemn parade of my own making, never realizing or experiencing the abundant life He desires for me. Instead of victorious living, my earthly journey might be eerily similar to those persons who operate without faith in a God they cannot see with human eyes. Without the hope and peace that only He can give in the midst of life's trials and tribulations, I cannot contemplate a future without the Architect of the Universe operating freely within my spirit in the present. Many people, I am certain, have searched diligently for the chapter and verse in which this quotation is contained, only to discover that the exact phrase does not exist in the Bible. However, there *is* a Scripture passage which supports the notion: "But by the grace of God I am what I am, and his grace to me was not without effect…" (1 Corinthians 15:10). As mentioned previously, this verse reinforces the spiritual principle that it is only by the grace of God—who made us in His image and loves us all equally—that we can be the people He desires us to be. And, as difficult as it may be to believe, our seemingly innocuous sins place you and me in the same category as the armed robber, the rapist, and the murderer. It is only God's unending grace and mercy, which He pours out liberally upon broken and contrite hearts, that can save us from ourselves—and our sin.

A young man who assisted in facilitating a marriage-relationship curriculum in which Fran and I participated years ago used a personal experience to illustrate how subtly a haughty heart-attitude can create significant impediments to building mutual trust and true relationships within the context of ministry—or life-in-general. A husband in one of his relationship classes had, in his past, ongoing problems with alcohol and drug use. Issues surrounding his substance abuse eventually led to him spending a period of time in prison. The couple was struggling in their marriage, and my friend—a former Division-One collegiate quarterback—was having difficulty "connecting" with this ex-con so that he might better be able to assist the husband and wife with their marital problems. The facilitator, believing that his motives were pure and that his intentions were good, spoke with his mentor— the man who had written the curriculum—about the dilemma. The wise older gentleman, who tended to view life and living through a finely tuned "spiritual lens," listened, smiled slightly and replied, "Do you know what your problem is? You think that you are better than he is." Somewhat taken aback, but willing to explore that possibility, my friend concluded that his mentor's assessment was correct. As he approached the couples' relationship needs with a new-found perspective, my compatriot was able to exhibit a less judgmental and exceedingly more humble attitude toward the husband. As a result, he was better able to forge an authentic relationship and assist in building Christlike character within the ex-offender so that his marriage might be restored.

Any fledgling relationship goes through an initial "feeling out" process as individuals begin the journey of getting to know each other. You or I would not bear our souls or share our deepest, darkest secrets with a stranger. Relationship-building requires time and effort, whether it takes place within the context of true romance, a workplace friendship, camaraderie at the local fitness center, or ministry at a county jail or state penitentiary. In the development of *all* personal relationships, numerous factors come into play, such as the duration and frequency of contact or interaction; whether or not the individuals are related by genealogy, marriage, or other family ties; mutual likes, interests, and beliefs; the end results or desired goals of the relationship; etc. The formula for relationship-building, within the context of prison ministry, may not differ dramatically from nurturing friendships in the outside world. However, such an intentional commitment may call for greater caution and discernment within the confines of "the Big House," as we will explore shortly.

It stands to reason that the rapport a traveling evangelist is able to establish with a given congregation differs dramatically when compared to relationships built by a pastor or minister who is able to interact with and support his or her flock with far greater frequency. On a daily basis, over an extended period of time, such relational factors as nuances within individual personalities, deep-seated issues or unmet needs can be explored and addressed far more efficiently *and* more effectively than through a "hit-and-run," sporadic contact between interested parties. But it should be noted that both short-term and long-term relationships can and do have a place when it comes to ministry opportunities within the prison system. During my two-and-a-half decades in ministry, I have learned to appreciate the differences between *evangelism* and *discipleship*. In simplest terms, the intention of the evangelist is to preach the good news of the Gospel of Jesus Christ— including Christ's death and resurrection for the remission of sins. Often, the role of the *evangelist* revolves around preaching the Word "in season"—perhaps during traveling concerts, special services, or revivals. The minister who takes on what is generally the longer-term role of a *disciple-maker* usually has opportunity, over an extended period of time, to breathe life into the Gospel message through study, teaching, and practical application of principles in the lives of seeking individuals who are intent on beginning or advancing their own spiritual journeys. In my life, I have taken on both roles—itinerant *evangelist* and *disciple-maker*—within the county and state prison systems and, to a lesser degree, in federal penitentiaries.

Ministry to incarcerated men and women is much like walking a tightrope. Initially, you seek some sort of equilibrium, as you adjust to your eclectic audience of "social misfits"—those who have broken the rules of society and now reside in an environment which is foreign territory to most outsiders. The ability to separate the sinner from the sin—seeing each man and woman as a "blank slate" upon which a testimony, of some sort, will be written—will help to establish a firm footing upon which to build relationships as your journey across the wire begins. And as you settle in to the mission field your own honesty and transparency—within reason—will allow you to establish a cadence, a flow, and a clear direction that captive men and women will more readily respond to and follow. When the prison minister is accessible and "real" to the prisoners, when the evangelist or disciple-maker is able to be viewed as needing the same spiritual nutrition he or she is dispensing to the inmates, then God can use you and me as more-serviceable vessels to accomplish His will. Ironic as it may seem, incarcerated individuals—many of whom exhibit a lifestyle characterized by manipulation and deceit—appreciate the presence of a "straight shooter" in their midst. At any given time, they may need you to take on the role of warm and welcoming friend, facilitator, moderator, tough-love administrator, order-keeper, peacemaker…and spiritual leader. It is incumbent that you and I—as missionaries in this foreign land—endeavor to be equipped and available to assist hurting people in their fight for spiritual freedom, even while they are in captivity. You can be the bondage-breaker who risks it all, spanning the chasm between spiritual death and a new life in Christ—striding across that tightrope—with an unseen, supernatural safety net: the strength, mercy, grace, and discernment that only a loving God can give.

Looking back on many years of building relationships through ministry to prisoners, I could fill an entire book with faith journeys and "adventure stories." Here is one such account.

Rufus described himself as "a good, ol' boy—an 'old head'" straight from the Florida bayou. He was a six-foot-four "tall drink of water," and thin as a reed. Nappy, unshorn salt-and-pepper hair, with scraggly beard to match, created a notable contrast against his burnished brown skin. His sly smile was punctuated by dark spaces, because Rufus didn't have too many good teeth. When he spoke, the words dripped out of his mouth like slow molasses. Therefore, it usually took an extended amount of time to hear what he had to say. I loved this guy immediately. And Rufus seemed to enjoy me as well. Perhaps our camaraderie developed as it did because Rufus sensed that I was "the real deal." That is to say, he watched and listened as this prison pastor came to "his" jail, week after week, preaching and teaching the Gospel of Christ, but also sharing himself in the process. He observed a certain openness and transparency in the way I often used myself—as opposed to other people—as my own "best worst example." He laughed, along with the rest of the inmates, as our discussions of "past-life behavior" brought out the foolishness and folly of our ways, when compared to the standard of Jesus Christ. If I could read Rufus' mind, I might imagine him thinking, *This Pete Einstein seems to be an approachable guy. I think I'll hang out with him while I'm in this place.* Slow as he was to articulate his thoughts, in that lazy, southern drawl, I always appreciated how Rufus could excise a spiritual lesson from our Bible reading and readily apply it to his own life in a way that would also make complete sense to the other men in the room. I'll never forget the poignant inquiry he directed to me one day during a group-discussion session. He asked, "Pete, how do I quiet the noise of the world which resides inside my head?" Think about it. Have *you* ever asked *yourself* such a question? Another reason I knew that Rufus and I had forged something more than just a teacher-pupil relationship was that he always had my back. At times, to spare me the effort of "tough-love" instruction, when he sensed that another inmate was trying to manipulate me or the discussion in a self-serving way, Rufus—as the senior citizen of most of our gatherings—would gently offer the offending party a molasses-delivered word of correction or rebuke to get matters back on track. On several occasions he asked me for a private word of prayer, particularly near his release when he was waiting to hear about an opening in a long-term Christ-centered drug rehabilitation program. At the end of each session, as he headed toward the door, Rufus would turn and approach me. Silently, he would bend

147

his slender frame downward, clasp his long, boney fingers in mine and give me a "shoulder-bump," as if to say. "Until next time, my friend."

I heard through the grapevine that Rufus had enrolled in the drug rehabilitation program that we had prayed would become available to him. But several months later, when Fran and I were invited to that particular facility to provide one of our concert/services to the men, he was nowhere to be found.

As I write this, I have never seen my friend Rufus again. I think about and pray for him often.

Like my friend Rufus, inmates come and go. Much like the ebbing and flowing of a tidal surge, men and women serve their sentences, then find a semblance of freedom, upon release, in cities and towns throughout the nation. Or, if they have satisfied their legal requirements at the county level, a number of offenders change "address and location," as they continue their saga of incarceration within the state or federal penitentiary system. Within the regimented, daily routine of prison life, the cast of characters is in a constant state of flux. Different people, different needs, different questions. The same answer: Almighty God. The Rock. A Fortress. Our firm Foundation. He alone is the constant that can be counted upon in a world that is constantly changing.

In the next chapter, this idea of "constant change" will be examined in greater detail as we continue to explore *The Inmate Within*.

Upon release from an extended prison stay,
many ex-offenders are caught in a
technological time warp, having to learn
such disciplines as how to operate a
personal computer, a mobile phone, an
automated banking machine or gas pump.

Chapter Fifteen

LOST IN THE MAIL: ADMINISTRATIVE RELATIONSHIPS AND PAPERWORK

"So I say to you: Ask and it will be given to you;
seek and you will find; knock and
the door will be opened to you."

(Luke 11:9)

Ask, seek, knock, and the door will be opened. I have seen that truth, contained in Luke 11:9, come alive in my life and in the lives of others in a myriad of ways. But, specifically, when it comes to entering a state or federal penitentiary for volunteer service, you can do all of the above and *still* not gain entrance. Why? If you do not go through proper administrative channels, if your paperwork is incomplete or incorrectly filed in a timely manner, those prison doors, indeed, **may not** be opened to you.

People often ask me, "Pete, how do I get started in prison ministry? What's the 'best way' to minister to men and women behind bars? Whom do I contact to take that first step, to see if this type of ministry service is right for me?" These are all legitimate questions that I myself faced years ago. And the answers to the first two questions may never be discovered if the third "Ghostbuster" question remains unanswered. That is, to get started on this unique journey, "Who you gonna call?" Throughout the course of our prison experience, we have initiated contact for ministry utilizing a rather narrow cast of characters within the system. This approach seems to work well for us.

Our initial foray into ministry at the state penitentiary level was facilitated by an evangelist (now a retired church pastor) friend who had ironically done many years of "hard time" in prison himself. Through nothing less than extraordinary favor from God, my comrade-in-arms was granted prison ministry privileges within a year or two of his release from a state facility—a feat that is virtually unheard of in the annals of service to incarcerated offenders. This man knew Fran and me personally and understood my heart for ministry. He was familiar with SonPower Ministries, having served on our board of advisors for several years during the formative stages of our adventures in evangelism. With that knowledge in hand, he confidently approached chaplains he knew and had partnered with, paving the way for us to accompany him and provide music during those penitentiary services for which he delivered a prepared sermon or message. He affectionately referred to the three of us as "road dogs," traveling the highways and byways of Pennsylvania and beyond, delivering the message of the Gospel to "the least of these" behind towering walls, impenetrable iron bars, and razor wire barricades. Observing the rapport I was able to establish with the inmates, this gentleman expressed to Fran that, for a person who had never served a sentence within a state penitentiary, God had gifted me with an uncanny ability to authentically connect with the prisoners who populated the "gated communities" we visited with regularity.

Initially, I wondered what compelled me to care about the plight of incarcerated men and women. Why did I feel it was important to personally connect with them? Looking back over the formative years of my life, I intentionally cultivated friendships with a wide circle of people, including the underdogs and those less-popular classmates who were not part of the "in crowd." Add to that, singing and traveling with a "black" soul group in the midst of racial unrest, my secular music experiences in Miami, Boston, and Los Angeles, my misadventures with New Age occultism, and I believe God was, even then, equipping me for the ministry opportunities and challenges that were to come years later.

Our evangelistic liaison continued for several years. At that point, our friend had become an ordained pastor and was birthing a church. As he spent less time on the road, Fran and I continued our travels, having established personal relationships and ministry accountability among a network of Pennsylvania state-penitentiary chaplains.

Within the county prison systems, several of my initial conversations were with wardens or assistant wardens. In one instance, the head administrator was known to me previously. In another case, the deputy warden was a personal friend. Still other contacts were made as the result of our ministry efforts receiving personal references and/or recommendations from mutual acquaintances, church pastors, and other prison administrators.

Aside from personal connections or third-party commendations, prison ministry inquiries can begin with something as simple as a letter, an email, or a phone call. A good person to start with is the prison chaplain. Because the practice of numerous religious persuasions is accommodated, particularly within state and federal prisons, it is imperative that "Christian" ministers interact with whomever is in charge of "Protestant" services. More often than not, the contact person would be the FCPD—Facility Chaplaincy Program Director—or the "head chaplain." You may be referred to another chaplain on his or her staff, but, unless you *do* have a personal relationship with another chaplain within a given facility, the FCPD is the proper connection to begin your entry process into prison ministry. As mentioned previously, a person seeking access to promote the Gospel of Jesus Christ should be aware that there are *other* religious disciplines present within the prison system, including Catholicism, Judaism, Islam, Mormonism, Quaker Friends, Native American (Spiritism), and Rastafarianism. Most recently, under the guise of "religious freedom," inmates have lobbied to have the "Wiccan Religion"—or witchcraft—introduced into the prison environment. As Christ-followers, this is the challenge that awaits me— and perhaps *you*—as we attempt to break through religious clutter to administer the good news of Jesus Christ to our unique target audience.

Feeling called or compelled by God to do His work in creative ways carries with it the weight of discipline and discernment. Please do *not* labor under the assumption—as some ministry neophytes have—that you will gain entry into the prison system and be able to convert incarcerated Muslims by striking an agreement (or what I refer to as an "unholy alliance") with a prison Imam, or Muslim religious leader. This same premise applies to the other aforementioned religions. The thought may seem to be noble, but you will be deemed naïve, or a troublemaker—and chances are that access to a penal facility for *any* type of ministry or volunteer service would be denied to you. Instead of striving to integrate a doctrinal belief system which runs counter to God's Word, consider how the power of God's Holy Spirit can and does work within the context of Christian ministry. I have had Muslims, Buddhists, Jews, Rastafarians, Native American Spiritualists, witches, agnostics, and atheists among those attending both our large-venue concert/services, as well as weekly, small-group Bible studies. Over a period of time, and within the context of building more intimate relationships, some of those professing non-believers in Jesus Christ have allowed the Gospel of Truth to illuminate their hearts. One example of such a transformation included a seemingly intellectual young man who began attending my county-prison small-group study session with the express purpose of convincing all within earshot that *there is no God*. Within a month, he left that facility knowing in his mind and spirit that God *is* real and that, through the death and resurrection of Jesus Christ, he has a personal relationship—for eternity—with the Creator of the universe! That is conversion as only God can do. This particular incident reminds me, to this day, that God can *use* willing hearts to serve Him, but He doesn't *need* us to accomplish His work. Why? Because He is God…*and we are not!*

In passing, I have spoken about creating interpersonal connections with those in charge of religious services within the prison system. Now I would like to explore further why relationship-building with prison chaplains is so important. First, the chaplain must be assured that any volunteer entering "his" prison domain will be presenting a relevant, scripturally-sound, Gospel message. To that end, chaplains must develop a working knowledge of who you are and what your ministry is about. Personally, I take it as a compliment when a prison chaplain takes the time and effort to see SonPower Ministries in action. By observing or taking part in a service with us, chaplains can capture the tone and personality of who we are and how we go about presenting the Gospel message to inmates.

At the conclusion of a chapel service, it is encouraging to hear a chaplain remark, "Wow! The men *really* responded well to your message this morning. We identified those who made first-time commitments of faith and will follow up with them during the coming week." And it is equally gratifying to receive a message like, "I've been receiving a number of good reports from the inmates as a result of your visit last Sunday. They related well to your practical style of preaching and *loved* your music."

On the other hand, you and I, as outside volunteers, will also have opportunities to observe how prison chaplains provide ministry and care to their congregations of incarcerated men or women. Experience has shown Fran and me that, for any number of reasons, some chaplains are able to establish a greater rapport and higher levels of trust and respect among the inmate population than others. Factors influencing the chaplain/prisoner dynamic may include the openness and vulnerability of the prison pastor (while he or she still maintains a proper professional distance with the prison population). Some chaplains seem to have a heightened sense of empathy and compassion for those in their care, and this is reflected in closer associations with the inmates. Still others can "hang loose" and enjoy the prisoners' company, within the construct of a firm-but-fair policy which governs day-to-day relationships. One thing is certain: Over time, it will become apparent to any outside observer that prison chaplaincy is not without flaws. Prison chaplains tend to be overworked, understaffed, and sometimes are required by the powers-that-be to do far more than they are able to physically (or spiritually) accomplish. Also, we should understand that, within the prison system, there will be those chaplains who choose to deliver a lukewarm or watered-down Gospel message to their constituents, but—praise God—they are the exception rather than the norm. My experience has been that prison clergy are intent on delivering a concise, Christ-centered message of salvation through the shed blood, death, and resurrection of Jesus Christ to those inmates under their spiritual care.

There is another important reason why building rapport with the FCPD and his assistants is crucial for outside ministry volunteers. On any given Sunday—or any other day of the week during which religious activities are scheduled—a chaplain must relinquish the time he or she would normally use to preach from the pulpit or conduct some other type of religious service to accommodate a visiting person or organization. To the outsider seeking access, it may appear that prison clergy are somewhat selective or territorial, but it should be noted that, for every opportunity chaplains make available for guest ministry, they tend to have many more requests than they can accommodate. If you, the reader, determined to make *yourself* available for such service within a jail or penitentiary, you can understand why it is important that a chaplain would have confidence that you or your organization could deliver a message that was spiritually on-point. In addition, he or she would want to be assured that you could communicate a given lesson or principle to the inmates in such a way that they could relate to what was being said and be able to apply the principles to their own minds, hearts, and lives in real and practical ways.

It is my hope that in this and the following chapter, you will gain understanding that creating good relationships with prison chaplains seems to produce a beneficial trickle-down effect throughout the system. Navigating what may seem to be a cumbersome process, administrative problems are bound to arise at some juncture of the prison ministry experience. Whether a given complication might involve paperwork, pre-entry procedures, personal background and equipment checks, or schedule and timing issues, having the chaplain's support can often pave the way for a speedier and more amenable resolution to the problem-at-hand.

Similarly, having a good, working relationship with the higher echelon of prison administrators *also* has its advantages. Having access to "upper management" in a decision-making process is helpful when it prevents a chaplain—or the ministry volunteer—from getting "caught in the middle" of unforeseen situations. Through the years, there have been several instances where administrative input by a warden, deputy warden, or commanding corrections officer on the prison block has hastened decision-making in the midst of unusual or extraordinary circumstances. For example, a member of my family spent a short amount of time serving a sentence in our local county jail. In some facilities, the reality of having a blood relative incarcerated within their walls would prohibit me from conducting ministry there— or, at least, it might limit the scope of ministry I was able to perform.

Through earnest conversation with the warden, his assistant, and the prison chaplain, and by pre-planning for the eventuality, I was able to continue ministering in that facility—uninterrupted and without limitations—throughout the duration of my family member's sentence. In fact, prior to his being transferred to the work-release program, my family member attended SonPower Ministries' weekly discipleship session on several occasions.

Finding favor with God should be the paramount quest in our lives as believers. Due to a track record of open and honest communication with prison administrators, strict adherence to the rules and regulations in each institution, and the *good fruit* being borne from SonPower's ongoing ministry efforts, I have been doubly blessed, finding favor with men and women within the prison system as well.

"Sorry, your paperwork has been lost in the mail."

The email arrived a week prior to our scheduled concert/service at a major penitentiary, a facility where all male offenders were first sent for physical, mental, and criminal classification before being parceled out to other prisons across the state. The message was short, but not sweet. In essence, it said that, because the state facility had not received updated clearance information and other required paperwork from Fran and me, our ministry could not conduct the services scheduled for the following Sunday. My heart sank. We had scheduled this day of music and ministry almost a year in advance. We had completed all necessary forms. I had driven the package to the post office and made specific arrangements for delivery and tracking months in advance of the appointed date. Not only did this cancellation throw a wrench in our plans, the change in schedule would affect the chaplain as well.

During the course of three services spread throughout the day, an average of 800 men would have the opportunity to hear and respond to the Gospel message. God *always* did mighty works during these ministry opportunities. Dozens of men received the gift of salvation during our services. But now we would not be there. Not on *that* particular Sunday, at least.

Upon double checking with the post office, my disappointment would have morphed into anger without God's steady hand providing equilibrium. Why? Because the tracking code for our package indicated the date and time-of-day our materials *had been delivered* to the institution! I carefully composed an appropriate response before I phoned the chaplain to report my findings. He was apologetic and promised to pursue matters as best he could. But, try as he might, he could not come up with the missing paperwork. My hope was that our personal information had been misplaced somewhere within the confines of the cavernous prison administration building, because the idea of an inmate with impure motives having access to our social security numbers, personal phone numbers, and home addresses was unsettling, to say the least!

The chaplain graciously scheduled us for another ministry date, and to ensure that he received our clearance information in a timely manner, I drove fifteen miles to the prison. Once there, I met my pastor friend in the visiting area and personally handed the package of materials to him. Several months later than our initially intended visit, we facilitated three services at the institution. If memory serves me, more than *three dozen* men received Jesus Christ as personal Savior and Lord of their lives. Was such a harvest worth the wait? Absolutely!

Our original package was never found, and it remains a mystery to this day.

In this age of computer automation across the landscape of business and industry, one would imagine that paperwork, in general, would be minimized. Eventually, we might assume hard copy of documents and forms could virtually disappear. That is not always the case within the prison system. In Pennsylvania, there exists a centralized computer system which stores voluminous amounts of data, including information pertaining to all visitors/volunteers who provide service—

from mechanical contracting, to vending machine replenishment and repair, to religious services—throughout the state prison system. With more than two dozen penitentiaries for male offenders in Pennsylvania, one might believe that—when it pertains to prison ministry—chaplains would draw needed information regarding ministries such as ours from the central computer files. This is not necessarily so. While it would seem logical and most efficient to fill out one set of paperwork for each twelve-month period of time, Fran and I find ourselves updating all required paperwork and forms for every facility we visit within any given year. Why is this the case? More often than not, prison chaplains, particularly at the state and federal levels, are subject to periodic audits and, therefore, feel compelled to have hard copy—*paperwork*—for all personal and clearance information in their files for accountability purposes. And so, the antiquated process continues, even in the midst of ever-increasing high technology.

If you, as a person actively engaged in, or preparing for, prison ministry *have* mastered the paperwork process, you may discover instances in which factors outside of your control scuttle your best-laid plans for entry into a particular penal facility. Imagine, if you will, my reaction when I received the following telephone call from a state penitentiary chaplain several days prior to our scheduled arrival at his prison: "Pete, there's a possibility that an execution may take place on the day of your service. If it *is* carried out, the prison will be closed to all outside visitors, including you and Fran. But if the governor issues a stay of execution…you're good-to-go! I'll give you a call either way." Praise God, the execution was postponed. Fran and I made the journey to that state penitentiary and a number of once-hardened hearts were changed for eternity.

Understanding that filling out more than a few forms and documents will be a constant component of the prison experience "equation" will enable ministry volunteers to guard against an improper heart-attitude and elevated blood pressure! "Go with the flow" and "be prepared for anything and everything" applies here in every way. For those of you seeking more definitive information regarding prison-clearance forms, documents are available online through your state's "Department of Corrections" website. There may be minor variations among states, but basic information is somewhat consistent throughout the nation.

Speaking of "constant components" within the context of prison ministry, we'll be exploring another constant in the upcoming chapter. That constant is **change.**

To overcome the hurdles of post-prison
employment, many entrepreneurial ex-
offenders have used their unique skills and
experience to create successful enterprises
in such areas as health and fitness,
retail/finance and service industries.

Chapter Sixteen

ONE OF THE BIGGEST CONSTANTS: CHAPLAINS AND CHANGE

"Therefore, my beloved brethren, be you steadfast, unmovable, always abounding in the work of the Lord... know that your labor is not in vain..."

(1 Corinthians 15:58)

The two young, enthusiastic—make that *zealous*—corrections officers were determined that *no* drugs, *no* contraband, *no* inappropriate materials of any kind would enter the prison on *their* watch. To that end, the COs grilled Fran and me regarding the nature and purpose of the various pieces of sound equipment as they checked each item off a master list we had submitted a month prior to our visit. Standing in the crowded guard shack, which bustled with activity, we politely answered their endless barrage of questions to the best of our ability. "No," I replied, when asked about access to the interior of our speaker cabinets. "Those cabinets were sealed during the manufacturing

161

phase and the back panels cannot be unscrewed. In fact, there *are* no screws in the cabinet design at all!"

When queried about two sets of cords coiled in a storage cavity behind what we call the "power head," Fran explained patiently, "Yes, these cords are necessary to connect this particular piece of equipment to our mixing board." I resolved to remain calm, assuring myself that this unanticipated—but not completely unexpected—ordeal would soon end, and then came a statement that—even with years of prison ministry experience under my belt—left me flabbergasted.

The two guards glanced at each other, looked at us and stated, "You're going to have to take the CD player apart."

"Excuse me," I responded, trying not to sound indignant.

"That's right," the one young man continued, as if completing a telepathic thought between the two COs. "How do we know there are no drugs or paraphernalia hidden in there?"

As if on cue, a new and much calmer voice of reason entered the conversation. It was the prison chaplain who had been dutifully standing by, in silence, as the guards went about the equipment check-in process. "Gentlemen," he said, "Pete and Fran Einstein have been conducting worship services and bringing their sound equipment into our facility for many years. Over this time, they have shown themselves to be visitors with the highest regard for the rules and regulations of this institution. And besides," the chaplain added, "even if we had the tools on hand to disassemble the CD player, who would have the time and expertise to put it back together so that it would be available—and *operational*—for this morning's service?" Respecting the chaplain and the humble manner in which he had approached the situation, and thinking more deeply about the ramifications of dismantling sound equipment in such a chaotic environment, the two young guards relented. Soon, Fran and I had loaded all our gear on a wooden platform dolly borrowed from the prison kitchen. And, with the chaplain in the lead, we began to make our way—on time—to the prison chapel.

As mentioned earlier, the penal environment is by necessity a structured and orderly place. Very little is left to chance. More often than not, the prison schedule and regimentation serves to benefit both the inmates, prison staff and administration. But even within this calculated system of operation, there remain fluid factors which can and do change the status quo, sometimes at a moment's notice. Some of these "agents of change" include new laws or legal precedents at the state or national level; more aggressive enforcement of *existing* laws, rules, and regulations; findings and recommendations from credible commissions and/or studies; and internal or external events and stressors (within a given facility or throughout the prison system) which necessitate an immediate response or reaction. Unfortunately, for those involved as volunteers or outside agents, the continuing call for greater accountability within penal institutions usually results in *more* cumbersome layers of administrative oversight and *more* paperwork as additional information is required of those who wish to serve within the prison system. Our experience has been that, as the years go by, there are more impediments to prison ministry, not less. But God always seems to provide opportunities for us to step out in obedience and to do His work in spite of the challenges. He does this as only the Creator of all things can: making a way, where and when there seems to be no way. "This is what the LORD says—he who made a way through the sea, a path through the mighty waters…Forget the former things; do not dwell on the past. See, I am doing a new thing! Now it springs up, do you not perceive it? I am making a way in the wilderness and streams in the wasteland" (Isaiah 43:16-19).

When it comes to promoting outside religious-service providers within the prison system, Fran and I, once again, want to sing the praises of the jail and penitentiary chaplains—the "go-to" men and women—for orchestrating visits by willing individuals and/or organizations such as SonPower Ministries. Particularly within state and federal penitentiaries, the chaplain is the first line of communication prior to entering a facility and, usually, the primary facilitator for volunteers or guests leading into and during the performance of ministry-oriented events. The chaplain provides spiritual equilibrium in an environment filled with dynamic tension. He or she holds a unique position within the hierarchy of prison life, representing or ministering to the spiritual needs of inmates, without compromising the rules and regulations of the system or a particular facility. The chaplain's position, and required demeanor, clearly illustrates the "fruit of the Spirit" in action. "But the fruit of the Spirit is love, joy, peace, forbearance, kindness, goodness, faithfulness, gentleness and self-control…" (Galatians 5:22-23). As the "prison pastor" negotiates those perilous waters connecting the needs and desires of inmates, corrections staff, and administrative personnel, an overriding attitude of humility is the rudder that insures "safe passage" amid the constants—and often unexpected changes—within the prison system. The chaplain's example provides a real-life model and a navigational map for you and me to follow as we pursue serving within this same system.

Let's take a moment to put a face to these men and women who bear the title of *prison chaplain*. Who are these people? What are their qualifications? What motivates them to do what they do? The typical prison chaplain has been ordained as a minister or clergy by a recognized church or denomination. More often than not, a master's degree in divinity (theology) is required for chaplaincy candidates. In addition, three units of Clinical Pastoral Education (C.P.E.) are preferred by those involved in the hiring process. The C.P.E. units consist of intentional, hands-on training and pastoral work within a supervised group setting (a church, organization, hospital, etc.) which involves discussion, evaluation, and written discoveries related to the individuals' experiences in the field.

At the county level, chaplains may serve on a part-time or full-time basis, depending upon perceived need and budget constraints. County prison ministers often are classified as "independent contractors"

("Contract Chaplains"), who are hired and paid through special committees formed from a local consortium of churches or a ministerial board. These chaplains are paid by the county. They also may receive additional funding for such things as Bibles, study materials and supplies from individuals or organizations within the communities they serve. State or federal penitentiary chaplains tend to be full-time state or federal employees. Their qualifications and hiring criteria mirror those of prison clergy at the county level.

As opposed to a stepping stone, prison chaplaincy tends to represent a goal or end-in-itself. While many ministers feel called to such distantly different surroundings as the prison environment, there are also those pastors who choose to use their years of experience in pulpit ministry to transition into prison chaplaincy in the mid-to-later years of their lives, as part of a pre-retirement plan.

The prison chaplain tends to have a broad range of responsibilities within his or her job description. Not only is he or she conductor and administrator of all religious services within the walls of a given facility, the chaplain oversees all volunteer ministry and visitor activities entering the prison. As mentioned several paragraphs ago, spiritual support to the inmates is a priority. Such support might include grief counseling, such as when a prisoner loses a loved one on the outside. Individual pastoral counseling to resolve personal or spiritual issues is commonplace, as is "spiritual fathering" (or "mothering"), particularly to young men who have grown up with no positive role models in the home. Also, prison chaplains make themselves available to prison staff and administration, offering personal counsel to COs and other staffers. And, last but not least, as time permits, they act as community ambassadors, disseminating information, seeking alliances, and sharing how religious instruction positively impacts the inmate population. Prison chaplains are ordinary people with an extraordinary calling: they attend elementary school PTO meetings, compete in YMCA adult recreation programs, volunteer at the neighborhood food bank and, when possible, worship at your church. Simply put, they are men and women much like you and me.

Throughout our decades of prison ministry, Fran and I have enjoyed the opportunity to develop closer and more personal contact with several prison chaplains. During our times together, we have been able to crack the veneer of formality which sometimes characterizes fledgling relationships, in whatever scenario they may occur. We have been able to laugh, cry, and pray with and for a particular female prison minister who, through the years, has battled multiple sclerosis, cancer, and various physical maladies in a seemingly endless succession of struggles. But in the midst of personal challenges, her love for God and the women in her spiritual care has kept her spirits buoyant and bright (at least to those of us on the outside looking inward). Through times of physical pain and exhaustion—not to mention the mental anguish which often remains unseen—this woman of God soldiers on, pouring her heart and soul into the lives of the ladies under lock and key. Another male chaplain at a state penitentiary became an instant friend for a number of reasons. First, we could see and appreciate his love for the men he pastored and the respect he was given in return. He was also gracious and accommodating to us far beyond the prison pastor-volunteer relationship—quick to go out of his way to assist with equipment transport, to engage in substantially meaningful conversations, and to extend the offer of a "free lunch"—at the prison mess hall, or at the church in a neighboring community. One of the most enjoyable aspects of our friendship was that the chaplain and I could trade "war stories" of our times on the road as secular musicians, and later, as traveling evangelists in the Christian-music scene. Fran and I were able to share a special bond with another black chaplain, who has since retired from his work within the prison system. After his initial surprise at the style of music and ministry we presented ("That white boy's got some *soul"),* he hosted us enthusiastically through the years at the facility in which he pastored. A musician himself, with deep gospel-music roots, we would sneak opportunities to enjoy each other's company in our own unique way. "Chap" would seat himself at the keyboard of a stately Hammond organ in the sanctuary and I would play drums or sing along during impromptu jam sessions in the prison chapel, often alone, or sometimes accompanied by other inmates on the praise-and-worship team.

The stories could go on and on, but one thing remains certain: As God allows us to pursue our journey in ministry to incarcerated men and women, we will endeavor to forge deeper personal relationships with the prison chaplains also, so that we are better able to minister to *their* personal and spiritual desires, as well as to the needs of the inmates.

The task of providing spiritual insight within what can easily be a spiritually vapid environment often makes the chaplain's job a seemingly thankless endeavor. ***But, with God working behind the scenes as only He can, a chaplain (and his invited ministry guests) can, over time, truly effect change within the confines of a jail or penitentiary.*** During my many years of prison ministry, I have observed this phenomenon again and again through what I call a "trickle-up" theory: A chaplain—or outside minister—displaying that "fruit of the Spirit" heart-attitude as described in Galatians—plants seeds of mutual respect among his rag-tag congregation of prisoners. By continually exhibiting unconditional love and compassion, tempered with firm but fair authority, the chaplain, and others under his auspices, can nurture strong allegiance among the inmate population. This alliance, rooted in Christ-centered (Kingdom) principles, encourages more righteous ("right-living") behavior among prisoners as they walk out their faith in tangible ways. Changes in conduct among a percentage of convicts is not lost on an observant corrections staff or administration. A more compliant, courteous, well-behaved inmate population can only aid in keeping the delicate balance of prison life intact. The respect earned by the chaplain among the inmates will tend to be recognized and upheld by prison staffers, whose burdens may be lightened considerably as inmate behavior improves. And, as long as the chaplain or religious volunteers "play by the rules," more often than not, they will be encouraged in their efforts to provide spiritual nourishment to a thirsty audience behind prison walls.

As vital as the chaplaincy is to the welfare of prisoners, the job remains a high-stress, high-turnover proposition, particularly at the state level. In the year leading up to the publishing of this book, Fran and I experienced the resignation or retirement of six chaplains within the Pennsylvania state prisons in which we ministered. And there was additional pastoral attrition in several prisons where we had not been for a period of time. This represents not only marked change to the inmates in affected facilities, but to ministry volunteers as well. Regarding the inmates, they must acclimate themselves to a new ministerial regime with a new personality at the helm. The incoming chaplain may have a markedly different way of building rapport or conducting religious services and discipleship opportunities among the prison population. For religious volunteers, changes in prison chaplaincy personnel may affect the perceived need for outside service providers and could limit possibilities for organizations such as SonPower Ministries to preach the Gospel. In some cases, Fran and I had to introduce our ministry to people whom we had never met and, perhaps, did not share a like vision for evangelism or discipleship. (For example, a prison chaplain might favor a church or parachurch organization which presents music or a preaching style that is in keeping with his or her personal preferences or ecclesiastical upbringing.) In other instances, we found ourselves reintroducing SonPower Ministries to individuals who may have had passing or prior knowledge of who we were or the way in which we approached prison ministry. Once again, with the power of almighty God at the helm, we have been able to re-establish ties with most of the prisons in which we have enjoyed fruit-bearing ministry as we begin to foster fledgling relationships with the current crop of new or transferred chaplains.

If you are at all interested in learning more about—or actively participating in—service within the prison system, there are a number of personal characteristics and attributes which can be cultivated to ensure effectiveness and efficiency in your endeavors. Again, we can reference the aforementioned Scripture passage, in Chapter 5 of the book of Galatians, for insight. God knows what you and I require to succeed. Over time, for my good, He developed in me—among other needed attributes—the Christlike characteristics exemplified in the following two words: ***"flexibility"*** and ***"patience."*** Why these two words specifically? Because, even in the best-run prison systems, many carefully calculated schedules tend to operate on a "hurry-up-and-wait" basis.

Perhaps you can relate to this "hurry-up-and-wait" phenomenon. Think about your daily commute to work. Your new-business acquisition meeting is at 9:00 a.m. The driving time from home to office is thirty minutes. You leave your residence at 7:45 a.m., knowing that upon your arrival you will enjoy the benefit of additional time to fine-tune your presentation. What you do *not* plan for, however, is the tractor-trailer pile-up on the freeway which traps you and 10,000 other commuters in a deadly four-hour gridlock! Maddening, isn't it?

And so it is in the prison system. Within the context of a ministry schedule, what could possibly go wrong? To quote Elizabeth Barrett Browning, "Let me count the ways."

First, there is the process of (volumes of) paperwork, which we discussed in the preceding chapter. Suffice it to say, if needed paperwork for your entrance into a facility is incomplete or misplaced, you are going to "hurry up and wait." Or if, by chance or ignorance, some sort of contraband is discovered on your person or among your possessions, you are *definitely* in a "hurry up and wait" situation. Perhaps the chaplain has been called off the prison grounds or is tied up attending to an internal matter, such as informing an inmate of a death in his or her family. You wait. And what about the seemingly never-ending head count…a constant factor in every penal institution? If one inmate is unaccounted for—if a single prisoner is "missing in action"—*nobody* hurries anywhere…*everybody* waits!

It certainly took me a while to understand the prison ministry experience for what it is with respect to time and timing. From entering a facility, through the check-in process, to registering and transporting needed sound equipment—even to the pastoral announcements and introduction of our ministry leading into the worship service—I found myself on edge. Instead of enjoying a sense of wellbeing and a peace which surpasses all understanding, I found myself anxious and somewhat stressed. In the back of my mind, I knew that, if the start of the concert/service was delayed, the ending time still would remain the same. That would mean less time—for *me!* It took a year or two before I truly embraced the spiritual lesson behind the physical "hurry-up-and-wait" events God unrelentingly presented to us during our prison adventures. The lesson: None of this prison ministry stuff was about me…it was all about *Him!* God didn't need me to sing my songs or even to preach His Word. I am sure He was delighted that Fran and I had made ourselves available for service, but I am equally certain He was distressed that I let my own agenda dilute the joy to be savored within the prison ministry moment. So instead of allowing me to continually "blow my note" (a phrase employed years ago by my musician friends to describe getting "bent out of shape"), God, instead, encouraged me to **go with the flow…**providing constant reminders that, inside or outside prison walls, *His* perfect will would be done, in *His* perfect time. As much as I can be waylaid by the unexpected, nothing surprises God.

And, now, much more humbly, I realize that what our heavenly Father ordains, He will perfect —with or without my assistance. Having said that, I am grateful He has allowed me to join Him on what has become the roller-coaster ride of a lifetime!

To paraphrase the prophet Jeremiah, as you and I seek the will of God and draw near to Him, we will be better able to cultivate the desire in our hearts to serve. Then the Lord will speak to us and *through* us to prosper us (Jeremiah 29:11-13). God may also employ us to offer a "hope and a future" to other needy souls through our ministry to them as *His* ambassadors.

With such heavenly power and protection —and with the assistance of a few benevolent chaplains along the way—we needn't allow changing constants or the messiness of unexpected twists and turns to thwart our mission of bringing the light of the Gospel of Jesus Christ to incarcerated men and women across the nation and around the world.

In the next chapter, as we continue our journey inside the walls of a state penitentiary near you, we'll take a look at how we can dress-up to avoid a mess-up!

Pending legislation in several states throughout the nation would allow corrections officers, within the cell blocks, to carry pepper spray. The purpose: to protect themselves against personal attacks or aid inmates who are being assaulted.

Chapter Seventeen
DRESS TO ACCESS: ACCEPTABLE ATTIRE

"Unto Adam also and to his wife did the Lord God make coats and skins, and clothed them."

(Genesis 3:21)

"**Y**ou can't enter this prison in *those* shoes." Fran looked at the officer, a uniformed, diminutive, thirty-something woman who sternly gazed back at my wife.

"Excuse me?" my wife replied.

"I said, you can't be going in there with those open-toed shoes," the officer repeated. Actually, Fran and I shouldn't have been surprised. The events unfolding before us seemed a fitting conclusion to a rather trying twelve hours preceding this showdown.

I had secured a room at a name-brand hotel—located at the edge of a blighted community that I called "the back door to hell"—less than a mile from the prison. Upon our arrival Saturday evening, we both noticed immediately that the hotel was "in transition." Not only was the place under new ownership, the entire facility was in complete disarray due to extensive construction work and remodeling.

If it was part of his job description to welcome us warmly to the establishment, the agitated and disheveled gentleman at the registration counter failed miserably, content to avoid eye contact and conversation as I registered for the room and received the key. It was a hot and humid summer day, so Fran and I welcomed the relief that the air conditioning in our third-floor abode provided. After settling into the surroundings and freshening up a bit, we made our way downstairs to the adjoining restaurant. The place was puzzling, to say the least. Imagine a diner/coffee shop/fine-dining amalgamation all in one place. It was right out of the classic TV show *Rowan & Martin's Laugh-In*. The color scheme throughout was brilliant orange, sunshine yellow, and chocolate brown. The well-worn, matted shag carpet picked up the color accents, with additional hues contributed by stains from years, if not decades, of food and drink mishaps. And the cast of restaurant patrons, seated in ornate chairs at several of the round, linen-clad tables and perched on swivel-stools at the counter, was an eclectic blend of grizzled locals mixed with a broad assortment of hotel guests, whose attire ranged from oddly-patterned Bermuda shorts and loud Hawaiian-print shirts, to summer dresses and sport coats. It was a sight to behold! All that was missing was a mirror-ball and go-go dancers on elevated platforms frenetically dancing to disco hits from the 1970s.

After a truly unremarkable meal, we returned to our room determined to turn in early so as to be rested and relaxed for our upcoming concert/service. But we encountered a significant problem: What had been a refreshing cool breeze from the air conditioner had turned into an icy blast. Checking the control box, I realized it was not operational. Climbing upward and balancing on the headrest of an overstuffed chair, I could reach the louvers in the air vents, but all were stuck in the full-open position.

Because of the height of the vents, I had no way to block the now fifty-some-degree air flow, nor any means to deflect the blizzard that cascaded upon us. I called the front desk and explained the situation.

Unfortunately, but predictably, I was told that nothing could be done. Fran and I huddled under the covers. After an hour of frigid, sleepless torture, we phoned the front desk again. Unbelievably, all rooms in this falling-apart hotel were booked! The male voice on the other end of the line promised he would send up some blankets, and four fleece blankets arrived shortly afterward. We spent the rest of the night and early-morning hours tossing, turning and freezing under an avalanche of blankets, blasted by arctic air, in the middle of the summer, on the outskirts of "the back door to hell."

In retrospect, Fran and I can look back on that fateful night as just one in a series of formative ministry mishaps. At the time, however, a good night's sleep would have been appreciated. (FYI—upon returning home from our "hotel from Hades adventure," I wrote a letter to the owner of the establishment but never received a reply. Chances are *very* good that we will not return.)

Fast forward to the next morning in the lobby of the state penitentiary. It was 7:30 a.m., and I was already drenched with sweat, having used a too-small, hand-truck to convey our sound equipment from the distant prison parking lot, through two sets of doors, into the visitors' center of the facility. Waiting to be inspected, our gear looked like a miniature mountain, stacked in a section of the lobby that had been designated as our check-in area. Now, as we waited for the guards to search and catalogue our equipment, Fran was being advised that "You can't be going in there with those open-toed shoes."

Ironically, not five minutes earlier, a young woman, whom I assumed to be an attorney or someone on official business, approached that same corrections officer, signed in, and presented her credentials. Immediately, the duty staffer pressed a button, filling the air with the now-familiar "buzz" as the heavy steel doors disengaged. As she walked past us on her way inside, I noticed that she was wearing a neatly tailored jacket and skirt combination, beautifully accessorized with matching **high-heeled, open-toed shoes.** Being a helpful sort of guy, I was quick to remind the female officer that, "the woman who just went into the prison was wearing open-toed shoes." My statement was met with a glare that could have curdled milk. To considerably shorten a very long story, I asked if our host chaplain would be able to join us in the lobby. After I explained the situation to the chaplain, he, in turn, requested to speak with the commanding shift officer, who proclaimed that "just this once" Fran would be permitted to gain admittance. "But," cautioned the officer, "Don't let it happen again."

The lesson? Ladies (or men), if you are wearing open-toed footwear of any sort, take a back-up pair of close-toed shoes with you! (Another lesson, which I have illustrated frequently in other chapters, is to be prepared for *anything*—expect the unexpected.)

I'm certain that most of you have heard the expression "dress to impress." Usually, the phrase is an encouragement for those attending an event or entering a particular venue to wear attire befitting the occasion. Within the context of prison ministry, a more appropriate derivation of this time-worn phrase might be "dress to gain access." By adhering to the "prison dress code," your entrance—and exit—from jails or penitentiaries might be easier and more pleasurable, as opposed to more laborious and frustrating.

The clothing conundrum confronting the prison visitor is a tug-of-war between that which is deemed acceptable by penal institutions versus what is preferred by the wearer—the person seeking entrance. When it comes to ministry attire, a number of old-school male pastors and prison volunteers still subscribe to the notion that being about the Lord's work *requires* a coat and tie, no ifs, ands, or buts about it. For ladies, that would translate to a modest dress or over-the-knee skirt and blouse. For evangelical believers, keeping in mind that our mission behind bars is to honor and glorify the name of God and the person of Jesus Christ, may I submit that the tone and personality which characterizes your particular ministry also might significantly influence your choice of wardrobe.

For our own SonPower Ministries, my intention is to set the stage for real, relevant, and relational interaction without compromising the Gospel message. When I am conducting a concert/service in front of a larger inmate population, my ensemble tends to gravitate toward a dress shirt, open at the neck with no tie, and a pair of dress slacks. On some occasions, as the Spirit leads, I might wear a pair of "fashion" jeans. Depending upon the time of year and/or the temperature in the facility, a sport coat or leather jacket may be added to complete my ensemble.

Because she often sets up and operates the sound equipment, Fran's wardrobe must be appropriate *and* functional, as she stoops and bends to wrangle speaker cords, etc. Usually, Fran will wear a modest top or blouse with a pair of women's dress slacks or long skirt. In the event that our sound system is not required, she is more likely to don an unpretentious but fashionable dress or tailored suit.

During the weekly Bible study and discipleship class which I facilitate at the local county prison, I dress more casually. At these small-group sessions, jeans or slacks and a button-down collar shirt or pullover tend to be the order of the day. To me, this style helps to create a more relaxed atmosphere and aids in stimulating conversation because I am not perceived by the inmates as the formally attired minister who is "preaching" to his congregation.

Virtually all penal institutions have standardized rules and regulations which comprise a dress code. A document regarding proper dress is usually issued to prospective volunteers well in advance of scheduled ministry dates as part of the clearance process. In general, the information covers issues of modesty, professionalism, and safety. To reinforce dress-code expectations, virtually every institution Fran and I have visited throughout our many years of ministry has onsite signage prominently displayed near the visitors' entrance highlighting the "dos and don'ts" of what to wear and what not to wear when entering their facility. If you are preparing to visit an inmate, are new to prison ministry, or are entering a particular facility for the first time, it would be a good idea to inquire about their dress code in advance. Not only will doing so make you more comfortable in choosing your attire, you also can avoid the inconvenience and embarrassment of not being admitted for an appointment due to your improper choice of clothing.

In an effort to provide insight, without belaboring the dress issue, the following are examples of some of the acceptable—and *unacceptable*—wardrobe components, excerpted from a document issued at the state penitentiary level along with some comments of my own: Neat appearance and professionalism are stressed, to insure a good working relationship with inmates and staff; to ease entrance into the facility, it is recommended that women and men do not wear an abundance of jewelry, as these items will activate the metal detector. In addition, women are cautioned regarding metal hair pins or buttons, as well as metal in underwire bras, supportive undergarments, etc. In the wrong hands, flexible or sturdy metal wire could cause havoc within the prison, whether as a lock-picking (or jamming) device or as material to be fashioned into a weapon. Men must wear long trousers and a shirt with sleeves; women must wear a dress, skirt or slacks with a modestly-appropriate top… the dress or skirt should fall close to the knee, covering at least two-thirds of the thigh; pajamas or boxer shorts (worn as outerwear), see-through apparel, halter tops, spandex outerwear and torn, ripped or revealing tops are never permitted. Men and women must wear shoes! Women must wear bras or proper undergarments. Clothing adorned with drug references, sexual or vulgar language, provocative or biased statements or symbols will virtually guarantee that the prison visitor or volunteer will be denied entrance.

In county jails, rules and regulations may be a bit more lenient. For example, during the warm-weather months, shorts which cover an appropriate amount of the thigh and upper leg are permitted in many county facilities but would not be allowed, under normal visitation circumstances, in state penitentiaries.

In my travels throughout the county prison systems, I have seen more than a few examples of visitor apparel which would be absolutely forbidden at the state and federal levels. And, in spite of the best-laid plans of prison administrators, I have also witnessed "creative" and brazen behavior during prison visitation that defies all rules and regulations, but so tragically illustrates the lasciviousness that can be entertained within the human heart. On one occasion, while waiting in a communal visitation room to counsel with a young man at a notoriously troublesome urban county prison, I became distracted by activity in the booth next to mine. A heavy-set woman, who had dressed "appropriately" to gain entrance into the facility, was in the midst of unbuttoning her blouse, unhooking her bra and exposing her ample bosom to the delight of a male paramour on the other side of a glass partition. Glancing in my direction with a sly smile, she continued the exhibition for a moment longer. Somewhat taken aback, all I could think of was, "Smile—you have *got* to be on *Candid Camera!*" The sad scene brought to my mind the desperate wickedness of the human spirit, seeking solace and fulfillment apart from God's grace. As it is written: "There is no one righteous, not even one; there is no one who understands; there is no one who seeks God" (Romans 3:10, 11).

Indeed, there are limitations within the penal system regarding personal attire but the prison minister enjoys ample leeway within those parameters. Over time, you will be able to settle into a style of dress which…

1. satisfies prison regulations
2. allows you to be physically comfortable during the course of ministry
3. honors God
4. honors the spirits of the inmates to whom you minister without being a distraction.

It would seem that if you and I simply obey the rules and regulations, we should enjoy relatively smooth sailing within the context of our ministerial pursuits. Or will we? Sometimes things just don't work out according to *anybody's* plans. You'll discover this truth as you explore the upcoming chapter. Fasten your seat belts. The roller-coaster may get a bit bumpy as we navigate the unexpected twists and turns of "When Things Go Wrong …"

Criminal aliens accounted for nearly
75% of federal drug sentences (2014),
40% of murder convictions in FL and
95% of outstanding homicide warrants
in Los Angeles.
(Immigration and Customs Enforcement (ICE) statistics)

Chapter Eighteen

WHEN THINGS GO WRONG...
AND THEY WILL

*"We are troubled on every side, yet not distressed;
we are perplexed but not in despair; persecuted
but not forsaken; cast down but not destroyed..."*

(2 Corinthians 4:8, 9)

With calculated cunning, the pack of jackals surrounded its prey, circling and moving ever closer, cutting off all avenues of escape. The hunters' eyes gleamed with cruel intent—the hunted stood wide-eyed, seemingly unaware of what was about to transpire.

The scene I just described was not taken from a television documentary about life and death in the animal kingdom on the plains of the Serengeti. No, this was my "worst-case-scenario" perception of a real-life encounter taking place prior to a concert/service at a prison known for being an "edgy" place where, at times, there seemed to be a thin line between discipline and chaos. The "jackals"—the hunters— were four to five inmates in bright orange prison jumpsuits. The "prey" was none other than Fran who was stationed toward the back of the room behind the mixing board. Moving quickly, I rushed to Fran's side, making no attempt to "play nice." "Gentlemen," I said, "this is **not** the place for you to be. Please step away from my wife and the sound equipment and find a place to sit in your assigned area." Perhaps, as you read this, you might be thinking, "Now, Pete…don't you think you were overreacting just a bit?" Perhaps I *was* being overly cautious, overly protective, but in the moment it seemed like the most effective course of action.

The prisoners may have, indeed, just been curious about our sound system. Or, they may simply have wanted to steal a bit of conversation with an attractive member of the opposite sex. But I perceived their actions to be symptomatic of a larger lack of oversight throughout the room. What was to have been an outdoor concert had been moved to an indoor gymnasium due to a thunderstorm. The gym, while certainly more than adequate to hold the crowd, was not set up in any way for a church service. The prison chaplain was trying to encourage the men to sit on the floor in designated areas of the basketball court with little success. Instead, many inmates took the opportunity to move to the far corners of the room, to catch up on conversations with friends and acquaintances, perhaps utilizing the shadows for far more nefarious alliances. At any rate, they blatantly disregarded the chaplain's instructions. I expressed my concerns to the prison pastor, then I approached a CO in the hallway, asked him to position himself within the room, in close proximity to Fran. With tighter security and a greater sense of control, the service commenced as scheduled.

Inevitably, within the context of prison ministry—or life in general—things will occur that seem to be totally out of our control. Unforeseen circumstances arise at a moment's notice, necessitating the alteration of our best-laid plans. And, if you are like me, situations which disrupt the status quo also have the ability to test your heart-attitude, determining whether or not we respond to some stressor in a Christlike manner. I firmly believe God, in His infinite wisdom, presents us with "pop quizzes" to help develop our character and decision-making capabilities, while building within us the attributes He finds pleasing and necessary as we grow in His image.

Our God is a *personal* God. He knows our needs. And He knows exactly *what* we need for spiritual growth in every life situation. That is why I believe every person's personal *or* ministry challenges will be "custom-tailored" for each of us. To illustrate this point, instead of listing hypothetical scenarios, I am going to present—as in the above example—some of the true-life misadventures Fran and I have faced during our prison ministry tenure. I will not simply note the problems, but will also include the viable solutions which God orchestrated for our good and, I believe, for the benefit of all who were participants in these events.

The Rebellious Young Man

At the beginning of every concert/service, I open with prayer, invoking the power of God to be upon the room (the sanctuary) and upon every person in attendance. Also, I invite the Holy Spirit of God to open the minds and hearts of the inmates (*and* any corrections officers in the chapel) and to have His way in their lives during our time together. I was in the midst of praying such a prayer at the onset of a men's county-prison service, when I was abruptly interrupted by a loud proclamation from the back of the room. A young man seated near the back wall of the chapel, had risen to his feet to announce that I didn't have to worry about God showing up on this particular evening. The reason was simple, he declared. ***The inmate was, in fact, Jesus Christ and he had everything under control!***

Several months prior to this outburst, the same prisoner had tried to disrupt another worship service in a similar way. At that time I had extended him grace and allowed him to remain in the chapel. This night, however, I knew immediately in my spirit that his second calculated verbal assault could not be tolerated. I perceived his actions to be an affront to Almighty God and a test of my willingness to defend the Person of Christ. It was fortuitous that the rebellious young man was one of the last to arrive and stood near the chapel door. Stifling what, in days gone by, I might have described as "righteous indignation," I called upon the name of the one and only Jesus Christ of Nazareth, rebuking the inmate's claims of deity. Summoning ministering—even warring—angels to cleanse the chapel of all unrighteousness, I demanded that the inmate leave, stating that by his insistent efforts to put forth his own agenda he had forfeited the right to attend the service. After a moment of dumbstruck hesitation he complied with my "request" and was ushered back to his cell.

As calm was restored, it was still obvious that a number of the men were both surprised and upset by the inmate's behavior and what had transpired (some having seen him act out on prior occasions). I sensed that God wanted to teach everyone present additional spiritual lessons from this unsettling event. And so, after a time of soothing prayer to refocus the prisoners' minds and hearts, I was able to use this disruption as an example of how the enemy will go to any lengths and use any available means to draw men or women away from the saving knowledge of the Gospel of Jesus Christ. With that thought firmly in mind, the evening continued without further interruptions. Toward the end of the service, I allowed additional opportunity for prayer and decision-making. That night five men behind prison bars received the gift of everlasting life through the shed blood of Jesus Christ. Freedom for eternity!

The "Duct Tape Thief"

In most of the state penitentiaries that we visit, Fran and I are permitted to use duct tape to adhere our speaker cords to the tile flooring or carpet in the chapel. This is done to lessen the possibility of inmates tripping and, perhaps, injuring themselves or yanking the cords from a power source or the speaker cabinets. At the end of any worship service we make it a point to gather every piece of tape, fashioning the strips into a sphere and then handing our "silver ball" to a corrections officer for proper disposal. On one Sunday morning, we had just concluded a particularly successful concert/service at a men's state penitentiary. After conversing and praying with several of the prisoners, Fran and I began the sometimes-arduous task of breaking down the equipment. As the inmates began to exit the chapel area, my attention was drawn to a solitary form—an extraordinarily tall middle-aged man—still seated at the end of one of the long, rather antiquated wooden church pews. Because the service had been a somewhat emotional affair, I surmised that the gentleman, with his head bowed and gaze cast downward, was simply having one final moment alone with God. Upon closer inspection, however, I saw far more than a quiet time of prayer. A "code-red alert" sounded in my brain, instantly confirming within my spirit the reality that absolutely no good could come from this man's actions!

As inconspicuously as possible, the inmate had slowly eased his gangly arm toward the linoleum floor beneath his scruffy, prison-issue boots. Ever so carefully, he maneuvered his boney fingers to gently peel off several strips of the sticky, waterproof tape that covered the wires by his feet. Experience had taught me all too well that duct tape, in the wrong hands, could be employed to jam locks or to keep unlocked doors or windows from re-locking. Also, I had seen examples of duct tape being wrapped around the butt end of a sharpened piece of metal to form the handle of a *shiv*—a jailhouse knife—or other assorted hand-made weapons.

Without a second's hesitation, I informed a nearby CO of what I had seen. Immediately, he approached the prisoner, searched him, confiscated the contraband, and ushered the "duct tape thief" from the premises. As a result, a potential catastrophe was averted.

Circumnavigating Perversion

One of the saddest, most disheartening examples of "when things go wrong" occurred more recently in our ministry travels, during a chapel service at a facility for adjudicated, juvenile offenders. The chapel was, in fact, a quaint nineteenth-century church located in a forested area within a complex of dormitory housing and free-standing buildings—all painted a pristine white. These somewhat-historic structures, with adjacent basketball courts and athletic fields, served the educational, recreational, and administrative needs of the detention center. Had it not been for the secure sally port entranceway and the razor-wire reinforced chain link fence encircling the grounds, one might have imagined themselves as visitors at a church camp or Christian conference center.

The church sanctuary was a simple structure with aged hardwood arches forming a cathedral ceiling and providing excellent acoustics. Colorful, pictorial stained-glass windows lined one side of the building. On this night the windows were open, allowing a fresh breeze and the scent of blooming wildflowers to enter the room, accompanied by a chorus of crickets, katydids, and tree frogs.

As part of the extraordinarily regimented schedule, an announcement of our presence had been made fifteen minutes prior to the start-time: "Religious service in the chapel. 7:00 p.m." (No mention of our names or ministry affiliation was permitted, due to privacy laws.) And so they came—boys in all sizes, shapes and colors, from twelve to nineteen years of age. Virtually every young man sported the same uniform: a white tee shirt with black athletic shorts. They arrived in threes and fours, each group representing a dormitory of voluntary attendees, always accompanied by a counselor. The boys congregated in designated seating areas, with the ever-present facility staff seated behind or alongside them in old-fashioned, high-backed wooden church pews.

I presided from a raised pulpit in the front of the sanctuary, allowing me to gaze out—and downward—over my audience of twenty-four adjudicated teenagers. Truly, I had a birds-eye view of everyone in the room, including the juvenile offenders; the smiling, kind-hearted chaplain who seemed to love the kids more than they loved themselves; the counselors, looking on with varying degrees of interest; and my sound person, Fran, inhabiting the farthest pew in the back of the room. I saw her with head bowed, and knew she was praying for God to change hearts and lives during this evening's service.

As the musical portion of the service began, the teens immediately responded to the up-tempo, rhythmic songs and the message of hope and victory contained within the lyrics. Several of the more animated adolescents clapped their hands and moved to the beat in their hard, wooden seats. But the slower, story-telling ballads affected this audience in a deeper way. Those songs allowed the young men—some of whom came from horrendous family situations and circumstances—to contemplate what their destiny might look like as they moved forward *with or without* God in their lives. The stage was set—now was the time for a message of healing and a new birth in Jesus Christ.

When I speak, I enjoy making eye contact with my audience. And in this particular chapel, the boys in the front row, on either side of the aisle, were easily engaged because their bench seating was fully open to my view. Several minutes into the message, I noticed two young men, inching ever closer to one another until, their bare legs touched. To my amazement, one teen was stroking the bare inner thigh of his shorts-wearing companion. The second youth responded by reaching over and rubbing the genital area of his more-aggressive mate. These two "lost boys" were within several feet of me, in full view, and acted as if they—or I—were completely invisible! Because of the height of the seat backs, their actions were hidden from the counselors and the teens seated behind them.

Can you even imagine this scenario? Here I am, preaching the Word of God, and these two young men are acting out sexually right in front of my eyes! To make matters worse, the seemingly-dominant boy had his eyes fixed on me, with a taunting smirk on his face that seemed to say, "Okay, preacher…what are you going to do about it?" The dilemma was this: how to put an end to such abominable behavior without completely distracting the others in attendance and/or disrupting the service?

Following the Holy Spirit's leading, I focused my attention on the rest of the audience in the sanctuary and within a matter of seconds completed the topical point being presented. Then, returning my gaze to the young offenders in the front row, I *quietly* asked the sneering lad to move away from his companion. He shifted about a foot down the pew, still with a challenging look of contempt. Raising my voice slightly, I instructed him to move five feet away from the other teen. Realizing that he was now the center of attention, he complied. At that point, I resumed preaching the Word of God, thanking Him for making a way through a dicey situation.

When the service ended and the teens and counselors had vacated the chapel, I informed the chaplain about what had occurred. I stressed to him that the situation should be reported, through *his* office, and dealt with immediately so that any sexual contact between the two young men would not be allowed to escalate or continue. Also, I cautioned that, because of the seating logistics in the sanctuary, the counselors should be instructed to take precautionary steps to thwart such inappropriate behavior in the future. The following week, I received a telephone call from the facilities director. During our lengthy conversation, he expressed gratitude for the way the situation was handled. He assured me that additional mechanisms and procedures were being enacted as a result of the incident being brought to his attention.

The "Silent Song"

Just as in our everyday lives, not all things that go wrong during ministry behind prison walls are earth-shattering events or disasters-in-the-making. Some happenstances are simply unexpected annoyances—one of those aforementioned "pop quizzes"—which are designed to further develop our Christlike demeanor. Such was the case during a state penitentiary concert/service several years ago.

More often than not, within the context of a prison concert, the music which accompanies my vocals emanates from studio-produced CDs of my original compositions as well as selected songs from other recording artists. As mentioned earlier, God empowers me to employ contemporary, lyrically-sound music as "spiritual ammunition" to help pave the way for preaching His Word. The job of operating the sound equipment inevitably falls on Fran's shoulders. If, as sometimes happens, an inmate is running the mixing board, Fran will be nearby to lend her "musical ear," as she is the one most familiar with the sound quality we both desire.

Logistically, more often than not, things go as planned. Not on this particular Sunday.

At the beginning of the musical portion of our service, Fran selected the appropriate piece of music from our prepared song list, cued the CD, and soon the sanctuary was filled with song, setting the course for that morning's worship experience. Midway through the opening number—without warning—the CD began skipping wildly! It was impossible to vocalize to the starting, stopping, and stuttering soundtrack. After what seemed like an eternity (actually less than ten seconds), Fran was forced to mute the music completely, leaving just me, myself, and I standing on the platform, in front of a multitude of quizzical inmates. What to do? God, in His grace, mercy and wisdom had presented me with an unexpected teachable moment. So, without missing a beat, I continued to sing the song lyrics a cappella, putting forth the same passion and emphasis as I had done when accompanied by a "full orchestra." The reaction was instant and spontaneous. At the song's conclusion, my "captive audience" erupted in applause, many prisoners rising to their feet in appreciation. By making the best of a humbling situation, I had illustrated to this congregation that SonPower Ministries' primary objective in serving them was to glorify God, even in the midst of unforeseen circumstances. And, as an added value, the men could see that Pete Einstein was just an ordinary guy—one who could laugh at his missteps, remain relaxed in the Lord, and not take *himself* too seriously.

As our lives and ministry continue through the days, months, and years, the stories of "things gone wrong" tend to multiply, creating a mini-mountain of chaos, dismay and despair, or healthy challenge, opportunity, and achievement—depending upon the spiritual condition of our minds and hearts (See Romans 12:2, 3). It is refreshing and good to remember that a mountain can present either an insurmountable obstacle or a privileged perch from which we can view even greater possibilities on the horizon. This holds true for you and me, as we walk in "freedom" within our society, as well as for those incarcerated men and women on the *other* side of the iron gates and razor wire.

Next on our journey, we will explore three short chapters of special situations, which directly apply to prison ministry…but which may affect your life in some way as well.

Currently, there are about one-half million correctional officers employed throughout U.S. prison systems.

PART THREE

UNIQUE SITUATIONS WITHIN THE PRISON MINISTRY EXPERIENCE

Chapter Nineteen

A SPECIAL WORD TO MUSIC MINISTERS—MINISTRY BEFORE MUSIC

*"Sing to the Lord a new song; sing to the Lord
all the earth. Sing to the Lord, praise his name;
proclaim his salvation day after day."*

(Psalm 96:1, 2)

*M*usic has been ever-present throughout the history of
mankind. It has helped define peoples, cultures, even entire
civilizations. Today, music, in both secular and religious contexts, still
plays an integral part in the societal fabric of lives around the world. In
modern-day America, if you were to ask evangelical pastors or music
ministers if "contemporary music" plays an important role in their
worship experience, a vast majority would acknowledge that it does.

In this chapter, we will explore Christ-centered music as it impacts
worship and ministry. It should be noted that there *is* a place and a role
for Christian musical *entertainment* within and outside the Body of
Christ. But because the central theme of this chapter is caring for

imprisoned men and women from a spiritual perspective, we will focus our attention on the concept of *music as ministry.*

The Bible contains 839 references to music. And no biblical text gives greater perspective of sacred music's value within ministry than the Book of Psalms. Although the attributes of music and singing are mentioned throughout scripture (i.e., 2 Samuel 6:5, 2 Chronicles 29:25, Ephesians 5:19, Colossians 3:16, etc.), the Book of Psalms can be an exhaustive study in and of itself. As we read from Psalm 1 through 150, it is notable that, when they were penned, many of these writings were presented as "spiritual songs" accompanied by musical instruments, such as the lyre, the harp, or the timbrel. Ministerial music was utilized in ancient days, as it should be used today, to praise God for who He is and to thank Him—for what He's done, what He *is* doing, and what He *will* do. Indeed, spiritual songs have the ability to pave the way for worshipping almighty God. And in the midst of such worship experience can come a call to repentance, forgiveness, deliverance— much like a healing balm to soothe the needs of a dry and thirsty soul.

It truly can be said that he who sings prays twice!

Music and song play an important role in my life and in the ministry to which I have been called to serve. Instrumental and vocal performance can add color and texture to *any* worship service, particularly within the context of prison evangelism and discipleship. As you consider the thoughts and principles conveyed in this chapter, please be aware that they apply principally to Christian versus secular music. That is not to say there's no place for Motown or some rousing soul music within the prison population. Interestingly, those sonic qualities sometimes appear within the melodies I present during a SonPower Ministries concert/service. But the lyrics of the songs I sing, without fail, have a Christ-centered focus, with emphasis upon proper *agape* love and relationships.

God gifted each of His "wonderfully and fearfully-made" creations with unique temperaments, talents, abilities, and gifts. Perhaps some of you are skilled musicians; others may possess excellent singing voices. If God has given you a talent for singing or playing a musical instrument, His heart's desire is for you to use those gifts for *His* glory. But make no mistake—our heavenly Father is more concerned about your *character* than He is about your musical expertise. In fact, God is most interested in the progression of each of our personal journeys, at a *spiritual* level, as we travel the "narrow road" toward Christlikeness (Matthew 7:14). Our inclination to reach out to others through some form of ministry will flow naturally from a heart intent on serving God first, as He allows His fruit of the Spirit to flourish within our innermost being (Galatians 5:22-23).

God seeks good stewards of the gifts and talents He has given us; He is not looking for Christian rock stars!

One particular verse that allows me to keep music and ministry in proper perspective is Matthew 6:33: "But seek first His kingdom and His righteousness, and all these things will be given to you as well." Throughout this adventure story of ministering to men and women who are hurting and in bondage—both inside or *outside* prison walls— I have mentioned, on more than one occasion, that music can and will "set the table" to enable those with hungry hearts to feast upon the good news of the Gospel message. With this perspective in mind, remember that, for the music minister, an attitude of servanthood should prevail during the course of preparatory worship. Therefore, regardless of vocal or musical style, the "spiritual ammunition" you discharge to pave the way for preaching the Word of Life should be three things:

1. God-conceived
2. Christ-centered
3. Spirit-led

As a minister within the penal system, you take on the weighty role of spiritual warrior, contending for the hearts and minds of needy men and women in whom society, for the most part, has given up hope or chooses to ignore. Therefore, the heart's desire of those ministering through music (as well as the spoken Word) should be that of ascertaining and pursuing one's direction and **calling,** following the Lord's leading, as opposed to promoting one's *career* through Christian musical endeavors. Let me reiterate that there is a place in God's plan for Christ-centered material that provides comic relief and/or entertainment value for the listener. During the course of ministry— in whatever form it takes—God desires that you and I exercise discernment when presenting our message to a given gathering of people, many of whom may be seeking answers to questions which seem far beyond their ability to comprehend or resolve.

With this thought in mind, we should remember that a prison concert opportunity is *not* the time to intentionally dazzle the audience with your musical prowess in a way that makes you the center of attention. You become nothing more than an elegant distraction when your performance overshadows the higher, more righteous purpose of rescuing lost and dying souls from the travesty of eternal separation from God! Another thought for consideration is this: There is *never* a right time to steal the spotlight by compromising the Gospel message simply to tickle the ears of those hearing the music. An example might be those misguided ministers who create a worship program by reworking popular and easily-recognized secular songs, sporadically inserting Christian lyrics to achieve some desired spiritual effect. Several times over the years, a former state penitentiary chaplain, whom I love dearly, repeatedly requested that I create customized musical selections for his prison-chapel attendees by simply inserting Christian lyrics or phrases into the tunes the men could listen to on secular radio stations. And always, knowing in my heart that my Father in heaven wanted something infinitely finer—something more Kingdom-creative for *His* pleasure—I politely declined that chaplain's request.

Why is it so important for the music minister to fervently seek God's will for his or her life and calling? One vitally important reason is that following the Lord's leading decreases the likelihood that hidden agendas or subtle egotistical notions will infiltrate our worship, turning the "joyful noise" into simply…noise. In the 5th chapter of Amos, the Bible describes how the Jewish temple singers fell under the influence of the Egyptian's vocal style and began to imitate this mode of expression for personal recognition and financial gain. Watching this perversion of worship, God responded in Amos 5:23, rebuking the musicians: "…Take away from Me the noise of thy songs; for I will not hear the melody."

So there you have it. Worship music that is spiritually-flawed, disingenuous, or presented with less-than-God-honoring intentions, regardless of genre or style, is nothing more than another example of a fallen humanity's chaotic clamor to our Creator God—the One who has knitted together the spiritual tapestry of melody and harmony since the beginning of time on this green, granite planet we call Earth.

One word before we continue: If the substance of your prison-concert ministry runs no deeper than the latest chart-topping songs, a hip style, cool beats, or impressive performances, as opposed to introducing the hearer to the person of Jesus Christ and His endless love for people who search desperately for spiritual truth, you will fail to meet the needs of those who are lost and dying in their sin. You will fail, even if you are applauded, elevated in status, and deemed a success in the eyes of the world.

When I entered the realm of Christian music, as a new believer, I was still a rather selfish and spoiled individual. To my egocentric way of thinking, I pictured myself as having an opportunity to be "a bigger fish in a smaller pond." For years, I had been intimately involved in the world of secular music, always striving for excellence, but having that noble intention irreparably tainted by a subtle but insatiable quest for power and fame.

Prior to beginning my journey as a new creation in Christ, I had returned from a somewhat spiritually-dark period of living and playing music in Los Angeles, which ironically means "the City of Angels." I encountered very few angels during my stay there. But, being heavily involved in the deception of New Age occultism, I was not on the lookout for angelic beings from a truly Christ-centered worldview. As opposed to "the peace of God, which transcends all understanding…" (Philippians 4:7), what I found was a self-centered motivation to triumph, even at the expense of others. My life was a constant battle to find order within the chaos that surrounded me and the turmoil which had taken up residence in my soul. In the eyes of the world I was "living the life." I was a lead singer and percussionist in a very talented band. I made enough money to live in my own little bungalow in North Hollywood. My back-door neighbor was Will Geer, who played Grandpa Walton on *The Waltons.* I attended soirees thrown by notable celebrities, including an after-concert get-together hosted by Kris Kristofferson and Rita Coolidge, where I had opportunity to talk briefly with Bob Dylan. And the reminiscences could go on and on. But the bottom line was this—for all the supposed glitz and glamour that surrounded my life as a secular musician, I was forever trying, without success, to fill a spiritual void in my heart—an ever-elusive hole in my soul.

On my circuitous return trip from Los Angeles to my hometown of Carlisle, Pennsylvania, I spent time in Tucson, Arizona. It was there that I developed a love for Native American culture and art. As a result of this interest and an entrepreneurial tendency inherited from my father, I birthed a Native American jewelry business which my dad and I operated for several years upon my return to the East Coast. Always remaining involved, in some way, with the music scene, I became a deejay at a happening (albeit short-lived) discotheque in Carlisle. It was in that place of glitter and sound that a providential meeting took place: Late one October evening in 1978, as I observed the colorfully decorated mass of humanity undulating on the dance floor, my eye was captured by a lithe spirit flowing amidst the strobe lights. For a moment, I thought it might be an ethereal image from heaven…an angel sent from above…but it was, in fact, Fran Wilson, the beautiful woman God had chosen to be my partner-in-life, my help-meet, my completer. That night, we talked until the wee hours of the morning. We were married within nine months. I adopted her then four-year-old son, and began a new life as a husband, father, and advertising/marketing executive.

For more than twelve years I strove for success in the business world and remained unfulfilled. And then, in April of 1992, I made still another life-changing decision. I left the advertising profession (two weeks after Fran had quit her job as a swimming and aquatic-fitness instructor), to begin a new adventure in ministry.

Because the Christian music industry was a minuscule entity compared to the secular music market, my still-selfish sense told me that my odds for success within the realm of music-as-ministry (read: Christian-music recording artist) should be exponentially increased. I would quickly learn, however, that at the highest levels, *the Christian-music industry was no different than the secular-music world from which I had just emerged!* Talk about a letdown!

At age forty, I was already far too old for industry big-wigs to be interested in me or my musical career. To add salt to my wounds, I realized that the heads of Christian music labels—most owned and controlled by secular corporations—were searching for beautiful-looking, sixteen-year-old boys and girls with passable-to-good singing voices in whom they could invest a modicum of up-front time and money in the hope that one of them would be the "next big thing." This mindset was no different than that of their secular counterparts. For a time, the realization that my best-laid musical blueprint was not going to develop as planned proved to be more than a bit disappointing to me, a man who was used to getting his way in life. But what appeared to be, on the surface, a major setback, God used as a foundational building block in my development as an others-centered follower of Jesus Christ. He began to teach me that He alone was to be the author of my destiny. Over time, I began to experience His Word and His principles affecting and directing my life and living, realizing, once and for all, that His Holy Spirit was the healer…the comforter… that His "still small voice" within me had filled the hole in my soul.

In 1992, a bit more than ten years after I became a Christ-follower—when God knew I might have something worthwhile to say—He put a burden on my heart to speak out against the dangers of New Age occultism under the banner of SonPower Ministries. Music did not become an element of the ministry He had birthed in me until 1½ years later. At that point, I enlisted the help of two talented singers—former band mates and friends from my junior high school days. We sang soulful, rhythm-and-blues-tinged "Contemporary Christian Music" in an era when many churches were still not comfortable with that style. During this time, I began writing and recording my own unique brand of Christian soul music. Because of the amount of orchestration and the complexity of the arrangements, we presented our music accompanied by studio-recorded performance tracks, first on audio cassettes and then CDs. At the end of our concert performance, I would present a topical Christian message.

After a period of three years, it became obvious that the Lord wanted more of *Him* and less of us in the mix. With that in mind—and with the blessing of the SonPower Ministries board of advisors—Fran and I struck out on our own, with CD performance tracks in hand, to minister in a more intentional way. Music, while still an important component of our services, was positioned as a vehicle to pave the way for more intensive—and *intentional*—evangelistic preaching and teaching.

And so it remains to this day, some twenty-five years later.

Through an extensive and sometimes painstaking growth process, God has shown me that there is no secret formula for effective music ministry, but there are foundational truths which can be applied to musically-oriented, or *any* type of ministry.

1. Love God more than yourself and the things of this world. Once we learn what it looks like to "Love the Lord your God with all your heart and all your soul and with all your mind…" then He will begin to reveal how we can more authentically "…Love your neighbor as yourself" (Matthew 22:37, 39).

2. Develop a heart and a passion for the ministry you have been given. Spiritual motivation helps build faith in the believer, allowing us to press onward even during tough times, when trials and tribulations seem to overshadow behind-the-scenes work God is orchestrating, on our behalf, in the midst of our mess.

3. Endeavor to grow in all things spiritual. A well-rounded believer will gain balance and perspective in his or her life.

4. Make yourself available. *Do something…now!* God does not desire that His children should sit on the sideline, watching silently as a multitude of lost people parade before us.

Then I heard the voice of the Lord saying, "Whom shall I send, and who will go for us?" Then I said, "Here am I; send me" (Isaiah 6:8).

As you develop a clear vision for ministry, you will begin to live your life with a new sense of destination. Hopefully, in time, your desire to use music as a healing balm or a two-edged sword, will become as natural as breathing, as constant as a heartbeat. Then you will become more fully aware of the ways in which God orders your steps and directs your path. Learning to balance **inspiration** with **preparation,** God will not only use you for His service, He will stretch you to your limits—in a very good way—through Kingdom-work opportunities! As His Word proclaims, God loves obedience even more than sacrifice. Be ready and willing to respond and He will bless your music and ministry efforts.

In our next step, we will tackle a reality that exists throughout our nation and around the world. Even if our upcoming topic hasn't affected you personally, it has almost certainly had an indirect impact on you or your family. The next chapter epitomizes, in a very literal way, one specific aspect of *the inmate within*.

Both male and female offenders are *especially* appreciative when musical instruments and/or music are incorporated into the worship experience provided by a visiting ministry.

Chapter 20

WHEN A LOVED ONE
IS INCARCERATED

*"Let the redeemed of the Lord tell their story…
Some sat in utter darkness, prisoners suffering in iron
chains, because they rebelled against God's commands
and despised the plans of the Most High."*

(Psalm 107:2, 10, 11)

Virtually every individual throughout the United States—and around the world—has been affected in some way by the concept, and the reality, of "imprisonment." Sons lose fathers. Fathers lose sons. Daughters lose mothers. Mothers lose daughters. Parents are separated from children. Children are separated from parents. And so it continues, day after day, month by month, year upon year.

Clearly, crime and punishment does more than simply affect the person responsible for perpetrating the offense. Immediate family, relatives, loved ones, and friends are *all* impacted by incarceration. It is the "trickle-down" effect at its most insidious. Whether the sentence constitutes a sixty-day stay at the local county jail for a DUI conviction or life-without-parole in a state penitentiary for first-degree murder, the imprisonment of one individual intrudes into the lives of many others.

While it may be convenient for the world-at-large to disassociate itself from one person serving a prison sentence, numerous factors—often spawning far more questions than answers—enter into the equation of incarceration for those who are close to the offender. There is much to consider when you are related to or a friend of someone who is incarcerated. Should bail, fines, or court costs be paid to help ensure release of the family member or friend or should those funds be withheld, so as not to enable the individual to continue along a path of self-destruction? What about approved clothing, toiletry items and basic necessities that must be paid for by the prisoner? Who should foot the bill? Over time, how much money, contributed or *sacrificed,* is enough? Should funds be continually deposited into the inmate's commissary account for snacks and creature comforts? Armed with the understanding that there may be no single correct answer for any given situation, let's briefly explore some of these prison/family dilemmas.

Bail or "prison-release payment" is often required of a defendant facing a criminal charge or multiple charges. Bail may range from a small sum to a king's ransom, depending upon the severity of the crime; the criminal history; and the current psychological, emotional, and physical state of the offender. When all aspects of a particular case have been carefully examined, a judge of the court will determine the bail amount. Variables for consideration may include…

- The *seriousness* of the crime—was the defendant charged with shoplifting $40 in groceries from the local supermarket or attempting to kill another human being with a deadly weapon?
- The *frequency* of the crime—was this a first-time offense or has the individual been charged with similar crimes in the past?
- Is there a *pattern of criminal behavior* that has been exhibited over time?
- Were there *extenuating circumstances* involved during the commission of the crime?

- Was the subject *under the influence of alcohol or drugs?*
- Is there a *history of drug and/or alcohol abuse?*
- What is, or was, the *psychological state of the defendant?*
- Is there *evidence of mental illness* as a contributing factor leading to the commission of the crime?
- Should the accused individual be considered a *"flight risk?"* Does he or she have out-of-area contacts or connections which might make it improbable that the defendant would even show up for his or her court appearance?

As you can see, an exhausting number of considerations may present themselves during the court hearing or bail-setting process. When all case factors have been scrutinized, a judge might rule that your Uncle Bill should be released on his own recognizance. Perhaps a *secured bail*—or what might be referred to as a *surety* payment—(guaranteed by personal assets or arranged through a bail bondsman) of several thousand dollars or more might be required to grant Uncle Bill's release until his day in court. For unpaid child support a *purge*—payment of a portion or the entirety of delinquent monies due—could help insure his release. But if the crime is particularly egregious, Uncle Bill may well be held in county jail until his trial date, with bail set at one-million dollars! In the case of a homicide, no possibility of bail is available for the accused.

It should be noted that there is no one-size-fits-all formula in the bail-setting process. In every case—even with a commonality of factors—a certain amount of subjectivity enters into the proceedings as the judge rules on an amount of money that is considered sufficient to guarantee a defendant's freedom until his or her trial date.

For the minister or layperson, here is a bit more basic information pertaining to bail. Let's imagine a district magistrate sets bail, or surety, for an alleged offender at $5,000. If the individual accused of the crime has access to $5,000 in cash, he or she is, in fact, able to post (or satisfy) their *own* bail. Or, if that same individual has personal assets—such as an automobile or a home—with a value equal to or exceeding the bail amount, he or she can use those non-monetary assets to satisfy the bail requirement. Bail money or collateral is returned when the accused makes an appearance at his or her scheduled court arraignment. If someone accused of a crime is unable to satisfy the bail requirement, that individual may seek the services of a *bail bondsman*. A bail bondsman provides monetary bail, in its entirety, on behalf of individuals accused of a variety of crimes. For this service, the bail bondsman requires a nonrefundable payment—usually 5–10% of the bail amount—from his clients upon their appearance in court. *But what happens, you ask, when a person accused of a crime fails to show up at the court hearing?* That's a great question. When an individual "jumps (or skips) bail," he or she becomes a fugitive of the law and an arrest warrant is issued. At this point, all bail monies are forfeited and become property of the court. If surety has been posted by a bail bondsman, the bondsman may employ the services of a specialized detective, commonly known as a bounty hunter who, for a fee, will seek to capture the fugitive and return him to face criminal charges. This process helps ensure that the bail bondsman will not lose *his* money leading up to the hearing or trial of the accused individual.

Assuming that a family member has been convicted of a crime and *is* serving time in a county jail or state penitentiary, additional monetary factors come into play. In county or state facilities, basic necessities for general-population prisoners are purchased through a system of inmate commissary accounts. Monies are deposited into each inmate's account—by family, friends, or concerned individuals—to provide for a variety of items: socks, underwear, lotion, deodorant, contact lens solution, toothpaste, snacks and, perhaps, approved electronic items such as a portable radio or CD player. (Please note: As mentioned earlier in this writing, cell phones are *absolutely not* permitted to be in the possession of inmates within any prison setting!) For a variety of reasons, many individuals awaiting trial have limited or virtually no access to personal income. The accused may be indigent or without a job. Perhaps financial resources have been squandered, fomented by addictions to gambling, alcohol, or drug usage. At times, personal assets may be tied up in legal wrangling, either related to or separate from the crime for which an offender is awaiting adjudication. Far too often, those charged with a crime are unable to provide for even their most basic necessities while in prison. Therefore, the responsibility for funding an inmate's account inevitably rests upon the shoulders of individuals outside the confines of the penal institution. In years gone by, a hands-on system of monetary exchange, facilitated by a designated member of the prison clerical staff, ensured that funds would be properly credited to an inmate's personal or commissary account. More recently, the process has become modernized, with family members or friends accessing the inmate's account via a computerized kiosk, usually located in the lobby or waiting area of a given facility. Whether the funding function is old school or high-tech, the reality remains the same: depending upon an accused individual's crime or the backlog within the court system, the realities of supplying financial resources over and above basic necessities provided by the prison could constitute weeks, months, or even years of giving.

At the county level, certain inmates are granted work-release privileges. Through symbiotic relationships with local business and industry, inmates are transported throughout the community to productively engage in jobs to help pay fines, reparations, and court costs, while alleviating the monotony of ongoing prison life within the general population. Depending upon the job, various approved articles of clothing are permitted by work-release inmates—again paid for or provided by someone outside the prison system. Wages earned by work-release inmates are administered through the county jail to help ensure the individuals' obligations are met. Once all financial responsibilities have been satisfied, any leftover monies are then deposited into the inmates' prison account.

Another monetary factor which comes into play when a family member or loved one is incarcerated are telephone or communications costs. Every penal facility is serviced by companies specializing in *inmate communications*. These private vendors are responsible for providing, updating, and maintaining all phones and ancillary hardware, as well as any software associated with the operation of the telephone systems.

The penal facilities manage and administrate the inmate accounts. Traditionally, prisons negotiated a commission with telephone-system vendors, usually based on a formula derived from the size of the inmate population and the expected call volume. Amid cries of excessive charges, which led to a flurry of lawsuits, the FCC increased the regulation of telephone rates within the prison system where a half-hour call can cost more than fifty dollars! As a result, some prisons currently have done away with the commission model, instead factoring in a much lower cost-recovery fee into the phone-service equation to help underwrite administrative expenses.

For many years within secure institutions, telephone calls from inmates to the world beyond the prison walls consisted of outgoing collect calls *only*. In this scenario, individuals being called by an inmate would receive a recorded message informing them that they had a collect call from someone within a penal institution and that, by accepting the call, they would be responsible for payment of all charges. More recently, as technology has advanced, self-funded inmate telephone accounts have been introduced within some facilities, separate and apart from the inmate's prison commissary account. In this more modern system, funds are electronically debited from an inmate's personal telephone account as calls are made.

As part of the total security strategy within the prison system, all calls are recorded and many of the telephone exchanges are actively monitored. Again, the recipient of the inmate telephone call is advised of such practices via a recorded message which precedes the actual person-to-person communication.

Visitation of an incarcerated person is another area in which questions abound and answers are sought. In earlier chapters of *The Inmate Within* we touched upon such topics as entering a prison facility, proper dress, etc. If you fall into the category of someone seeking to visit an inmate this might be a good time to review and receive a refresher course. The rules and regulations that apply to the prison *minister* are equally applicable to the prison *visitor*.

But the prison visitor faces additional philosophical and personal questions that can be pondered here and now. For instance, is it healthy for families rife with child abuse, domestic violence, and dysfunction to bring younger children to visitation sessions with fathers or mothers who may have participated in or perpetuated abuse? If visits involving married adults, loved ones, acquaintances, or children *are* permitted, should they be conjugal, if allowed, or only through a glass partition? How often should such visits take place? As in life outside the prison walls, there are no secret formulas for successful decision-making, no easy answers. And through it all, many of the supposedly concerned people within an individual's sphere of influence are quick to offer advice—or harsh criticism—of any and all efforts to make the lives of a prisoner's family more bearable and more normal.

Throughout the prison experience, myriad mandates within the system seem to dictate the course of action (or inaction) for concerned parties seeking to communicate with inmates in a personal or spiritual manner. By design and necessity, ponderous institutional rules and regulations take away the autonomy of both the *visitor* and the one being *visited,* both the person being *ministered to* and the *minister* seeking to provide solace in the midst of despair. Shouldering our burdens alone can leave *all* of us—you, me *and* incarcerated family members or loved ones—with a sense of hopelessness and defeat. What, then, is the answer? How can we make a way where there seems to be no way? King David said to his son, Solomon, "Be strong and courageous and do the work. Do not be afraid or discouraged, for the Lord God, my God, is with you. He will not fail you or forsake you…" (1 Chronicles 28:20). For the inmate and the family and friends of the imprisoned, God is with us. His Word says He will *never* leave us or forsake us. As we seek answers to the questions that surround us, "the Spirit (of) God…does not make us timid, but gives us power, love and self-discipline (a sound mind)" (2 Timothy 1:7). And best of all, He is only a prayer—a simple, one-way conversation—away. We speak, and then we listen. We seek, knock, and in His perfect timing, doors will be opened…whether they are iron bars inside a state penitentiary or entranceways to the human heart. In all facets of life, God has taught me this simple truth: If I will humble myself, call upon Him and seek His face, first and foremost, God can make things happen—in my life and in the lives of those around me—that would never have occurred had I not come to Him in prayer.

In the midst of unsettling moments, paralyzing uncertainty, even utter chaos, brought about by the imprisonment of one near to us, there is *One* Firm Foundation, *One* Way-Maker in the midst of circumstances which are, often, far beyond our control. There is *One* All-Consuming Fire which can purify even the dirtiest, most impure situations—the Person of Jesus Christ. "Seek the Lord while He may be found; call on Him while He is near" (Isaiah 55:6). It is during these tough times of decision-making that we can be encouraged in our minds and renewed in our spirits, realizing that prayer can and should be our first line of offense…and defense.

The topic of an imprisoned loved one takes on a peculiarly ironic twist when individuals involved in ministry within the penal system find *themselves* in the position of having an incarcerated friend or loved one. Your immediate thought might be, "Well, there goes any opportunity to minister in *that* facility." But, as you will shortly learn, God not only makes a way where there seems to be no way (Philippians 2:13), He can turn what looks like a bleak situation into a spiritual lesson-learning opportunity.

Realistically—under "normal" circumstances—at the state or federal penitentiary level, if a spouse, family member, relative, or close friend were being held within a given facility, chances are you would *not* be allowed to volunteer at that particular prison. However, with proper relationship-building, a track record of obedience to the rules and regulations, and—most importantly—absolute reliance upon the supernatural power of God's Holy Spirit working in and through you—your ministry could continue unimpeded in other prisons throughout the system. At the more local county level, trusted and cordial relationships with wardens, assistant wardens and chaplains may help pave the way for more "creative" arrangements—as long as hard-

and-fast principles are not violated or compromised. If ministering within several different states, or across the nation, the reality of an incarcerated family member or loved one in a given state should not affect one's ability to minister to prisoners in other states. But, as in all areas of life, there are no guarantees.

As a disciple-maker, I believe that someone should exercise extreme caution not to expound upon or offer in-depth advice about a topic for which he or she lacks personal experience. And so it is with great humility that I present this chapter to you. Because, recently, I found myself—a minister within the prison system for more than twenty years—in the position of having a loved one—a close family member—incarcerated in a county prison in which I ministered on a weekly basis. For me, a theoretical example, a remote possibility, became a living-color reality in my life and ministry. *What on earth was I supposed to do? What was the correct course of action? How was I to address this unforeseen dilemma?*

I had been ministering weekly in this particular county jail—just minutes from my home—for almost fifteen years. I facilitated what I fondly refer to as a "Pre-Sentencing/Pre-Release Class" to any and all male inmates who were permitted and/or chose to attend. The premise of each session was simple: God would put one of the *Daily Bread* devotional lessons on my heart, we would read the scripture verses associated with that particular day's reading, and then examine the relevance and practical application of God's Word in our lives. During my time at the jail, the chaplain and I developed a warm and mutually beneficial relationship. I learned to appreciate the pressures the chaplain endured in his daily ministry at the facility, and I recognized the almost-thankless task he faced as he almost single-handedly sought to address the spiritual issues of an ever-growing number of needy men and women. The chaplain, in turn, seemed to appreciate the several evangelistic concert/services Fran and I presented throughout the year and the inmates' response to those celebratory sessions. Even more importantly, he enthusiastically supported my obedience and persistence in offering that discipleship class to the men on a weekly basis. As schedules and time permitted, the chaplain and I talked about the spiritual climate within the jail. With this relationship firmly established, I approached the facilities chaplain as the first line of communication regarding my incarcerated family member.

I suggested, and he agreed, that I should outline the fast-developing situation to the warden as well. This made sense because the warden would be the final authority, deciding what would or would not be permitted within the context of SonPower's ministry at the county jail. It also made sense to bring the warden into the mix because I had known him during the current chaplain's tenure and even for many years prior. The warden included an assistant specifically in charge of inmate programs, and an agreement was forged. After all the appropriate discussions were completed, arrangements were made whereby I could continue the weekly sessions within the facility. If I wished to meet with my family member, it would be during normal prison visitation hours, following the same mandates and restrictions as any other person visiting an inmate. The administrators wanted to ensure that there was no hint of favoritism, because in prior months another pastor had continually requested what the warden perceived as "special privileges" in visiting one of *his* family members at the same facility. In the final analysis, not only did the arrangement work to the satisfaction of all concerned, I believe God used what could have been a very problematic situation in a marvelous way to everyone's benefit: Prior to being assigned to the prison work-release program, my loved one was able to attend several of the Wednesday sessions with yours truly! This interaction helped pave the way for continued communication between us throughout the remainder of his sentence. In addition, the county jail was able to continue, uninterrupted, what had proven to be an extremely beneficial ministry for the entire male prison population.

What made the difference in this scenario? Why did things work out for the good, as opposed to my being presented with major obstacles or bureaucratic red tape? I believe the answer lies within the heart-attitude God enabled me to express throughout the course of events. "As a man thinks in his heart, so is he," "…for he is the kind of man who is always thinking about the cost" (Proverbs 23:7). Instead of dwelling on all of the negative possibilities, or becoming haughty and demanding "my way," I remained humble but expectant that God *would* make a way. As evidence of that attitude, both the warden and his assistant expressed appreciation that I had approached them with a cooperative spirit, seeking an amicable solution to the problem-at-hand, while always considering, first and foremost, the rules and regulations of the prison.

Here are some additional thoughts to consider for the minister or visitor concerning an incarcerated family member or loved one. In this age of "helicopter parents," some well-intentioned individuals cannot seem to resist the temptation to constantly insert themselves into the personal challenges, trials, tribulations, and *legal matters* of family members. Left to our own devices and desires, it is often easy to get caught up in the problems, the "injustices," and the "unfair" treatment surrounding those we love. Without proper perspective and God-given discernment, our misguided actions translate into nothing more than feeble attempts to rescue those near and dear to us from the consequences of sin. In our efforts to assist our loved ones, we become "enabling agents"—sometimes manipulated by the very people we seek to help!

Too often, inmates, beset by carnal mindsets, will regale family members with tales of being innocent casualties of a corrupt prison system, or victims of nefarious forces conspiring against them, even if they were caught red-handed in the commission of a crime. When a man or woman is in full-blown survival mode, who easier to manipulate or get on one's side than those who love them the most? In instances such as these, all is not lost. As we allow Him to work, God can and *will* manifest Himself within the dark places of the human condition as only He can. And sometimes He will choose to use us— as ministers and/or family members—to speak truth into the matter, encouraging an unrepentant or struggling loved one to allow God's work and will to be done. When an inmate remains determined to fight his or her own battles in their own power (their flesh), however, dire consequences may result. The problems being faced will undoubtedly be exacerbated—whether it is a beef with a fellow inmate, a disagreement with the policies of the facility, or enmity against the prison system at-large—they may win a battle here and there but they will ultimately lose the war. *So, what can you do?* You, as a catalyst for spiritual reason, can remind your loved one that his or her attitude and response to conflict—fortified by the power of almighty God—is the *only* variable over which they have the power to effect positive change. The unfortunate alternative would be to suffer the consequences of someone who is improperly acting out and perceived to be "bucking the system."

As individuals seeking the will of God, let us understand that He does *not* show favoritism. God shows *no* partiality. In the original text, there is no (elevated) respect of persons with God (Romans 2:11). He is sovereign over all peoples, all nations, all governments—and all prisoners, whether they be relatives or strangers.

Up next…when it comes to inmate correspondence, is there a right or a wrong way to write?

In some foreign countries, the principle food source for an inmate may often be prepared meals delivered to the prison by family members.

Chapter Twenty-One

THE RIGHT WAY TO WRITE: PRISON CORRESPONDENCE

"Continue to remember those in prison as if you were together with them in prison, and those who are mistreated as if you yourselves were suffering."

(Hebrews 13:3)

*I*was talking with a fellow believer, a successful businessman who, through various indiscretions in years gone by, had done time in a state penitentiary. In fact, I *met* him during a SonPower Ministries' concert/service at the prison in which he was serving his sentence!

During our conversation, we began discussing various aspects of *The Inmate Within* book project. At one point, he grew silent—a very unusual posture for my loquacious friend. Gazing at me with a rather sad look in his eyes, he posed this question: "Pete, do you know the time during which a prisoner feels most alone? It is after mail call, when the corrections officer has read the last name, delivered the final envelope, and the inmate realizes, once again, that he will not receive a letter…from anyone." He went on to explain that a number of incarcerated men and women, throughout the nation, *never* receive even

215

one piece of correspondence during the years, or *decades,* in which they are confined in a world very few people care to see. Despite my many years of prison ministry experience, the reality of his words penetrated painfully to the core of my being like the steely blade of a knife to the heart. A postcard, an uplifting note, one letter of encouragement—such a seemingly small gesture—could mean the difference between the spirit of an inmate soaring to new heights or that same person's life plunging into the depths of despair.

The truth of the matter is that, more often than not, incarcerated men and women *do* enjoy receiving letters from the outside world. Correspondence with a prison inmate truly exemplifies a tangible and practical way in which you and I can connect and build a relationship with another human being. Through such personal interaction, the souls of both the writer and the reader can be refreshed. This is true whether the recipient will soon be released, or if the inmate faces a much longer road of incarceration. Furthermore, the process of corresponding with a particular individual—or developing a pen-pal network—in itself can be the fulfillment of someone's call to prison ministry. At the very least, it represents Christ-centered service to the Kingdom of God. In Matthew 25:36, Jesus teaches His followers that, "…I was in prison and you came to visit me."

As disciples of Jesus Christ, you and I can exchange cards and letters with an inmate, providing countless "literary visitations" even as he resides within the six-by-eight-foot cell he calls home. Yes, prison correspondence can provide enjoyment and a sense of satisfaction for both the writer and the recipient. But, as in every other area of prison ministry, this discipline should be approached with both Godly wisdom and healthy caution.

If, within your immediate family, there is someone who is incarcerated, decisions surrounding correspondence are rather clear-cut. But when written (or telephone) interchange falls within the broader purview of prison ministry, and the inmate is by-and-large a stranger, the waters of communication become a bit more murky. For example, most of the inmate letters I receive are from men with whom I've come in contact during my weekly discipleship classes at the county-jail level or through the concert/services Fran and I conduct within the state penitentiary system. In the most general sense, I must always remember that those prisoners with whom I have met briefly—or even those individuals who may have attended my prison classes for weeks or months—are, in the truest sense, relatively unknown to me. That is to say, I do not understand them—their minds, hearts, or motivations—with the same intimacy or depth that I enjoy with a family member or close friend. In some instances, I may receive correspondence from a prisoner who has seen me only from a distance, during a prison concert. At other times, a letter may arrive from a complete stranger serving time in a prison Fran and I have never visited.

Although it is gratifying to read the scripture quotes, Bible-study excerpts, and personal testimonies contained in some of the cards and notes, I always must be aware that some letter-writers may have hidden agendas. As I address several *communication cautions,* I encourage you to put yourself in my position. By doing so, perhaps you will gain greater insight and a slightly different perspective when the topic turns to prison correspondence.

Some prisoners write seeking immediate favors. An inmate might see me—or *you*—as a viable "personal reference," whose endorsement might pave the way for leniency during a sentencing or parole hearing. In the past, I have been asked to go before a trial judge or magistrate on behalf of an inmate. I have also been requested to be a go-between to contact a wife or family member who may wish to have no communication with the inmate whatsoever. Or, a prisoner may write asking "the ministry" to provide money or other tangible goods and services for himself or for his family during a time of need. In instances regarding personal assistance, if I am familiar with the incarcerated individual and ascertain that the request is legitimate, I will usually check with other ministries or organizations which may be designed or better-equipped to consider the request. In doing so, my hope is that aid can be administered directly to the prisoner's family, even as the inmate continues to serve his or her sentence.

Still other inmates, with carnal hearts and less-than-honorable intentions, will send a series of cards or letters injecting subtle forms of manipulation within the content of their correspondence. The writers' messages may weave the web of a troubled upbringing, a particularly sad life journey, or a justice system that has falsely accused, imprisoned, and then abandoned them. In the broadest sense, such calculated correspondence is sent with the express purpose of garnering favors or money from unsuspecting, kindhearted recipients *or*—with more sinister intent—to groom the recipients and play upon their emotions so that they will provide financial assistance, housing, or even more intimate creature comforts to the inmate upon his or her release. "The heart is deceitful above all things and beyond cure. Who can understand it?" (Jeremiah 17:9).

More often than not, the letters I receive are earnest outpourings from brothers-in-the-Lord expressing their appreciation to Fran and me for what we do under the auspices of SonPower Ministries. These correspondents relish sharing their hearts with someone who has taken the time to minister to them while they are separated from the rest of society.

As mentioned earlier in this chapter, I periodically receive letters from inmates who are completely unknown to me. Most are requests for me to secure places to live or jobs for them upon their release from prison. If I am unable to fulfill their petitions personally, they inevitably ask that I supply them with contact information for other individuals or organizations who may be able to assist them. Contacts such as these represent pleas to fulfill the inmates' mandates for a *home plan,* the process through which incarcerated men and women draft a strategy for obtaining living quarters and income opportunities prior to their release from prison. Often, the home plan is a requirement for parole. Sadly, most requests of this type that I receive are simply eleventh-hour mass mailings by inmates to a laundry list of contacts in the hope that someone…*anyone*…will come to their aid. Often, the cry for help arrives several weeks or just days before their supposed release date. I typically do not respond to these letters, having no background or information regarding the criminal records or mental states of the individuals making the requests. SonPower Ministries is not designed or equipped to provide jobs or housing to ex-offenders, and I am hesitant to forward the names of persons unknown to me—persons with whom I have not developed some semblance of an ongoing, insightful relationship—to those agencies, which may offer post-release or aftercare services.

Obviously, correspondence with an incarcerated family member or loved one carries its own set of parameters, based on family history, current functionality or dysfunction within the kinship, etc. But, a person desiring to begin a type of pen-pal relationship with someone who is essentially a stranger, or even with licensed clergy exchanging correspondence within the context of more formal ministry, might do well to exercise a heightened level of discernment.

One guideline, in particular, was impressed upon me early on in my prison adventures: **Never, under *any* circumstances, should an individual give his or her home telephone number or street address to an inmate within the context of a pen-pal relationship.** This same rule applies when engaging in person-to-person visits within the prison system. The reasons for not doing so are numerous, but the most obvious reason is this: Why in the world would you want to divulge such personal information to someone who is virtually unknown to you…someone who has committed a criminal offense, and whose current accommodations are a jail or penitentiary cell? The ramifications of doing so could be more than problematic— they could be both *disastrous and dangerous!* For example, picture a kind-hearted, Christian pen pal who releases her home phone number or address to an inmate with whom she has been corresponding for several months. The inmate, in turn, forwards the pen pal's information, via a coded message or phone call, to an accomplice on the outside. The accomplice calls the pen pal's home. No answer. He then goes to her address and ransacks the residence, stealing tens of thousands of dollars in valuables. Or, in an even worse scenario, a disingenuous prison inmate, having such personal information, lies about his release date and shows up unexpectedly at the pen pal's door demanding money, transportation, or sexual favors. "Oh, come on, Pete," you might be thinking, "what are the odds of such an event occurring?" I don't know the answer to that question. But in my years of experience within the prison system, I have heard enough tragic stories to compel me to mention the possibilities.

Before I introduce my next cardinal sin about prison correspondence I will state up front that the rule I am about to present is consistently violated. Additionally, there are those, even within the circle of prison ministry, who may choose to disagree with the premise. Here it is: *I do not believe that a woman should ever correspond with a male inmate with whom she did not have a familial or personal relationship prior to the offender's incarceration.* The same principle applies to a man in the free world writing to a woman in prison. I am emphatic about this because of the possibilities mentioned in the above paragraph. In addition to being physically or financially exploited, a correspondent outside the prison bars may also suffer emotional turmoil at the hands of a calculating inmate with whom he or she is communicating. Such exploitation can occur both in secular or Christian contexts because, without divine discernment accompanied by spiritual maturity, the heart and emotions are very easily subject to manipulation.

A number of years ago, during the mid-stage of SonPower's prison ministry, a situation was brought to my attention that heightened my sensitivity to common-sense and prudent practices which should accompany prison correspondence—particularly in regard to pen-pal relationships. Through reliable sources, I became aware of a disciple-making ministry within the region which was primarily staffed by female volunteers to facilitate the sending and receiving of Christian-education and Bible-study materials. Although the group ministered to a number of female offenders, much of the correspondence involved intercommunication with male inmates from across the state. This somewhat suspect practice was even more egregious because the inmates' completed assignments were being sent to the *home addresses* of the women volunteering within the ministry! For the aforementioned reasons, it made absolutely no sense that this Christian organization would put kind-hearted volunteer workers and their families in what could potentially be very precarious positions. Thankfully, within a year or so of the initial report, I received word that the ministry's policy had changed and that all materials were being sent and received in a more secure manner (which I will address later in this chapter). So, when it comes to writing a prison inmate under the banner of Christian service or ministry, what is one to do?

What do you do, Pete?

I'm glad you asked.

If I am physically involved in ministry of some sort within the confines of a jail or penitentiary, I have one standard response when asked by an inmate for contact information. I direct him or her to the chaplain or other designated prison official who has access to SonPower Ministries' information. ***All inmate correspondence is directed to the SonPower Ministries post-office box address.*** In fact, *all* ministry communication—whether or not it is prison-related—is sent and received through our mail box at the local post office. This is a simple and safe way to ensure a modicum of privacy and to keep the clutter a bit more manageable in our condominium's in-home office!

What *does* happen when we send a letter to someone within the confines of a prison? Sending and receiving written correspondence or printed materials to incarcerated men and women is part of the ebb and flow of prison routine. Let's place incoming mail for prisoners into three categories.

First, there is *general correspondence:* letters and cards sent to inmates from family and friends, offering encouragement or advice, "newsy" updates, information from the home front, prayers, etc. All such correspondence is opened and inspected for content and contraband prior to being delivered to the intended recipient. Some prisons may place size restrictions on paper, photos, drawings, artwork, greeting cards, etc. As a matter of security and safety, all stamps are removed from the envelopes. This is to guard against incarcerated men and women being able to lick or ingest stamps which have been dosed with mind-altering drugs like LSD and suboxone. Popularized back in the 1960s as part of the psychedelic movement, most readers are at least familiar with the term "LSD." Suboxone, on the other hand, is a more modern drug of choice within the prison system. As a liquid, pill, or "breath strip," this drug—used to treat opioid addiction—can produce a high of its own. Some prisons, having experienced illicit substances rubbed on the sticky sealant, may dispose of all envelopes enclosing incoming mail. And in penal institutions in which authorities have uncovered a consistent pattern of intent, such enclosures as watercolor paintings, crayon art, and glossy photographs may also be screened for drug contamination.

The second category of mail is *privileged correspondence,* including legal or court documents, lawyer/client communiqués, notices from public officials, etc. In most jails or penitentiaries, the contents of such mail are logged by prison officials, then opened and inspected in the presence of the inmate designated to receive the information.

The third type of incoming mail is *courses and subscriptions,* including educational or trade correspondence courses, religious instruction or

Bible-study curricula, as well as newspaper and magazine subscriptions. These materials are scrutinized for content—particularly magazine subscriptions—to ensure that pornography standards and gang-related prohibitions are not violated.

Outgoing prison correspondence is often entered into a database to keep track of the "who, what, when, and where" of inmate mail within the facility of origin. Outgoing written communication emanating from a particular jail or penitentiary is not subject to review or screening under normal circumstances. If, however, prison officials have "probable cause," an inmate's mail can and will be subjected to scrutiny on a temporary or permanent basis.

As mentioned, by following common-sense dictates and God-given discernment, prison correspondence can be a source of joy and spiritual enrichment for both the sender and the recipient. There is nothing more gratifying than to hear how God is working in the hearts and lives of brothers and sisters in a mission field that much of the world never experiences. The stories of earnest seeking, spiritual growth, and *practical applications* of Biblical truths within the cell blocks can bring renewed hope to *the inmate within*—the focus of this book—while, at the same time, buoying the spirits of those of us on the outside, dealing with our own trials, tribulations, and transgressions. Whether approached as a beneficial way through which to maintain contact with an incarcerated family member or loved one, as a casual one-on-one undertaking to better serve mankind, or pursued as a full or part-time prison ministry in itself, there are many right reasons to write to those who have done wrong and are now paying the price.

Our journey within the world of prison ministry is rounding the far turn and approaching the home stretch. Hopefully, you are enjoying sojourning with me through this unique adventure while discovering sobering truths about *yourself*, prison inmates, and a holy God Who oversees us all. It is only as you and I continue to learn and grow that *we* can experience a greater sense of freedom from the bondage and "prisons" of our own making, thus allowing us to be more suitable for service in the days to come. "So if the Son sets you free, you will be free indeed" (John 8:36).

One more chapter to go. Is prison ministry worth it?

> When Mother's Day cards are displayed
> and offered to male inmates, on a
> common-area table, they quickly disappear
> and are utilized. When Father's Day
> cards are made available, they remain
> virtually untouched.

Chapter Twenty-Two
THE POSSIBILITIES
ARE PRICELESS

"…this is what the Lord says…He who formed you Israel. 'Do not fear, for I have redeemed you; I have summoned you by name'."

(Isaiah 43:1)

*P*rison ministry is often a "path less traveled" when compared to other more mainstream evangelical endeavors. My hope—my desire—is that the information contained throughout the pages of this book will resonate in human minds and hearts in such a way that positive change will result from practical application of the spiritual principles that have been presented.

My intention has been to minister to *you,* the reader—no matter who you are, no matter what you do for a living, or what your circumstances and situations may be in life. Undoubtedly, my target readers *do* include incarcerated men and women who may benefit from the broadening and deepening of their *own* understanding, which might be shaped or impacted by *your* service to the Kingdom of God on their behalf.

To curious readers whose view of prison life has been formulated through the lens of melodramatic, titillating print articles or cable television exposés, may the intriguing adventure stories contained throughout *The Inmate Within* reveal truths that transcend the sensational and embrace the gritty, gut-level realities experienced by the men and women behind bars. More than that, may you be able to see God at work—on the front line and behind the scenes of human experience—as only He can, purifying the filthy things of this world, sanctifying the wretched, giving hope of a brighter tomorrow to those living in seemingly helpless situations today. And may you, the reader, experience that *same* God impacting *your* life as well, breaking down strongholds, predilections, and the sinful devices which seek to enslave far too many searching souls in the outside world—freeing *you and me* from the bondage running rampant in our own lives wherever we may be. At this stage of our spiritual exploration, I trust you will agree that we are *all* in prison in some way.

For those young men and women on the road to destruction—actively engaged in rebellion against authority in the home, at school, within society, or even bending rules and regulations in small ways—may this book serve as a wake-up call. Our actions *do* produce cause-and-effect reactions. There are consequences for sin. Know also that there is an almighty God who loves us far beyond our ability to comprehend. He is full of grace and mercy. He can and does forgive the petitions raised to Him by transgressors seeking to repent or turn away from un-Christlike thoughts, words and deeds. But be aware always that God is just—He will not be mocked. He does not "wink" at sin (Acts 17:30).

The unlawful and rebellious things we do can imprison us. I have never spoken to an inmate in his right mind who did not regret the actions which placed him in a society where "three hots and a cot" was the best lifestyle option he might expect—in some cases, for the rest of his earthly life.

For readers dealing with fractured family relationships; alcoholism; drug addiction; physical, mental, or verbal abuse; or a nameless sense of desperation in a world gone mad—may you find yourself somewhere in the pages of this "journey toward humanity." More importantly, may you understand that you are not alone; there are answers to the problems that confound us. There *is* a love that is more than able to help you overcome the struggle, a solace that is greater than the pain. I trust that you have seen—or will *experience*—"the answer" alive and operating within the minds and hearts of flawed individuals in need of a Savior of their souls and a Lord of their everyday lives. The "answer"—that freedom nurtured through a growing, vibrant personal relationship with Jesus Christ—is available to all prisoners, *inside* or *outside* the walls of any penal facility built by man.

For individuals struggling with mental illness, anger issues, alcohol or substance abuse, there are specific organizations that can help you on the path to recovery. For those who seek a closer walk with God there are churches and other religious institutions that offer guidance, support, and fellowship. But the one thing that supersedes all else is that one-on-one relationship with the Creator of the universe.

As previously mentioned, this book is written for a special band of brothers and sisters who have run afoul of the law. I trust that herein is wisdom and practical advice for those who continually pay a price, whether you are an inmate currently serving a prison sentence or an ex-offender who may be struggling to re-integrate into a seemingly callous society. May the words of this text minister to you in a particularly special way. Will you choose to experience hope and peace through a first-love relationship with God that you may have encountered during your incarceration? Or will you continue that desperate journey of going it alone? Let that same Bible that guided you through the prison study sessions be the handbook for life and living in a world beyond those steep, stone walls topped with razor wire that you call home. And for those offenders who have not harnessed the supernatural power of God to provide joy within your journey...*what are you waiting for?*

The Inmate Within, in addition to being an intriguing adventure for the curious, can also serve as a blueprint for those who actively engage in the lives of incarcerated men and women throughout the United States and around the world. To the men and women seeking to minister in the prison system, the rewards can truly be priceless. For all of the frustrations, obstacles, and failures, involved in sharing the Gospel of Jesus Christ to imprisoned individuals, God will open up a world of possibilities to those willing to step out in obedience and venture inside the clanging steel doors.

Whatever your expectations may be regarding your impact on others, prepare yourself for the transforming power of God's Work in your own life as well. I believe you will find that the time spent in mental and spiritual preparation to serve will be a reward in and of itself. Then, when a lesson takes shape and is presented, not only can it be a life-changing message for the hearer, it becomes a double-portion of blessing to the one delivering the good news. You may begin your adventure in prison evangelism or discipleship, as I did, with various preconceived notions as to what might or might not happen within the context of what you feel called to do. But over time—as you let go of the rudder and allow God to steer the vessel—you will truly begin to gain insight into what *He* has planned for your life of ministry. Also, you will more clearly understand the truth of God's Word when it states, "'For My thoughts are not your thoughts, neither are your ways My ways,' declares the Lord" (Isaiah 55:8).

You will find favor and bring a smile to the Master's face as you step out in faith to minister to men and women who many have written off as damaged goods, incapable of being redeemed. As you teach compassion, you will learn in your own life what it means to be compassionate. While explaining the many facets of love, God's Holy Spirit will empower you with the ability and determination to love the unlovely. Like the apostle Paul, you will be able to weep with those who weep, but you will also relish the laughter that comes as hearts entwine in fellowship. Hope is contagious. Nourishing once-hopeless inmates through a river of life that can only flow from the all-consuming wellspring of God's love will compel you, the minister, to be exceedingly hopeful about your *own* life as you sow into the lives of those around you.

And the most exciting possibility of all: God can use you to proclaim to those in captivity that even though they may be imprisoned within a physical fortress, the shed blood, death, and resurrection of Jesus Christ has broken the bondage of sin. As a result of Jesus Christ's earthly mission and *His* sacrifice, the way was paved so that *all* captives can be set free for eternity. Because of this freedom, even as they experience a season of life within the confines of a prison cell, the spirits of incarcerated men and women can take flight and soar to heights never before imagined.

The journey never ends. Amen.

> Numerous surveys of prison chaplains
> overwhelmingly confirm that religious
> affiliation and (church) participation
> upon release is critical to the successful
> re-integration of ex-offenders.

PART FOUR

Food for Thought and Morsels of Motivation for Moving Forward:

ADDITIONAL CONSIDERATIONS FOR INTENTIONAL PRISON MINISTRY

*"You are the salt of the earth…
You are the light of the world."*

(Matthew 5:13, 14)

T hug life is a tough gig. On the street, "bad actors" don't see transparency or vulnerability modeled to any great degree. Instead, individuals hustling to survive see a macho world of posturing and perception—we used to call it "fronting" back in the day—where the biggest and the baddest dudes earn the most respect. And if you can't back up your talk, bad stuff happens.

In the prison system, you, as a minister of the Gospel, have a unique opportunity to shed light on a variety of spiritual matters to hurting—and sometimes hostile-hearted—men and women. Speaking and exhibiting the truth in love, you can be the example of Jesus Christ that incarcerated men and women may never have experienced in their lives. And to be the utmost blessing to God and to those to whom you minister, it is wise to remember that light is seen, not heard.

Regardless of the form or function of your ministry, be careful that you, as the leader of a worship service, Bible study, or discussion group, do not spend precious time showing off your knowledge or wisdom regarding spiritual matters and/or life in general. Remember, your captive audience has plenty of real-life experience. As the facilitator of a prison ministry session, understand that you may not be able to conjure up all the correct answers to the multitude of questions which may arise. Instead of worrying or feeling inadequate should you *not* be able to supply a ready response to a particular inquiry, simply be prepared to point individuals to the One who holds *all* the answers to the questions resonating throughout a world that He created. Utilizing the Bible as the guide and handbook that it is intended to be will help alleviate the pressure of trying to know it all and will pave the way for the prison minister to engage in meaningful dialogue *with* those in attendance, as opposed to preaching or teaching *at* them.

If you are considering some course of ministry to prisoners, I would like to provide some bite-sized tidbits of knowledge gleaned through several decades of prison ministry. Not all the information may have the same weight of relevance to you, but you should find more than a few practical pointers as God begins, or continues, to tailor the tone, personality, and substance of the vision for ministry He has birthed within your mind and heart. You may have encountered some of the thoughts expressed in the following paragraphs in other chapters of this book, but as we discovered in elementary school, a little bit of repetition never hurt anyone!

For those who seek spiritual insight and knowledge without intentions of applying the information in this book specifically to prison ministry, may I assure you that your time has been well spent. Why? Because the spiritual and relational principles contained throughout the chapters of *The Inmate Within* can and will bear fruit to all modes of interpersonal connection—*inside* or *outside* the prison system.

Session Preparation

Just as it is on the outside, behind bars there exists a colorful cast of characters with personalities ranging from domineering, aggressive, and boisterous to meek, voiceless, and subservient who, together, create a worldly yin-and-yang coexistence delicately balanced on the cusp of chaos. As the prison minister enters into such an environment—studiously prepared and "prayed up"—it is time to leave all ego and personal agendas at the visiting-room door. If God gave you a missional vision for such ministry as this, if He empowered you, if He perfected you, if He sent you, then *He* is in control. Even as He chooses to use your abilities, talents, and convictions to reach out to others, rest in this truth: Always remember, *He is God and you are not!* You have been gifted with an awesome responsibility. Prepare yourself accordingly.

Begin each ministry adventure with an end in sight. This might involve thinking or planning with a daily, weekly, monthly, or even a yearly perspective in mind. What would you like to see God provide through your efforts in regard to a one-day prison concert or worship service? What might *He* accomplish within the context of a Bible study or topical discussion session on a weekly or monthly basis during the course of a year? As an example of far-range thinking, as opposed to simply creating converts to Christianity, set as a goal the development of disciples or Christ-followers. In this way, you can better prepare men and women for Godly living on a daily basis, during their incarceration and after their release. Furthermore, you will be fulfilling the Great Commission that

Jesus invoked in Matthew 28:19 when He instructed His disciples to "…go and make disciples of all nations…" Transferring your thought process from what you want to what God might desire will provide a firmer foundation from which to build more meaningful relationships with incarcerated men and women during the course of ministry.

Be real. Be authentic. Just as a bona fide 1955 Rolls Royce Silver Cloud is exponentially more valuable than a modern-day, kit-car reproduction, so the down-to-earth, transparent prison minister, and the information he or she conveys, will be received as more valuable in the minds and hearts of the inmates being served. If you, as God's ambassador, come across as erudite or pompous—speaking down to your audience from an ivory tower—you will be seen as disingenuous or fraudulent by street-wise offenders. Many inmates and ex-offenders are adept at reading people and their intentions. Incarcerated men and women will scrutinize your words, body language, and actions to form first impressions, as well as longer-lasting, relational alliances—sometimes formulating their conclusions to determine whether they will attempt to use you, or if they will *follow* your lead. If you fail to appreciate the individuals under your ministerial care as spiritual brothers and sisters in Christ, the best-intentioned evangelistic or discipleship efforts may not bear fruit or, at best, might not yield the most abundant harvest possible. That is to say, you, and the prisoners you serve, may not receive the greatest blessing God has for you.

Everyone needs a vision, a path to follow in life. God's Word expresses this truth in the following manner: "Where there is no revelation (vision), people cast off restraint (perish); but blessed is the one who heeds wisdom's instruction" (Proverbs 29:18). Just as it is necessary outside the prison walls, that same vision is needed in the hearts and minds of those within the inmate population. This notion applies to one-time evangelistic and worship services, relationship-building classes, or study sessions over an extended period of time. That being said, the ministering party owes it to himself or herself to cast the biggest and widest "visionary net" possible. This requires deflecting the focus from himself (the minister) and directing the eyes, ears, minds and hearts of those being ministered to toward the person of Jesus Christ—our Savior, Sanctifier, Comforter, Healer, and Coming King. As vision-casting unfolds, and the first steps of spiritual interaction begin to take shape, basic rules and structure should be incorporated into your ministry endeavors. Be careful, however, that you do not get bogged down with so many dos and don'ts that you lose spontaneity. Within such a structured setting, remember that flexibility is a valuable asset. As mentioned earlier in this text, unforeseen circumstances and occurrences are bound to arise, but these distractions are nothing that your proper preparation, combined with God's supernatural intervention, cannot handle.

Ministering to incarcerated men and women—or aftercare to benefit those who have been released—may seem daunting or unfamiliar to you. I remember how the first several visits Fran and I made to state penitentiaries took me out of *my* comfort zone. But as I continued to focus on the vision *God* had given me for SonPower Ministries, I began to view each prison service as a challenging opportunity for my *own* spiritual growth, as well as a chance to minister to the hearts of the inmates. And you and I, as service facilitators, are doubly-blessed through the preparation *and* the presentation of God's Word.

Session Relations

Remember, your mission field is a prison environment. As you have read, things might be a bit different than in a normal ministry setting. Every so often, an inmate may test you to see if he can throw you off-track or ruffle your feathers in an attempt to thwart your efforts to share the Gospel of Jesus Christ. "For our struggle is not against flesh and blood, but against…spiritual forces of evil in the heavenly realms" (Ephesians 6:12). Within the course of scheduled activities and during group discussions or conversations, you may hear coarse or vulgar language or expressions which are totally inappropriate for *any* occasion, much less a ministry setting. Such occurrences provide a perfect opening for you, as prison pastor, in a loving but firm manner, to emphasize that this time should be an opportunity to:

- Honor God
- Respect you, the ministry volunteer
- Endow prisoners with the grace and sensitivity to respect one another

A vital point to remember is this: *You* set the tone for control and self-discipline among the men or women in your spiritual care. Your kind, compassionate response to a harsh or heated exchange directed at you, another inmate, or to the group in general, will go a long way toward creating the proper atmosphere for the duration of the ministry session. In fact, you should pray and prepare intentionally, *in advance of your ministry opportunity,* that God would enable you to maintain a friendly, calm, and self-assured demeanor *before, during, and after* your prison visit. In this way, you are equipping yourself to be God's ambassador to *anyone* who is ready to receive a blessing. This includes prison officials, corrections officers, chaplains, and, of course, the inmates. Whether you are facilitating a worship service, a group discussion, or a one-on-one conversation, make a point of *beginning and ending each session in prayer.* Modeling the lifting up of praise, then prayer, to God emphasizes the importance of such divine discipline during the process of developing spiritual maturity and understanding with others. Also, praying a simple prayer is an encouragement to inmates and others that *they can do it too.* And, within your role as pastor/minister, never hesitate to ask an inmate if you may extend a personal prayer for his or her individual situation or condition. Almost without exception, your request will be eagerly welcomed by those who are in need of spiritual comfort.

Throughout our text, relationship-building between those within and without prison walls has been a topic of more than casual discussion. As relationships between minister and inmate develop and grow certain precautions should be considered and exercised by prison volunteers. To wit, most penal facilities discourage hugging of male and female inmates by outside ministry volunteers. Under no circumstances should a visiting male embrace a female inmate, unless the imprisoned woman is a loved one or family member and the encounter takes place in a properly supervised setting.

On occasion, you may observe incarcerated men, in particular, fist-bumping one another in lieu of a more standard handshake. More often than not, this quick touching together of fists simply is one way to avoid transmission of germs, viruses, etc. from one person to another during a friendly salutation. As mentioned previously, throughout any given penal facility, such maladies as tuberculosis, influenza, MRSA and the HIV virus are ever-present within the inmate population. For outside volunteers, proper hand washing and sanitation measures are a *must,* particularly after ministry sessions with large numbers of prisoners. At one state facility Fran and I visit semi-annually, we choose to shake hands with every inmate at the conclusion of each of three worship services, often greeting more than 800 men in one day!

If your ministry travels take you to the same penal institution with any regularity—for instance, I conduct a discipleship group study at the local county jail on a weekly basis—make a calculated effort to learn the first names of some of the regular attendees at your events. Not only does being on a first-name basis allow you to become more familiar with individual inmates, it can pave the way for less-guarded relationships and, perhaps, deeper and more meaningful conversations. As a bonus, inmates within the group can also become more familiar with fellow prisoners when first names are used. In my Bible examination and discipleship classes at the local county jail, I have created a built-in mechanism which allows me to remember many first names in an ever-changing "band of brothers," numbering eight to eighteen or more on a given week. After an opening prayer, and prior to the beginning of our study session, we quickly go around the circle, each of us stating our first name.

Notice I referred to first names as opposed to full names. In the course of building relationships, an inmate may choose to divulge his or her last name, but I usually don't inquire. There are several reasons: First, an inmate's reticence to offer a full name may be a mechanism to safeguard his or her life from unwanted intrusion, especially within the context of a fledgling religious connection with someone from the outside. Also, an offender may be content to offer only a first name, if asked, to maintain a sense of anonymity when his or her crime is particularly egregious, distasteful (as in deviate sexual intercourse with a child), or if the offense has garnered more than its share of media attention and publicity.

Through the years, I have found that using an inmate's first name encourages that person to become more engaged in general conversations and more prone to participate within the context of lesson-learning exercises or group discussions. When offering prayer and/or seeking divine intervention, you, the prison minister, are able to pray for an individual personally…by name. What a marvelous opportunity to illustrate to incarcerated men and women that we serve a *personal God,* who loves us individually and unconditionally—a God Who is aware of our every need, before we even ask. "Do not be like them (the hypocrites), for your Father knows what you need before you ask him" (Matthew 6:8).

Reading back over the last two paragraphs, you may sense an ironic twist in reference to the "last name" conundrum, rendering the entire topic a moot point. In many of the state penitentiaries Fran and I visit, *all* inmates' last names are printed or stenciled on a cloth patch sewn onto the pocket of a shirt or jacket. In other institutions, offenders may be required to wear badges sporting a full name and/or photo with an inmate-identification number. So, by simple observation, the prison volunteer is supplied with a prisoner's *last* name and, in some instances, their *entire* name. As we have seen so often in our ministry journey, *nothing,* save the truth of God's Word, seems to be carved in stone. And a further irony is this: God's Word, through the Ten Commandments given to Moses, *was* inscribed in stone!

During many years of relationship-building with imprisoned offenders, I have made it a point to never violate the following premise: ***Never ask an inmate why he or she is incarcerated!*** If, by chance (or media exposure), you *are* aware of the charges lodged against an individual, make it a practice *not* to solicit details. Over time—as relationships emerge between prisoner and prison ministry volunteer—some inmates may choose to offer information regarding their criminal and/or personal lives. Learning more about an individual's life certainly can be a useful and empathetic building block of communication, but, as expressed throughout this text, added knowledge carries with it the weight of added responsibility. Care and discernment should be exercised by the prison minister so that he or she does not stray from the mission-at-hand. That mission is to be an ambassador of Jesus Christ to a needy prison population. The prison minister, by allowing himself to get caught up in personal history and/or current life situations can be manipulated by an inmate as a means to an end. Some prisoners simply may use diversionary interpersonal devices as a way to make themselves look better in the eyes of the prison minister, or as a tactic to minimize or excuse the sin in their lives. Other more cunning offenders may attempt to use such adroit misdirection as a means of cultivating their *mark* (you) to obtain special favors or unauthorized assistance. To guard against such relational missteps, it is incumbent that the prison minister be intentional in focusing—or redirecting—all efforts toward presenting the life-changing message of the Gospel of Jesus Christ to those in need of a Savior of their souls and Lord of their lives.

As it is in *any* group setting, so it is within the prison system—some participants will be more talkative than others. Just as some are quick to offer answers and opinions, or enter into tightly structured or more-fluid discussions, there are others who seem content to sit on the sidelines, watching and listening, without contributing one word to the conversation. Trying to force an inmate to participate against his or her will is *never* a good idea. In personal conversation or within a group setting, the more shy or quiet individual may feel embarrassed, put upon, targeted, or judged in some way and, instead of opening up, he or she may retreat further away from heartfelt communication. Sometimes, in a surprisingly short period of time, God's perfect timing can and will open up the minds and hearts of the more reticent inmates, and prompt them—in their own human spirits—with a newfound desire to willingly participate in conversations from which they may have shied away in the past.

Session Insights

As previously stated, I often use myself as my own "best worst example" to illustrate a point. To turn that somewhat negative premise into a positive one, you can use your personal testimony, illustrating to incarcerated men and women as to what the power of God *has* done, *is* doing, and *can* do, not only in your own life, but in theirs as well! Within the context of *any* ministry endeavor, be it a Bible study, group discussion, or sermon, take every opportunity to present real-life applications of the scripture passages or spiritual truths being explored. When possible, make the reading and/or discussion relevant to the here-and-now, touching on inmates' personal interests as you begin to interact with them on a more personal level. Even prisoners new to your ministry will appreciate you personalizing the message, without compromise, to some of their friends with whom you are more familiar. Not only may inmates more readily respond to your servant's heart, but they may become attracted and more easily drawn toward the Gospel message you proclaim, as well.

Throughout many years of ministry, I have continually been impressed by the percentage of inmates who have been raised in God-fearing, Christian homes. Many have attended church with regularity during periods of their lives, and some grasp basic and even advanced scriptural principles, being able to quote chapter and verse from the Bible during the course of conversation or discussion. But there are just as many inmates to whom the Word of God is a foreign language. Biblical concepts simply are not a part of their mental processes and therefore thoughts, speech, and actions do not reflect the Spirit of Christ to any appreciable degree. "The person without the Spirit does not accept the things that come from…God but considers them foolishness, and cannot understand them because they are discerned only through the Spirit" (1 Corinthians 2:14). To successfully span this "spiritual information gap," it is important that the prison minister tailor his or her message so that biblical ideas and principles can be understood, to the greatest degree possible, by the least spiritually-educated segment of the prison population. This will help to ensure simplicity and clarity during presentation of the Gospel, whether within a quick-hitting evangelistic service or an extended period of teaching or discipleship.

Disciple-making—inside or outside the prison system—is a long-term process. You, as prison minister, should be prepared to spend a significant amount of time, over a significant *period* of time, as you prepare and present spiritual ammunition to inmates in the way God directs. The following paragraphs reflect some of the "nitty-gritty" instructional details for insight, or practical application, within the context of prison ministry.

Within any informative assembly, questions are bound to arise. The prison ministry environment is no different. Make it a priority to go directly to the source for your answers. And what *is* that source?

For the prison minister who is intent on being utilized as a vehicle for spiritual change that source is the Holy Bible—what I often refer to as my "handbook for life and living"—the Word of God. You and I are living in a time in which our culture, and the mores and values which comprise it, is being shaped by the court of public opinion. Too often, biblical principles are relegated to a means of last resort, or are summarily dismissed as outdated concepts or, even worse, old wives' tales and fables. Our society has become enamored by—and bombarded with—intelligent-sounding personalities dispensing wisdom and advice that was generated solely in their own minds. Those who strategically position themselves in the public eye and speak loud enough and long enough often receive access to the podium of public opinion, whether or not their statements have merit. And today, as it has been throughout our history, a lie repeated often enough has a great possibility of being received as truth. As a result, believers, must contend with an increasingly humanistic worldview built on the shifting sands of secular intellectualism, as opposed to a bedrock of allegiance to the one and only God and a belief in something greater than ourselves.

What a blessing it is that people of faith have the infallible, everlasting, authoritative Word of God as *the* source from which the world's questions—or an inmate's inquiries—can be answered! The Bible is the text to which I turn for answers to the questions posed during prison ministry sessions. Because of inmates' street-wise discernment and the fact that a certain number of prisoners are well-versed in the Scriptures and spiritual constructs, it would be folly for me—or for *any* volunteer prison pastor—to assume that he or she should pose as the know-it-all authority during the course of ministry. This reality, again, addresses the aforementioned need for transparency and vulnerability in the heart of the prison minister. But more than that, it allows for spontaneity and creativity within the ministry process. How so? By searching the Bible for unknown answers to the questions-at-hand, the prison pastor is modeling a real-time illustration of a quest for spiritual knowledge to the session attendees. Also, by encouraging *the inmates* to join in the search for scriptural clarity or meaning, the outside volunteer is setting the stage for incarcerated men and women to put forth effort and to *take ownership* of their *own* spiritual quests. That is why I often use naturally occurring question-and-answer scenarios as opportunities to create homework assignments for the inmates, challenging them to study their Bibles and find the information they seek, either individually or as a group project with other believers in their respective cell blocks. Then I dutifully follow up with them during our next time together.

Bunny trails: almost every conversation has them, and you can expect some bunny-trail distractions during the course of your prison ministry. Especially during a Bible study or group discussion, it is not uncommon for an inmate to pose a question, or to make a statement, so off the wall that to pursue it would spin the conversation into an entirely new orbit. Sometimes such a diversion can usher in productive dialogue, but that's not usually the case. As the facilitator, you must decide how the discussion should proceed. At times, an inmate, endeavoring to show off his Biblical knowledge, or attempting to put forth his own agenda (i.e., a Muslim wishing to introduce divergent beliefs into the discussion), may intentionally seek to derail the conversation. But, more often than not, an inquisitive inmate might veer a group study or discussion off course by posing a question borne from:

- Naiveté or ignorance of the scriptural principle being discussed
- Over-enthusiasm or exuberance
- A lack of organizational thinking

When this occurs, and I believe in my spirit that the comment will hinder the teaching/learning process, I gently but firmly redirect the conversation. However, I *never* leave the questioner with the impression that he or she is being "hung out to dry," dismissed, or ignored in front of his or her peers. Instead, seeking to validate the individual and to create empathy, I may respond like this: "Thanks for your input. Perhaps if you can stay for a moment after church, we can more-fully pursue that idea." Or, "That's a great question, but we should save that thought for a later time, so that we can give it the attention it deserves." As relationships develop I have been pleasantly surprised at the increasing number of instances when other prisoners have offered—on the spot—to spend time answering questions or providing spiritual counsel to neophyte attendees after the ministry service has concluded. Not only does this willingness to serve illustrate leadership, but as Christ-followers, it exemplifies *the essence of discipleship*—reach one to teach one to reach and teach another one! "Then Jesus came to them (the disciples) and said, 'All authority in heaven and on earth has been given to me. Therefore go and make disciples of all nations…teaching them to obey everything I have commanded you. And surely I am with you always, to the very end of the age'" (Matthew 28:18-20).

Finally, within the topic of our "journey of distractions," there are times when *all* ministry session participants—prisoners and yours truly alike—get caught up in conversation, revelry, and fellowship which takes us totally off the beaten path. In moderation, this can introduce or build the beneficial component of friendship into the relationship-building process. But at some point—usually employing a somewhat humorous approach—it is incumbent upon me, as minister/facilitator, to rein in the discussion. "Gentlemen, I believe we are on a major bunny trail! Let's refocus our minds and hearts on the matters-at-hand." And the neatest result of such a time as this? God will immediately enable me to use our bunny-trail conversation to illuminate a spiritual principle which *He* wants us to grasp at that very instant on that given day!

Throughout our decades of service—particularly at the county and state levels—Fran and I have seen how the wearing effects of daily life within the prison system take their toll on the inmates, the chaplaincy team, the corrections officers and administrators alike. Over time, a sense of wariness, callousness, and negativity can color the minds and hearts of *all* the players in the world behind iron bars. As a result, earnest statements made by prisoners to those around them may tend to be minimized or taken at less than face value by those in authority. Hopefully, at this point in our literary adventure, such a revelation should not come as a complete surprise. Trust me, the prison staff has heard it all: All the promises, all the pleas, all the impassioned declarations, all the carefully worded cons, from those inmates seeking to survive or gain advantage within the prison population. And the reverse perception is true as well, as those behind bars constantly add entries to an ever-growing list of broken promises, injustices, and slights which they believe have been perpetrated against them.

To get by or get ahead in this game called prison life, some inmates may tailor their words to say what they think the prison pastor or chaplain wants to hear. With that thought in mind, when it comes to spiritual matters, you and I should make every effort to attune our spiritual eyes, ears, and hearts—processing all inmate conversation through a God-filter to discern with a power far beyond ourselves what is truly being said. This is especially true when the topic turns to first-time professions of faith in Jesus Christ or an inmate reaffirming his or her relationship with God. If we, as prison ministers, really believe that God can change a wayward soul for eternity, then such words of positive profession, spoken to us, should be received with celebration, as opposed to doubt. In less-caring, surface relationships, spiritual declarations made by prisoners are more easily discounted as simply "jailhouse religion." In growing more-intimate spiritual connections, the volunteer minister—with heavenly guidance—is able to build upon and nurture spiritual conversations so that, in time, the inmate will be able to experience a first-hand illustration of God using an ordinary man or woman to sow into his life. You and I can serve as living examples of what it means to be "hands and feet" within the Body of Christ. "If one part suffers, every part suffers with it. If one part is honored, every part rejoices with it. Now you are the body of Christ, and each one of you is a part of it" (1 Corinthians 12:26, 27).

Criticism: expect to hear it from the inmate population throughout the course of your ministry. Within the context of any conversation—particularly with men and women who have no spiritual foundation or God-centered accountability—prepare for negative commentary regarding every topic imaginable, from religion to the prison system to grievances regarding personal injustices which they feel have made them victims, even as they serve their sentences for crimes committed against society. God is never taken by surprise. He never allows you and me to face *any* challenge—in this case responding to various forms of criticism—for which He does not prepare us, and those in our circle of influence, for soulful, ecclesiastical lesson-learning. God will give us the words, wisdom, and wherefore to turn virtually any instance of negative commentary into a positive life-lesson. "…for it is God who works in you to will and to act in order to fulfill His good purpose" (Philippians 2:13).

One obvious area of contention for the prison minister will be the subject of religion itself. The caution here is not to "major on the minors," that is to say, don't get caught up in deep, murky theological issues or doctrinal beliefs. Keep the salvation message—the death, shed blood, and resurrection of Jesus Christ—the main refrain. Whether the topic turns to Christians as hypocrites (yes, it's true, we *all* mess up and fall short of the glory of God), church rules and regulations, "pastors who are only interested in getting my money," denominational nuances and differences, or misguided beliefs and even occult practices, criticisms will abound and even derail your ministry efforts if left unchecked. Time and space limit addressing the myriad possibilities which could arise, but suffice it to say, by directing or *redirecting* attention to the "ultimate handbook"—the Word of God—many critical ideas or assumptions regarding religion can not only be disarmed, but can be used to fortify practical spiritual truths. For instance, through examination and clarification of Scripture during many years of worship services or led discussions, I have been able to encourage a number of prison audiences to consider that it is not religion (a man-made concept) so much as personal relationship with God, through the sacrifice of Jesus Christ, which should form the cornerstone of our faith.

Another topic of concern leading to inmate anger or distress is the perceived lack of care or support from family members and other people on the *outside,* from prison administrators on the *inside,* or even from other inmates *within* the prison population. Such umbrage may be lessened by the prison pastor's biblical instruction regarding our sufficiency in Christ even in the midst of trials and troubling situations, or through scriptural admonition and teaching about accepting responsibility for one's actions.

Major sources of distraction, if left unattended, are griping and complaining about "the system," about the offender's current prison home and/or its administration, about an upcoming court case or impending legal actions. These issues, in particular, tend to dominate an inmate's psyche …sometimes, it seems, to the point of obsession.

Incarceration can make even the strongest of men feel helpless, hopeless, out of control. Without a foundation of faith—a belief in something infinitely finer than the current circumstances—dark thoughts churn in the mind and heart, boiling, bubbling, and building like molten lava under pressure. Spiritual oppression, coupled with physical bondage, tends to bring out the base, carnal natures of those in its grip, sometimes dealt with by inward seething or depression, but too often manifested as volcanic verbal or physical explosions. You and I must understand that these pressures are not that much different from the daily troubles which skew the thoughts, actions, and attitudes of numerous people in society-at-large. The One and Only God Who provides comfort, instruction, healing, and peace to the masses outside the prison walls is the *same* God who ministers (sometimes through our efforts) to *the inmate within.*

Yes, the prison minister must be vigilant—on guard against falling into the trap of engaging in jailhouse gossip or hearsay. Getting caught up in a prisoner's grievances or untoward affairs, or expressing opinions about the prison system, a particular penal institution, or an individual inmate's legal situation can lead to dire consequences. Because if—or when—word is relayed to prison administrators, legal authorities, etc. that you have spoken out of turn or advocated in any way on behalf of a troublesome or complaining inmate, there is a distinct possibility that your ministry credentials could be brought into question or revoked outright. To serve the cause of Christ within the prison system is truly a privilege. You and I have a calling which must transcend the mundane things of this world. "From everyone who has been given much, much will be demanded; and from the one who has been entrusted with much, much more will be asked" (Luke 12:48).

You and I, as ambassadors of Jesus Christ, are an extension of the prison chaplaincy. As emissaries within the system, we should not only embrace the opportunities of ministering to inmates through our *own* worship services or class sessions; we should encourage prisoners to avail themselves of *other* opportunities to worship and to study the Word of God. This might include, but certainly is not limited to, promoting Bible distribution, supporting a chaplain's Bible study efforts, or recommending another parachurch ministry's lifestyle discussion or counseling sessions to inmates in our sphere of influence.

There may be times when you feel discouraged by a seeming lack of progress as you travel the road set before you. For this reason, it is a good policy to keep your mission in proper perspective, realizing that, even with our best spiritual intentions, we tend to see the men and women in our care—the thieves, rapists, and murderers—as they are *today.* God, on the other hand, has unique insight into the "end game" of their lives, seeing those prisoners in their D.O.C. jumpsuits as they *can* be. Hopefully, this knowledge will provide a hedge against weariness for *all* those involved in serving the spiritual needs of inmates.

As you begin to develop relationships with certain inmates during your season of service, do not take it as personal failure if some men or women stumble and fall along the path to right-living. There will be times within the prison environment—just as there are on the streets of America or on avenues around the world—where individuals will backslide, falling into old destructive habits or succumbing to new temptations, even to the point of rejecting the gift of salvation, freely given to mankind, through the shed blood of Jesus Christ. As ministers, we can sow seeds, we can nurture the crop, but it is *God* who brings the harvest to fruition. The apostle Paul says, "I planted the seed, Apollos watered it, but God has been making it grow. So neither the one who plants nor the one who waters is anything, but only God, who makes things grow" (1 Corinthians 3:6, 7). There are certain burdens we can, and perhaps should, assume on behalf of others. The path to Christlikeness is not one of them. We can pray, we can encourage, we can offer leadership and instruction, but each man or woman is called upon to walk their own journey of faith. No one else on earth can walk that walk for them.

We serve a *personal* God who desires that all people have a *personal relationship* with Him. Each of us—inside or outside prison walls—who calls himself a Christ-follower chooses to embark upon a *personal* journey to Christlikeness which transcends to the heavens and eternity with Christ when our time on Earth is finished. Throughout that journey, during the joy and laughter, amid the sorrow and tears, God has specific personal lessons for each of us to learn.

Although, through our self-reliance and intellect, we often believe we know what we require in life to survive and be happy, the reality is that only God, in His infinite wisdom, understands what each of us truly needs to prosper and to fully enjoy the journey. Why is this?

Because He alone is God. Our lives are not about us so much as they are about *Him*.

If God has given you a vision to minister to incarcerated men and women, follow it. Pray. Prepare. Step out in faith, having no inkling of the results *He* has in store. Be obedient to the calling on your life. Offer *yourself* in service to those people He puts in your path. "Does the Lord delight in burnt offerings and sacrifices as much as obeying the Lord? To obey is better than sacrifice, and to heed is better than the fat of rams" (1 Samuel 15:22).

The rewards of prison ministry may or may not be endless, but one thing is certain: they are eternal. Now may be the appointed time for you to begin your service to *the inmate within*.

A Special Message
to Incarcerated Men and Women

There is hope beyond the hurt. There can be peace in the midst of pain. All things *are* possible, but not through mere mortal efforts alone. You and I—*we*—need something or *someone* bigger and better than ourselves. We need a Savior to take away the sin. We need a Lord to guide and direct our everyday lives. He is One and the same. His name is Jesus Christ.

Supernaturally conceived by God, in the womb of an ordinary teenage virgin named Mary, Jesus Christ entered this world as a lowly carpenter's son. As a young boy, growing up in the town of Nazareth, in a region called Galilee, Jesus exhibited an uncanny wisdom and knowledge far beyond His years. He confounded and intrigued the scribes and teachers of the law, even instructing *them* as He held forth in the temple.

How was Jesus Christ able to engender such respect and command such attention? One reason: Jesus is God. Entering manhood, the work-a-day world could never completely understand Him. During a vibrant three-year adult ministry, which changed the very spiritual fabric of this planet, Jesus received His share of adulation and acclaim. And so, you might say, just as in some stages of *your* life, Jesus Christ might have been perceived by some as being "on top of the world." But, as can so easily be the case, the world turned against Him. Jesus was criticized, scrutinized, chastised, so much so that He was referred to as a "Man of Sorrows" who was bruised and broken for our iniquities. "He was despised and rejected by mankind, a man of suffering, and familiar with pain. Like one from whom people hide their faces He was despised, and we held Him in low esteem" (Isaiah 53:3). Lied about and falsely accused during a mockery of a trial, this God-Man uttered not a word in His own defense. Why? Because Jesus *is God*. Jesus Christ was sent by His Father in Heaven as the stand-in, the substitute, the

251

propitiation for the sins of all mankind. He was torn to shreds at the whipping post and nailed to a rugged wooden cross during the Roman ritual of crucifixion. As His crimson blood cascaded from open wounds, washing your souls and mine white as snow—our sins forgiven—the Savior looked down upon the assembled crowd with an unconditional, otherworldly love. And with His dying breath, He petitioned the heavens saying, "Father, forgive them, for they do not know what they are doing" (Luke 23:34).

Jesus Christ's sacrificial death was a new beginning for mankind. True to Jesus' Word and His earthly mission, the devil couldn't contest Him. The grave couldn't hold Him. Death couldn't defeat Him. Even the chains, shackles, and fortress of hell itself were unable to contain the Son of Man, as He rose again, on the third day, to sit at the right hand of His Father in heaven. Jesus' resurrection was the culmination of God's promise to save you and me *from ourselves.*

To my brothers and sisters behind prison bars, my message is this: "There is power in the Name of Jesus and everlasting life—far beyond your current circumstances—through a personal relationship with Him." Many of you have heard this sentiment expressed in the past, perhaps even during the course of a prison service. Through the death, shed blood, and resurrection of Jesus Christ, you and I have been given an opportunity to receive the victorious and vibrant power of God's Holy Spirit to guide and direct our minds and spiritual hearts. Active and operational—every second of every minute of every hour throughout any given day—this is power that will not simply *change,* but a force that can *transform* a man or a woman from the inside out.

I waited thirty-one years to accept such a gift.

Some of you have waited much longer. In the meantime, we have relied on our *own* power and abilities—physically, mentally, and spiritually—to strive for and accomplish those things which we deemed to be of paramount importance and most suitable for our lives. My only question to you is the same one I asked myself many years ago: *"How has it been working for you so far?"*

There is the way, the truth, and the life, in Jesus Christ, which chooses to forget your past. "For I will forgive their wickedness and will remember their sins no more" (Hebrews 8:12). God's grace and mercy is fresh and available every day, to guide and direct you along the path to righteousness and right-living. There is hope and healing in abundance for those who hurt and are in need of comfort.

God's Word says that you and I are to "Make the most of every opportunity, because the days are evil" (Ephesians 5:16). In older biblical translations, this admonition encourages us to "redeem the time," or put the minutes, hours, and days which we have been given to best use. If you are a man or woman currently serving a prison sentence, there is no doubt about it—you have been given **time.** The question is, *how are you going to use that time?* Through many years of trial and tribulation in my *own* life, God has taught me that there is no such thing as coincidence. I believe that the same premise holds true for you. God, combining both infinite wisdom and a measure of mercy, sees a man or woman careening crazily through life, caught in a web of sinful desires, addictions, deception, or criminal behavior. To arrest, to a degree, the headlong rush toward destruction, I believe God chooses to place some individuals in county jails, state penitentiaries, or federal facilities, not only to slow them down, but to allow those with criminal intent to determine who they are going to be...*with or without* Him in their lives! Ironically, I have seen, time after time, how our Heavenly Father places someone in **prison**—behind steel bars—so that, in the midst of developing a heartfelt, personal relationship with Him, the prisoner can become *free* from the bondage created by a sinful lifestyle.

To repeat: In this earthly life, within the unique timeframe each of us has been given, God's eternal inquiry to you and me remains the same: "Who are you going to be, *with* Me or *without* Me?"

As Fran and I continue our ministry, I constantly hear declarations from inmates which are both encouraging and disheartening at the same time: "When I get out of here, I'm going to become involved in Christian music recording and ministry." "When I've done my 'bit,' I'm going to provide counseling for ex-offenders dealing with substance abuse and addictions." Or, "When I finish my sentence, I want to prepare myself to become a pastor or an evangelist." I'm sure you'll agree that all of these statements express noble intent. And throughout our travels, experience has taught me to answer each inmate's avowal with the same question for consideration: "That sounds great, but what are you going to do *in here*…during the next hour, the next day, the next week, month, or year of your stay?" You see, we—you and I—are called upon to redeem the time, no matter *where* we are, no matter *what* the situation. You must take action and change your life *now!*

In a prison environment, that means receiving and developing a heartfelt, personal relationship with the Son of God; to become infused with a supernatural power greater than your own. It means obtaining a Bible and reading, studying, and meditating upon the Word of God on a daily basis. How do you know the direction in which to go if you do not have access to the definitive guidebook which you can consult at a moment's notice? Through such spiritual discipline and with God's help, you will truly become a "new creation" (2 Corinthians 5:17), able to change the way you think, speak, and act, so that you become more like Christ and less like your "old" self. Always remember that the yoke by which we are connected to Christ is for learning and guidance, not punishment (Matthew 11:30). And, like any new venture, we, as Jesus' disciples, will go through periods of unease and consternation, never receiving all of the answers to all of our questions along the way.

In practical, gut-level terms, the spiritual growth of any inmate involves creating a relationship with the prison chaplain and taking advantage of the counsel, studies, and activities that he or she has to offer. Understanding that your Christlike journey is a marathon, not a one-hundred-meter dash, you should avail yourself of services offered by outside volunteers and ministries—as well as inmate-organized spiritual initiatives within the cell blocks—to better enable you to become a more well-rounded, mature Christian.

Also, the spiritual sojourn of *the inmate within* would have you distance yourself from conversations where there is gossip, vulgar language, or where the name of God is taken in vain. Avoid the arguments, the dirty jokes, and the negative thinkers, the poker sessions, the dice games and other forms of gambling. Refrain from using *any* contraband substances. Choose not to view questionable television programming, or reading materials which sometimes make their way behind the prison walls. Purpose not just to *do* better but, through the power of God's Holy Spirit working in you, to *be* a better inmate, a more desirable cell-mate, and a more understanding friend. Utilize the time God has given you in "the joint" to better strengthen and prepare your mind and heart so that you will be better suited for Kingdom-life and service upon your release. And if release is years or decades away—or, perhaps not in your future—consider it a challenge *and* a privilege to make that prison home *your* mission field, to carry out the works and the will of your Heavenly Father, until you meet Him face-to-face for eternity!

Here is a secret weapon to employ as you fight the good fight: Each day, after acknowledging Jesus Christ as Savior and Lord, arm yourself with "the armor of the Lord" (Ephesians 6:10-18), paying special attention to that shield of *faith*—which is the belief in things we cannot see. The world says, "Show it to me and *then* I'll believe." In studying God's Word, we learn that there will be more than a few mysteries in our lives for which we may never receive revelation or complete understanding. We, as human beings, will always have unanswered questions because "…now we see only a reflection as in a mirror; Now (in this life) I know in part…" (1 Corinthians 13:12). But throughout Scripture, we are provided with numerous examples of ordinary people stepping out in faith—having no idea what lies on the road ahead—and thus being used by God in extraordinary ways. The one element which crushes our faith is *fear*. The painful emotions stirred up by mental alarm, a disquieted spirit, or an impending sense of foreboding or doom, can paralyze us—*inside* or *outside* the confines of a man-made prison cell.

And so it is that we are faced with still another choice to make. *Which of two powerful constructs will determine the course of our lives?* Will it be a childlike *faith* through which we live, and move, and have our being, or an all-encompassing *fear*, fomented by the things of *this* world, which so easily can dominate every facet of our existence? Fear and faith cannot take up residence in the human heart and mind at the same time. One will always push the other aside. The path of faith is the choice God prefers for His people. Fear should not be allowed to become our default mechanism. God's Word underscores that truth emphatically: "For the Spirit God gave us does not make us timid (fearful), but gives us power, love and self-discipline" (2 Timothy 1:7).

Finally, my incarcerated brothers and sisters, do not become weary in right-living. Sin is easy. The standard of the world—lying, cheating, stealing, murdering—presents to you and me the *lowest* common denominator known to man. Let the standard of Christ be your standard. Jesus, Himself, taught that, *"…my yoke is easy and my burden is light"* when compared to even the best things this earthly life, devoid of relationship with Him, has to offer.

Last, but certainly not least, remember and rely upon these words of assurance, penned by the apostle Paul, while *he* was chained and imprisoned: "I can do all things through Him (Jesus Christ) who gives me strength" (Philippians 4:13).

May you find joy and jubilation in your journey! And may you not just survive, but prosper, even as your soul prospers. "…if the Son sets you free, you will be free indeed" (John 8:36).

A Final Word: Righteousness or Rebellion—It's Your Choice

Perhaps some of you reading this book have done so to avail yourselves of the opportunity to peer behind prison walls, "to see how the other half lives," thinking, "This could *never* happen to *me!*" What a noble delusion! It reminds me of a visit to a video store a number of years ago when I literally ran into a well-known local pastor as he emerged from the adults-only area in the back of the showroom. With an embarrassed smile he sought to conceal the x-rated video cassettes in his hand. Then he said, "Well, Brother Pete, you know how it is. We always have to be aware of how the 'other half' lives." I simply returned his gaze then walked silently away. Looking back on that day, I now realize that I missed a God-given opportunity to speak the truth, in love, to my pastoral acquaintance. If I could relive that moment, I would say this to my friend: *"I don't need pornography to remind me of how the 'other half' lives. Any time I allow my mind and heart to drift away from communion with God, my own carnal nature—my flesh—will rise up, in an instant, in an attempt to lure me to the uttermost depths of human depravity."*

That, my friends, is the nature of rebellion. It is a glimpse into what "spiritual death," or separation from God, looks like. Rebellion can take on a variety of faces. Many of us have witnessed or experienced bold, in-your-face defiance. Perhaps some of you can relate to that mindset. In 1979, the hard-rock group AC/DC released a top-selling recording, with the lead song mirroring the album title—*Highway to Hell*. The album cover featured a full-color photo of the Australian bandmates, with one member sporting a satanic, horned headpiece and caressing a forked, "devil's tail" in his hand, as if showing off his most esteemed appendage. At least they were honest. Here's who we are…here's where we're going. We're on the Highway to Hell! In-your-face. Nothing left to the imagination. So what's that got to do with *me,* you might ask? The answer, for some of you, is "more than you could ever imagine."

257

As I walk the streets of America today, God grants me a birds-eye view of the good, the bad, and the ugly of our collective spiritual condition. A "sacred malaise" manifests itself in any number of ways. I see men and women—individually or within the context of gangs or movements—who seem totally devoid of any sense of spiritual purpose or reality. I am referring to people *outside* the walls of our jails and prisons, living life on their own terms, doing whatever is expedient or necessary, not just to get by or survive, but to secure advantage for themselves. Some people are brazen in their attitudes and actions, openly mocking the laws of God *and* the mores and foundational principles of man, making light of the possibility of eternity in a place called hell, because "all my friends will be there!"

Other people, exhibiting a carnal spirit, are more subtle, more insidious in the ways they exhibit or *conceal* characteristics of defiance. This is the *furtive,* secretive face of rebellion. These are the men and women who, to the outside world, present themselves as pillars of virtue, making every effort to be seen as *doing* the right things for the right reasons. But their hearts are far from God. There is no Kingdom connection. Instead of "treasures in Heaven" built upon a solid foundation of spiritual truths, they are consumed with amassing earthly possessions and material pleasures, often at the expense of their very souls. "What good will it be for someone to gain the whole world, yet forfeit their soul?" (Matthew 16:26). Over time, the end result for both categories of rebels looks very similar. Instead of contentment and a peace that passes all understanding, too frequently the harvest of hard-hearted, callous people more closely resembles chaos, confusion, unfulfilled desires, spiritual oppression, and a prison sentence of their own making. The irony is that, measuring their lives according to the standards of this world, many individuals living life on their own terms—directing their own destinies—tend to see themselves as better than others…and certainly cannot identify with the "losers" in society, particularly those wretched transgressors behind prison bars. Perhaps

God is allowing you to catch a glimpse of *yourself* as this passage unfolds. I can assure you that *I*—without the presence of His Holy Spirit guiding, guarding, and directing my life—can revert to a rebellious state of mind in an instant. But, by the grace of God, I don't live there anymore.

Rebellion is a condition of the human mind *and* the human spirit (the heart). Rebellion was birthed in the midst of a God-created paradise—the Garden of Eden. It was there, in the garden, that God created a man, Adam, in His own image. Seeing that man should not be alone, God blessed Adam with a woman named Eve. The woman was spiritually designed to be a "completer" or "helpmeet" to the man. "The Lord God said, 'It is not good for the man to be alone. I will make a helper suitable for him.'" (Genesis 2:18).

God also gave Adam and Eve free will—decision-making capabilities—which differentiated them from the animals. These two created beings, made for communion with God, were cajoled by Satan (the serpent) to taste forbidden fruit against the edict of their heavenly authority. "…you must not eat of the tree of knowledge of good and evil, for when you eat from it you will surely die" (Genesis 2:17). This act of disobedience—or rebellion—ushered in the spiritual fall of man and sin entered the world. This indwelling, carnal nature plagues us to this day. But even in the midst of Adam and Eve's transgression, God, in His infinite grace and mercy, offered provision, protection and a "way out of the wilderness" for men and women separated from Him by their sin.

For many years I marched to the cadence of rebellion. My thoughts, my words, and my actions were selfish, self-centered, and self-aggrandizing. The world, and all therein, revolved around me and what I could receive as rewards for my accomplishments. The seeds of rebellion undergirded and motivated my philosophy toward life and living. A better-than-average communicator when it suited me, I was able to develop friendships among a wide variety of my peers. Within the context of those relationships came the reputation of "Pete Einstein, nice guy." Throughout my self-orchestrated journey, I did seem to have a place in my heart for others—particularly those who might be perceived as "underdogs"—and people of lesser station in society. But even I realized, in my mind and heart, that the "good-guy" image was too often clouded by a dark and critical spirit which dictated that I continually put myself before all others. God's Word describes my heart condition in these terms: "The heart is deceitful above all things and beyond cure. Who can understand it?" (Jeremiah 17:9). For thirty-one years I lived an existence of subtle—and sometimes not-so-subtle—rebellion, with music and song irrevocably woven into the tapestry of the path I had chosen. Looking back on those days brings a rueful smile to my face as I realize that, in spite of thinking myself a caring, conscientious, courteous person, I was always number-one on my Hit Parade, placing myself above all else, above all the people whom God had providentially placed in my life. To confound matters, from my youth through early adulthood I cultivated a head full of knowledge concerning "God," much like the Pharisees and teachers in biblical times. By relegating Jesus Christ to simply an historical figure, and, later, by manipulating God within the context of a "religion" of my own design, I was able to enjoy what I believed to be the best of both the secular and spiritual worlds. As time passed, however, I discovered that my "best-of-both-worlds" notion was utter foolishness, simply a "cosmic distraction" which prohibited me from experiencing something infinitely finer, purer, and greater than anything I could conjure up myself.

During His brief time on Earth, Jesus Christ reserved some of His harshest rebuke for the Pharisees, Sadducees, and "learned" teachers of the day. These esteemed Jewish rulers had much knowledge of the Mosaic Law, with its many rules and regulations. But these same men had no humility or room in their hearts for the true and living God. "Woe to you… hypocrites! You are like whitewashed tombs, which look beautiful on the outside but on the inside are full of the bones of the dead and everything unclean" (Matthew 23:27). "You snakes! You brood of vipers! How will you escape being condemned to hell?" (Matthew 23:33).

Looking back on my life, I now realize that I was on the "Highway to Hell," and *enjoying the ride.* Please understand: No matter who you are, no matter what you've done—***you don't have to be that person. You don't have to follow a path to destruction!***

Here's where the deception lies. Without the highest standard (Jesus Christ) alive and operating in us, we actually believe that we *are* inherently good and that we *can* become even better by *doing* even greater things through our own efforts. The irony is this: in order to achieve these self-serving, self-directed objectives, we have to use the intellect, gifts, and abilities that God gave us in the first place! In our urge to succeed, sin—in whatever form it may present itself—continues unnoticed and unabated. Through it all, you and I, when compared to the lower standard of the world, can always emerge as sounding good, looking good, and *being better* than many of those around us. But in the midst of our striving, God seems nowhere to be found. His Word, His truth is "lost in the shuffle." Although we may enjoy accolades, material gain, and/or ever-elusive "fame" for a season, in light of eternity, the victories of a spiritual rebel are hollow indeed.

Rebellion—sin—is easy. Why? Because left without discipline, structure, or accountability, you and I can just "do our own thing." Many of us are familiar with the lyrics popularized by the iconic jazz singer Frank Sinatra when he sang "My Way." To hungry hearts, Sinatra presented an anthem which extolls virtues like self-sufficiency, free-spirited independence, persevering against all odds, pulling oneself up by the bootstraps, to soldier on and to win this race called life. That message connected in years gone by and it still resonates today with those searching for meaning, fulfillment, and success in an increasingly problematic world. Perhaps you, like I did in the not-too-distant-past, champion Sinatra's mantra as the best way to live and prosper. After all, "my way" certainly appears to make the most sense, doesn't it? On the surface, doing things "my way" would seem to satisfy the checklist of what matters most to…***me:***

- Obtaining the things *I* want and achieving the goals *I* desire in life (check)
- Instant gratification…obtaining and achieving *my* desires sooner, rather than later (check)
- Being free of the fetters, the constraints, the rules and regulations which seem to burden others and short-circuit pathways to *my* success (check)

Our list could go on and on. Living life on our own terms, defying spiritual and/or man-made boundaries, may seem to be a panacea for what ails us in the short term. Looking back on my life, I realize that by following this credo I was able to be very innovative and creative in attaining my goals. Also, I now understand that, even without God in the picture, I was utilizing the gifts and talents He had bestowed upon me to carry out my own agenda. I could "soar for a season," but inevitably run out of physical, mental, and spiritual fuel over time, only to self-destruct on a runway of my own design.

Life's journey can truly be ironic in that, try as we might to be "free" in and of ourselves, our best efforts tend to culminate in some sort of bondage or imprisonment. In my own history, this resulted in a cyclical, circular pattern of continuous ups and downs. When I describe this mode of living to incarcerated men and women, almost without exception they can relate to what I am saying. Jokingly, but somewhat ruefully, I compare persons living out this syndrome to Bill Murray's character in the movie *Groundhog Day.* Left to our own designs and desires, we seem determined to make the same mistakes—follow the same pernicious patterns—over and over, never being able to destroy the "gopher" that drives us to distraction. It's as if God allows us to relive the same physical events, time and time again until, finally, we break down and seek Him to take the lead for the help we need. "There is a way that seems right to a man, but its end is the way to death" (Proverbs 14:12 ESV).

Some of you might wonder, "Ok, Pete, what are you intimating here? Is the equation as simple as, 'Give your life to Jesus, or you'll end up in jail'?" My answer to that question is "no." Like many of you may be doing at this point in time, I, too, lived my life with reckless abandon, with little regard for others—or myself. Through it all—the lying, cheating, stealing, questionable activities—I never once found myself on the inside of a physical jail cell, looking outward. However, I *did* experience the bondage that comes from living a "settle-for" existence, always striving for, but never attaining, the finer, nobler, purer things in life. I was aware of the confinement that conformed my mind and spirit to the limitations of this world. I *did* suffer the heartache, as a prisoner of my own making, condemned by my humanistic nature, to an eternal death sentence.

I was admittedly cannonballing headlong down my own "Highway to Hell"—and you may be, too! It's time to end that dangerous journey, before you crash and burn—destroying yourself and those around you. There is a single, illuminated exit on that "Highway to Hell," yours for the taking. It is clearly marked *Jesus Christ*. You can take that off-ramp, pull over to the side of the road, and find rest for your soul, or you can put the pedal to the metal and speed away into the darkness, hurtling toward destruction on your "Highway to Hell." It's your choice. It was my choice. I took the exit.

Without a Savior of our souls we are *all* prisoners. In the court of life, our own human nature, devoid of personal relationship with God, declares that we are *all* guilty of sin. Left to our own devices, we *all* fall short of His glory (Romans 3:23). Like a TV melodrama, you and I need a high-priced lawyer to plead our case. We have that in Jesus Christ, our advocate with His Father in heaven. He, alone, was qualified—sinless, pure, and righteous—to be the atoning sacrifice for not just our own sins, but for the sins of the world (1 John 2:1, 2). Through His death and resurrection, Jesus Christ paid our bail, and so much more. Our death sentence has been commuted, and, instead of probation or parole, we receive eternity in a place called heaven. And that is **priceless!**

Freedom from captivity. It is life-saving. It is life-encompassing. It is available to all throughout the highways and byways of our lives, in our neighborhoods, our nation, and our world, and in the cramped prison cell of *the inmate within*.

GLOSSARY

Useful Prison Terms, Acronyms and Expressions

"5.0 Cop"
An inmate's slang term for "There's an officer on the block." (See "Block")

83 Form
A form or document used by inmates to file a Civil Rights Complaint against a correctional facility and/or its staff.

"Bad Actor"
Reference (often used by law enforcement) to describe the perpetrator of a crime.

"Bag & Baggage"
The intercom or person-to-person departure announcement directed to an inmate at the time he/she is scheduled to leave a particular facility.

Bail
Monetary or other security given to obtain an individual's release from imprisonment and to insure his or her appearance for an upcoming court hearing or trial.

Bail Bondsman
A person whose profession revolves around providing bail money or "posting bond" for individuals accused of various crimes.
(This payment to the court insures "freedom" for the accused leading to his or her court appearance.)

Bit
Refers to a prison sentence, the length of incarceration for an individual convicted of a crime.

Block
A secure housing unit or living area for inmates.

Block–Runner
An assigned inmate who assists officers by delivering meal trays and other items to inmates on the block. (See "Block")

Bounty Hunter
An individual whose job it is to apprehend persons accused of crimes who, after posting bail through a bail bondsman, fail to appear in court for a criminal proceeding.

(The) "Bubble"
Inmates' term for the officers' secure staff station or control room. (See "Guard Shack")

"Bufing" (Buffing)
Introducing contraband into a correctional facility by concealing it in one's anal cavity.

"Celly"
Nickname referring to a prisoner's cellmate.

Chaplain
An ordained minister serving within the prison; the chaplain may be a member of the facility's staff or may be an independent contractor.

"Chit"
A pocket-sized, metal disc carried by a corrections officer to identify themselves as they perform security checks throughout a jail or prison facility.

CI
Confidential Informant. An inmate who provides correctional staff with information about another inmate's wrongdoings or unlawful actions. (Also see "Snitch")

C.O. (or CO)
Corrections Officer.

"Code Blue"
Emergency response; part of the National Incident Management System Compliance. This code most often indicates that an officer needs assistance.

"Code Red"
Emergency response; part of the National Incident Management System Compliance. This code usually involves a fire or structural situation within a facility.

Commissary
Basic necessities, such as toiletry items, underwear, socks, etc. and some snack-type items which are purchased and issued through the prison system.

Con (noun)
Slang for a person charged with a crime and sentenced to prison. (See "Convict")

Con (verb)
To perpetrate a crime or hoax against another person, usually for personal gain; to "Run Game." (See "Running Game")

Contraband
Anything not issued to an inmate by the prison, not authorized by prison officials, altered from its original condition or employed for purposes other than the intended use.

Convict (noun)
A person charged with a crime and sentenced to a jail or prison.

Count Times
Periodic times during the day when every inmate is accounted for by prison staff. (See "Head Count")

"Diaper Sniper"
Derogatory term for a child molester.

"D.O.C."
Acronym for Department of Corrections. The "DOC" initials are often emblazoned prominently on inmate shirts, jackets and overcoats.

"Dry Druggie"
Although a person may not be actively addicted to alcohol or drugs, the compulsive and manipulative behaviors associated with such conditions may dominate the individual's personality.

DUI
Driving under the influence of alcohol or drugs.

Earned Time
A program approved by the courts whereby an inmate earns an established number of days per month off his/her sentence by remaining on "good behavior" and complying with recommended treatment programming. (See "Good Time")

EBID
Electronic Body Immobilization Device; a hand-held stun-gun device used for control purposes.

FCPD
Facilities Chaplain Protestant Denomination.

Felony
Any offense of a graver nature or character than those labeled misdemeanors; commonly accompanied by a prison sentence of more than one year. Examples of felonies may include robbery, rape or murder. (See "Misdemeanor")

Fish
New inmate arrivals at a correctional institution.

Frequent Flyer
A person who is a habitual offender and repeatedly returns to prison, usually for minor offenses.

"Getting Paid"
Taking something of value (i.e. money, drugs or personal possessions) from another person, often accompanied by the use of force.

"Going to the Store"
Ordering items from the inmate commissary.

Good Time
A program approved by the courts whereby an inmate earns an established number of days per month off his/her sentence by remaining on "good behavior" and complying with recommended treatment programming. (See "Earned Time")

"Guard Shack"
The central control station within a jail or prison.

Head Count
Periodic times in a given day when the inmate population literally is tabulated by prison staff.

Hooch
An alcoholic beverage made from fermented fruits and juices; jail-made wine.

(The) Hole
A designated location within the prison for solitary confinement. (See "Lock-Up" and "In the Bucket")

Home Plan
The place an inmate will reside upon being paroled and released from a correctional facility; this residence must be approved by the supervising Parole Officer.

"Homie"
A slang term of endearment (derived from "homeboy"), which describes a friend, who may or may not be from another individual's neighborhood; a best friend or buddy, who is welcome to share the food, drink or possessions of another.

"Hot Trash"
Describes televisions, radios or other electronic devices which are sold illegally – by inmates, or sometimes by guards – within a jail or prison. These contraband items may be smuggled into the facility or left behind by other inmates upon their release.

"Hut"
A term used to refer to an inmate's cell.

Imam
The religious leader or officiating priest who ministers to the Muslim (prison) population.

"In the Bucket"
When an inmate is housed in disciplinary detention.
(See "Lock-Up" and "The Hole")

Incarceration
To be confined in a secure facility such as a prison.

Inmate
A man or woman incarcerated or confined in a county, state or federal prison facility.

Inmate Grievance
The procedure by which an incarcerated man or woman may seek a formal review of a complaint relating to any aspect of their confinement.

Jail
A facility (prison) especially for the detention of persons awaiting trial or convicted of minor offenses (i.e. "the county jail").

Jail Break
Escape from a prison or other correctional facility, usually by forcible means.

Jail House
(An older term) Refers to a building that is used to house those convicted of (minor) offenses or crimes.

"Jail Kite"
A message folded into a triangular-shaped packet that is slid along the floor toward its intended destination (i.e. to the door of another inmate's cell). The "tail" of the kite is an attached string, so that the kite can be retrieved if it misses its target or "return mail" can be received.

Jail House Lawyer
An inmate who does not possess a law degree but has learned the procedures involved in filing court motions and other legal actions, on his/her own behalf or on behalf of other inmates.

"Jail Purse"
Refers to the vaginal or anal cavity; inmates will carry and conceal drugs and other contraband in body cavities to avoid detection during routine searches.

Jailhouse Religion
A term used, usually in a derogatory manner, to refer to an inmate who has professed faith in Jesus Christ as Savior and Lord while in prison.

"Jumping Bail" (Also "Skipping Bail")
The action of an individual, accused of a crime, when he or she fails to appear at a court hearing, after posting bail money or a "surety" payment.

Kiting Mail
An unauthorized method used by inmates to correspond with one another via the US Mail. Mail is sent to a third party who then mails the same letter back to the correctional institution for its intended recipient.

Lead Officer
The administrative officer or "White Shirt" in charge of all corrections officers (and the inmate population) during a particular shift. (See "White Shirt")

Lockdown
A thorough search of the prison facilities for safety and security reasons. During the lockdown inmates remain in their cells, outside visitors are prohibited and entrance in and out of the prison is limited. (See "Shake Down")

Lock-Up
Refers most often to disciplinary detention. (See "The Hole" and "In the Bucket")

"Max Out"
To serve the entire duration of one's sentence in a correctional facility.

Misconduct
The formal paperwork an officer prepares to document and report an inmate's infraction of rules and regulations.

Misdemeanor
A lesser crime that is deemed not as serious as a felony. Examples may include driving under the influence (DUI), failure to pay child support, trespassing. (See "Felony")

Mule
An inmate who is known to transport and deliver contraband (see "Contraband") to other inmates; a trafficker of prohibited items.

"Old Head"
An elderly or more mature inmate; often those from a period "back in the day," when there was a more defined "code of honor" among criminals.

Out–mate Trusty
An inmate that has court-ordered authorization to perform tasks and selective jobs outside the confines of a prison or jail. These tasks may include lawn care or landscaping, snow removal and outside painting. (See "Trusty")

PO
Abbreviation for "Parole Officer." (See "Parole Officer")

PV
Parole violation. (See "Parole")

"Panic Button"
A personal safety device similar to a car alarm key pad which may be issued to volunteers for their protection within a prison facility.

Parole
The conditional release of a person from prison prior to completion of the maximum sentence imposed.

Parolee
Refers to a person who is released from prison on parole. (See "Parole")

Parole Officer
An individual within the judicial system charged with overseeing the conditional release of offenders from prison prior to completion of their maximum sentences.

"Pay Rent"
A term used when a weaker inmate pays a stronger inmate for protection.

"Perp"
Someone who "perpetrates" or commits a crime or wrongdoing against another.

"Pipe"
A metal appliance used by corrections staff to insert in specially, wall-mounted receptors to record time and location during security rounds in a penal facility.

Programming
The classes and programs offered by a correctional facility to benefit inmates, including drug & alcohol counseling, anger management, high school equivalency (GED) education, life skills training, etc.

Rap Sheet
A (accumulated) list of crimes committed by an individual, usually over an extended period of time.

"Running a Store"
Refers to inmates who barter, loan, sell or trade prison-purchased commissary items or contraband for profit. An exchange rate of 2–3 items for every one item loaned is common.

"Running Game"
To perpetrate a crime or hoax against another person, usually to obtain an advantage or for personal gain. (See "Con")

SCI
State Correctional Institution.

Sally Port
An enclosed, fortified area outside a prison entrance into which vehicles can be driven to be searched prior to being admitted into the facility. Traditionally, the end sections of the sally port are electronically-controlled sliding gates.

"Schooling"
Teaching someone a lesson, usually at the other person's expense. This is as opposed to "getting schooled," when the tables are turned and the lesson-learning is at your expense.

Shake Down
The systematic search of an entire correctional housing unit; all cells, inmates and common areas are thoroughly searched. (See "Lockdown")

Shank
An "old school" term referring to the blade or cutting portion of a (prison-made) knife. (See "Shiv")

Shemale
A male inmate undergoing a sex change, i.e. a man with developed breasts.

Shim
A female inmate undergoing a sex change, i.e. a woman with a deep voice and facial hair.

Shiv
A homemade knife.

Snitch
An informant; a person who discloses information about someone else to another inmate or to the administration.

Stash (noun)
A place where something or someone is hidden, always modified by another object word (i.e. "stash-house," "drug stash" etc.)

"Stoolie" or Stool Pigeon
See "Snitch"

Stress Box
A term used to refer to the prison telephone.

"The Big House"
Nickname for a prison facility, usually at the state of federal level.

"Three Hots & a Cot"
Three meals a day and a place to sleep (while "housed" in a penal facility).

Trusty
An inmate who is assigned a particular job within the confines of the prison; kitchen and laundry workers, janitorial functions, etc. (Also see "Out-mate Trusty")

Turtle Suit
A suicide smock; an outfit worn by an inmate on suicide watch.

"Up State"
Inmate reference to going to or coming from a state prison. (i.e. "I came from Up State to answer these county charges.")

"Urban Yard"
A secure, non-climate controlled, outdoor enclosure… shielded from the elements by overhead, protective roofing.

White Shirt
A ranking uniformed correctional employee (officer) such as a Corporal, Sergeant, Lieutenant, Captain or Major.

Work Release
A supervised program within the county prison system which allows those inmates convicted of non-violent offenses to obtain jobs within the community.

Peter K. Einstein

About The Author

From his earliest recollection, Pete Einstein has marched to the beat of a different drummer. A self-taught singer, drummer, and percussionist, he created a unique rhythm track that flowed throughout his life. Growing up in Carlisle, Pennsylvania, Pete cut his musical teeth on jazz, pop, and rhythm-and-blues. Beginning at age twelve, Pete's soul groups enjoyed success based on their musicality and tight vocal harmonies. During his mid-teens, one of Pete's groups served as a backup band for many of the Motown acts that performed in the region. His travels in the 1960s and '70s spanned the nation, from Miami to Boston to Tucson and Los Angeles. During that musical journey, in search of "spiritual enlightenment," Pete got caught up in the snare of New Age occultism.

Returning to Carlisle in 1978, Pete pursued a career in advertising and marketing. He met and married, Fran in 1979; they dedicated their lives to Jesus Christ in 1981. After a ten-year period of spiritual growth and seasoning, Pete began to write a new type of "soul music," under the banner of SonPower Ministries. In 1997, he recorded his first CD of original music entitled *Work To Do,* which included two Billboard International Songwriters' award-winning songs. In 2005, Pete released *Jubilation Journey,* a music CD which explores the joy *and* struggles of the contemporary Christian experience. To help promote his music and the message it conveys, Pete graced the stage with nationally-recognized gospel artists at numerous Christian music festivals and special events.

Today, Pete and Fran travel as "stateside missionaries," ministering in churches and at conferences and retreats. They find their greatest joy, however, in presenting the Gospel to incarcerated men and women throughout the county, state and federal prison systems. As part of SonPower Ministries' *Inmate Initiative,* Pete facilitates a weekly discipleship class at a local county prison facility.

The Inmate Within: Prison Ministry, a Haven of Hope, based on more than twenty years of prison experiences, is his first book.